PATIENT ENDURANCE

THE GREAT FAMINE IN CONNEMARA

KATHLEEN VILLIERS-TUTHILL

CONNEMARA GIRL PUBLICATIONS

To William and Graham.

First published in 1997 by
CONNEMARA GIRL PUBLICATIONS
90 Pine Valley Ave, Rathfarnham,
Dublin 16, Ireland.
(tel:01 4945414).

ISBN 0 9530455 0 1

By the same author
HISTORY OF CLIFDEN 1810-1860
BEYOND THE TWELVE BENS:
A History Of Clifden And District 1860-1923

Printed by Temple Printing, Athlone.

Cover design by Bernard Kaye
Cover Print courtesy of the National Library of Ireland.
NLI R24,728

Contents

List of Illustrations

Acknowledgements

My thanks to the staff of the National Library of Ireland, in particular Colette O'Daly and Anita Joyce of the Prints and Drawings Department; archivist Gregory O'Connor and the staff of the National Archives; Ruth Willoughby for allowing me use the Fanny Bellingham drawings; Anthony Dopping-Hepenstal for the photograph of his ancestor John Dopping; Marie Mannion of the Galway Family History Society; Brian Mitchell, Inner City Trust Derry, for allowing me to make use of his maps, Bernard Kaye for graphics, layout and typesetting and also to Ryan Air.

My thanks also to friends and family who have provided help and support along the way, especially, Tom and Angela Moore, Margaret Critchley, M.J. Lavelle, George Villiers-Tuthill, Dr William Casey, Patrick Melvin, Adrian and Shirley Lead, Terry Sweeney, Dr Noel Kirby and most of all my ever tolerant husband John.

I am especially grateful to Prof Gearóid Ó Tuathaigh for reading the manuscript and offering advice and encouragement.

My sincere thanks to my sponsors, listed at the back of the book, for their generous contribution towards the publication of this work.

Preface

The original impetus for this work came from reading the many recent publications and listening to television and radio documentaries on the effects of the Great Famine on the political, economic and social history of Ireland. This material left me wondering about the experiences of my own ancestors throughout those terrible years. Both my father's family, the Lavelles, and my mother's, the Joyces, lived in Connemara for an unknown number of years prior to the Famine: the Lavelles in Inishbofin and the Joyces somewhere in the heart of the Connemara mountains. Both families, like the majority of the people of Connemara, were small tenant farmers totally dependent on the potato and, in the case of the Lavelles, a little fishing when the weather permitted.

They, like their neighbours, would have experienced fear and panic at the realization in 1846 that their staple food, the potato, was rotting in the fields for the second year in succession. They would have endured hunger, humiliation and pain as the Government of the day failed to do its duty and bring an adequate supply of cheap food to a starving people. To have suffered starvation, fever and typhus and to have witnessed the death of loved ones, in the most inhumane conditions, must surely have left horrific memories with the survivors.

In an effort to come closer to a realization of what they had experienced I began my research in early 1996, the results to be used in a talk given in the Connemara National Park later in the year. However, the sheer volume of information available on Connemara for this period prompted me to go one step further and publish the following work.

The aim of this work is to give a detailed account of the effect of the Great Famine on the people of Connemara. From the partial failure of the potato crop in 1845 through to the "official" end of the Famine in 1849 the book traces the struggle of all classes in one of the poorest regions in the country.

Twenty years of research into the history of Connemara has shown how difficult it is to give detailed information of the tenant class, particularly in the years prior to the 1860's. This can be particularly frustrating for the amateur genealogist and family historian, a growing interest for many in recent years. The genealogy of the landed gentry is covered by Burke and other such sources. The middle classes can be traced through Title Deeds to property, newspaper clippings and family records. But the tenant farmers owned nothing, recorded little and left their names mainly on the small half covered grave-stones in the local cemetery.

I have tried to redress the lack of information on this section of our community in the following work. Wherever possible I name names and give the location of incidents covered.

Painstaking research has turned up more data than I had anticipated, yet still not all of it is conclusive. For example, it is not always possible to give the verdict in certain court cases. Neither is it possible to be accurate as to the number of those who died and those who emigrated from Connemara during this period.

However, even with all this data I still failed to uncover even one mention of a Lavelle and, as always with the Joyces, they were confusing by their multiplicity. Following the Famine both families moved closer to Clifden, the Lavelles to Streamstown and the Joyces to Coolacly, and future generations have remained in the vicinity right to the present day.

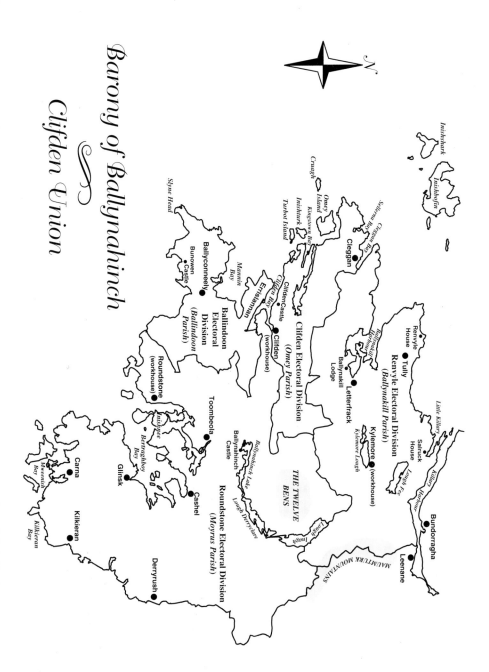

Barony of Ballynahinch

Clifden Union

INTRODUCTION

The Barony of Ballynahinch was created in 1585. It was bound on the north, west and south by the Atlantic ocean. Its eastern boundaries ran from the southern shore of Killary harbour through the Inagh valley and south to the townland of Derryrush (Doire Iorrais) at the top of Kilkieran Bay.

This is the region most commonly referred to today as Connemara and is the area of study for this book. It was also the area covered by the Clifden union, an administerative division set up under the Poor Law Act of 1838 for the purpose of relieving the poor. Therefore, at various points in the book the region is given different names. For example, in the early years of the Famine official records and contemporary sources refer to the Barony of Ballynahinch. However, from 1847 on most sources dealt with refer to the area as the Clifden union.

From the thirteenth to the seventeenth century the region was ruled by the western branch of the powerful Celtic clan, the O'Flaherties. However, in consequence of their support for King Charles 1 in the civil war of the seventeenth century, the O'Flaherty lands were confiscated and under the Act of Settlement were divided out among several parties.

Down through the centuries Connemara gained a reputation as a wild, barren place, cut off from the rest of the country by its natural boundaries of mountain, lake and sea. By the early years of the nineteenth century the Barony still had no roads, just mountain paths and bridleways running along the foothills, and there were no piers along the coast.

The region had become an asylum for army deserters and outlaws. Smuggling and poteen making were widespread but the law rarely investigated beyond Oughterard. It was considered a lawless wilderness and drew little or no attention from government or the political authorities of the County.

All of that changed, however, with the construction of new roads in the 1820's and 1830's. This network of roads, cutting through the heart of the Connemara mountains, linking Killary in the north with the deep harbours in the south, opened up the region to travellers, adventurers and speculators.

Many were attracted by the possibility of employment on the construction of the roads and by the availability of land. Small holdings were easily obtained in Connemara. Some roads ran through hitherto inaccessible areas and vast stretches of land, previously thinly populated, were now available for occupancy. But the quality of the land was poor and required a good deal of fertilizer. Seaweed, cut from the shore, was for centuries the most common fertilizer used and for this reason costal land was eagerly sought after, leaving the vast interior almost deserted. Local landlords, who in the past had lived outside the area, took up residence within Connemara itself; such as the Blakes at Renvyle, the Martins at Ballynahinch and the D'Arcys at Clifden. The setting up of the new town of Clifden and the village of Roundstone brought law and order to the district and created markets for home grown produce and the availability of imported goods.

All of these developments attracted people into Connemara and, taking into account the natural increase in the existing population, resulted in a steady rise in population figures in the years leading up to the Great Famine. The Barony of Ballynahinch's population increased from 19,408 in 1821 to 33,465 in 1841[1]. Although today these figures are considered not to be entirely accurate, they are an indicator of a significant increase in the population during this time.

Over the years the small stretches of arable land along the coast became densely populated and more and more mountain and bogland was reclaimed and brought into cultivation.

John D'Arcy, the founder of Clifden, attributed "the extraordinary increase of population ... to the building of the town of Clifden"[2]. In an effort to encourage people into the region he offered leases in perpetuity of a plot of ground in the town, on which a two-story house was to be built, along with four acres of mountain at Shanakeever[3]. His offer was taken up by men with capital, many of whom leased sizable holdings which they later divided into smaller lots and sub-let to less well off farmers.

However, along with the merchant, craftsman and farmer, came the poor:

> strangers, generally supposed to be tenants dispossessed of their holdings in other parts of the county, who are induced to flock towards the sea coast for the sake of the cheap food they can easily produce; they obtain...a half or quarter of an acre of land, on which they build a miserable hovel.[4]

As the demand for land increased the tenants began subdividing their holdings:

> if a man's daughter marries, they go and subdivide again...They are so fond of subdividing, that their holdings will not support the number of people that creep in upon them. Their object is to make the rent out of the fishery, and to support the family out of the potatoes.[5]

Constant subdivision had reduced holdings to an uneconomical size and retarded agricultural advancement. Efforts were made to stamp out the practice, but as the tenants were too poor to emigrate[6], any attempt at clearance simply meant pushing the tenant off one estate and on to another.

In the years that followed, the landlords were criticized for bad estate management in allowing this subdivision to take place. The overcrowding and poverty that resulted left the people ill equipped to face the onslaught of the Great Famine, and, it is argued, eventually lead to the death of thousands of tenants and to the financial ruin of many of the landlords themselves.

CHAPTER 1

NO BEGGARS IN CONNEMARA

The Great Famine as an ecological disaster began in 1845 and went on until 1849, but its effects lingered well into the 1850's. During that period the population of Ireland was reduced by over two million. It is estimated that one million died of starvation and famine related diseases and more than a million are thought to have emigrated.

It started with a fungus, *phytophthora infestans*, which attacked the potatoes in the field, causing blight. This fungus first appeared in Ireland in August 1845. The reason it had such a devastating effect on this country was because for over one third of the Irish people the potato was the mainstay of their diet. They ate it three times a day mixed with a little buttermilk, and if they lived along the coast they sometimes added fish.

The most common type of potato grown at the time was the Lumper. It was cheap and produced a bountiful harvest, it was also very nourishing. This resulted in the Irish rural population being generally healthy in their diet, and in the poor being technically well nourished.

Because the potato was so cheap, easy to grow, did not need processing and the expense that this might entail, [for example a visit to the mill to be ground], was nourishing and fulfilling and to a degree reliable, the poor needed little more than a plot of land on which to grow their potatoes in order to be self-sufficient. But their almost total dependency on the potato made their situation very vulnerable.

In Connemara, as in other parts of the country, the poor were totally dependent on the potato for their food. They literally lived from one harvest to the next. They had no cash, no reserves and made no provision for a bad harvest.

At this time there was no government system for offering relief to the poor. During times of crop failure certain steps were taken by the government to alleviate conditions, but this was just a temporary response to a temporary crises. A more permanent relief system was called for and this was provided under the Poor Law Act which came into operation in 1838.

Formation of the Clifden Union

Under the Poor Law Act of 1838, Ireland was divided into unions, each containing a workhouse for the administration of relief to the destitute poor. Relief was to be administered inside the workhouse only and a Poor Rate was levied on the inhabitants of the union to finance its administration and maintenance. The unions were to operate under the supervision of the Poor Law Commission and were administrated by a Board of Guardians; the majority of whom were elected by the ratepayers with the remainder being ex-officio Guardians.

The Clifden union came into operation on 24 August 1840. It covered 191,426 statute acres and had a population of 33,465. Geographically the union covered the Barony of Ballynahinch and was comprised of four parishes; Ballynakill, Ballindoon, Moyrus and Omey:

> Bounded on the North by the Atlantic ocean and the Ballinrobe Union, on the East by the Ballinrobe and Galway Unions and on the South and west by the Atlantic ocean.[1]

The best town in the union was usually selected as its capital and for this reason Clifden became the capital of the union and would in time be the site for the workhouse. For administrative purposes all unions were sub-divided into Electoral Divisions. Joseph Burke, the Assistant Poor Law Commissioner responsible for setting up the Clifden union, chose the parishes as the defining boundaries and divided the union into four Electoral Divisions; Clifden, Renvyle, Roundstone and Ballindoon.

An election soon followed the setting up of the union and a total of sixteen Guardians, twelve elected and four ex-officio, went on to form a Board.

The election was bitterly contested and claims of bribery, vote rigging and candidates 'using undue influence with the voters'[2] were made to the Poor Law Commissioners and published in the newspapers. One letter writer in the *Connaught Journal* declared his lack of faith in the character of those finally elected:

> Guardians returned, achieved their corrupt ends, and...such will be the way they will act towards the public in discharging their arduous duties henceforward[3].

The Clifden Electoral Division returned three guardians. It consisted of the parish of Omey, an area of 20,836 statute acres which in 1841 had a population of 7,953; this included the town of Clifden which was founded by John D'Arcy thirty years earlier[4].

Renvyle Electoral Division took in the parish of Ballynakill; it had a population in 1841 of 7,928, covered 49,053 statute acres and returned 3 guardians.

Roundstone Electoral Division returned four guardians; it covered 'the extensive parish of Moyrus, containing 101,503 statute acres'[5] and in 1841 had a population of 11,969. It included the village of Roundstone, set up by the Scottish engineer, Alexander Nimmo, in the 1820's.

Ballindoon Electoral Division consisted of the parish of the same name; it had an acreage of 20,033 statute acres, a population in 1841 of 5,615 and returned 2 guardians.

The union covered a region of great beauty; its mountains, numerous lakes, vast stretches of bog and a rugged indented coastline offering mystery and romance to the early 19c traveller but little sustenance to those trying to eke out a living from its poor quality soil and dangerous coast-line. Joseph Burke, in his report to the Poor Law Commission, painted a picture of a region with many advantages; fishing, possible mineral wealth and land suitable for reclamation, well capable of supporting its poor and, although prone to periods of scarcety it had, in his opinion, the ability to meet such emergencies.

Ever since the opening up of Connemara in the early years of the nineteenth century, travellers and commentators alike remarked on the vast stretches of bog and mountain waiting to be reclaimed and put to good agricultural use. This was compared with the densely populated arable land along the coast, where large numbers lived out their lives in very poor circumstances and in very overcrowded conditions.

To the outsider it seemed that all that was necessary to convert Connemara from a barren land to a prosperous one, was energy and capital; both of which appeared to be lacking in the proprietors of the time. Joseph Burke was no exception to this view:

> If the waste and uncultivated lands in Connemara were let and leased on favourable terms, their reclamation and improvement would prove a most profitable speculation for the expenditure of labour and investment of Capital.[6]

Down through the years efforts had been made by resident landlords to reclaim bog and mountain land and some of these had met with success. But reclaiming land was expensive and the landlords had little capital at their disposal and offered almost no financial benefit or encouragement to tenants to reclaim their holdings.

Local Landlords

The entire area was owned by a handful of families, many of whom had been in possession of their lands for two hundred years or more and almost all were resident in the area: Thomas Martin M.P., Ballyanhinch Castle, Hyacinth D'Arcy J.P., Clifden Castle, Henry Blake J.P., Renvyle House, John Augustus O'Neill, J.P., Bunowen Castle, Major-General Thomson J.P., Salruck and Robert Graham, Ballynakill Lodge.

By far the largest landowner was Thomas Martin of Ballynahinch Castle, the Member of Parliament for County Galway. His estate consisted of roughly 200,000 acres of mountain, bog and lakes and stretched from just outside Oughterard to the D'Arcy Estate, which ran along the coast at Clifden. Thomas was the son of Richard Martin, better known as *Humanity Dick* because of his love of animals and *Hair-Trigger Dick* because of his reputation as a duellist[7]. Although it is Richard who is best remembered from this family, it was Thomas who lived at the castle and worked for the development of the region.

The second largest landowner was Hyacinth D'Arcy. Hyacinth held 20,000 acres and was the son of John D'Arcy, founder of Clifden. He lived at Clifden Castle just outside the town and was a cousin of Thomas Martin.

John Augustus O'Neill of Bunowen Castle held 13,000 acres. He represented the English Borough of Kingston-upon-Hull in Parliament[8] and was spending less and less of his time in Connemara. All three of these estates were already in serious financial difficulty in the pre-famine years.

Henry Blake came to Renvyle in the early 1820's and his estate covered 12,000 acres. Although the estate had been in the family since 1678[9], Henry was the first member of his family to take up residence there.

Major-General Alexander Thomson, a native of Scotland, was a veteran of the Peninsular Wars. He acquired the 8,099 statute acre Cushkillary estate through his marriage to Anne Miller in 1815, but did not take up residence there until around 1835.[10]

Robert Graham[11], of Drumrallagh, County Fermanagh, purchased a 10,000 acre estate at Ballynakill in 1839. The estate had been in the hands of the courts for twenty to thirty years. Robert Graham's son, Francis John Graham, seems to have taken over the running of the estate and almost immediately made himself unpopular with the tenants when he demolished three villages and consolidated the holdings into large farms.

When the Grahams took possession of the estate it was said to be 'covered with paupers...the houses like Indian wigwams'. The property had been badly managed under the courts and was let out 'in running dale: twenty families upon five acres of ground.'[12] These clusters of families formed a rundale village or '*baile*'. They lived on the small stretches of arable land available and communally farmed the surrounding rough land, using the hills for grazing stock. This form of settlement was common in the northern half of the Barony in pre-Famine times and it encouraged subdivision and stunted agricultural development in the region.[13]

All rent arrears owed by Graham's evicted tenants were written off; some were offered rough mountain land for reclamation: free of rent for the first few years and at a low rate afterwards, but very few took it up the offer, preferring instead to move on to the Martin estate.[14]

In the years that followed, Graham leased out farms to men such as Thomas Eastwood of Addergoole, Thomas Butler of Rockfield House (Crocknaraw), Amerald Dancer, at Letterfrack and Thomas Young Prior, who reclaimed many acres and carried out improvements in that district. And he himself, in time, succeeded in winning the good will and respect of his tenants.

Tenant Agreements

The tenants of these landlords were for the most part very poor, living at subsistence level on the few stretches of arable land along the coast and on the reclaimed hills and bogland. They held their plot of land at the will of the landlord; there were no leases, just verbal agreements, giving the landlord the power to 'turn him out when he likes'.[15] The only exception to this was on the D'Arcy estate, as previously mentioned.

Stocking seller in Connemara
Mary Lynch sketched on the road to Maam 14 September 1842
W.B. Kerwan

Courtesy of the National Library of Ireland NLI 2085TX (7)

This lack of security of tenure caused

the tenants to let their houses and lands go into a state of dilapidation, fearing if they put them into a better state, as it frequently occurs, that their rent would be raised according to the value to which they might enhance their land.[16]

The lack of proper leases was recognized as a definite disadvantage to the tenant. However, the impoverished circumstances of the vast majority of the people meant that even if leases were offered to them they would not be in a position to take them up.

Rent was payable in May and November and averaged from 10s to 15s an acre for bog, £1 to £1.10s for rough reclaimable land, and from £2 to £3 for arable land.[17] The rent was not demanded by the landlord or his agents until one year after it became due and was usually paid 'on account'; when the fishing was good or the oats were sold, rather than outright in one lump sum. The usual method of recovering rent from defaulting tenants was to distrain them; their stock were driven to the pound and held until part payment was received:

but should they not have sufficient effects, they are processed and decreed, and put to gaol, until they pay the amount of the decree, otherwise to give up their farms.[18]

Generally, given time, the tenant paid what was due, but usually he was in arrears. The Connemara landlords, however, had few complaints about defaulting tenants. After nine years as proprietor of Salruck, Major-General Thomson told the Devon Commission, a government enquiry into the occupation of land in Ireland in 1844, that he had 'not lost £10 by defaulting tenants.'[19] Henry Hildebrand, who for seventeed years acted as agent for the Marquess of Sligo on Inishbofin Island, told the Commission that the 'Marguess of Sligo has not lost, during the whole seventeen years, more than from £100 to £150 for bad tenants.'[20]

Fishermen-Farmers

The chief occupations of the tenants were agriculture and fishing. The 1841 census records 5,909 families in the Barony of Ballynahinch. Out of this 5,909 families, 4,881 are listed as deriving their income from their own manual labour, with 4,665 employed in agriculture.[21] This meant that almost every family in the Barony, in the years leading up to the famine, was self-sufficient, living off the land, fishing and taking day labour when ever it could be had:

The heads of families were in general holders of small farms, averaging five acres arable, with some acres of mountain, and waste...the tilling of their small farms gives them employment for a very short time, there is no constant employment for them or for those who have no holdings.[22]

Fisherman's wife and family at Killary awaiting the return of the boat

W.B. Kerwan

Courtesy of the National Library of Ireland NLI 2085TX (3)

They maintained themselves by what they raised on their own farms, which was the potato: 'The only resource is the potato-crop, and sometimes a fishery.'[23]

Few in Connemara depended solely on fishing for their livelihood. The majority were fishermen-farmers the fish provided the rent and the potato provided the food. But neither proved fully reliable. Just as the potato crop had failed previous to 1845, so too had the herring deserted the coast. In the years leading up to and throughout the Famine the herring fishing was poor and at times non existent and the quantity of other fish available was insufficient to feed the people.

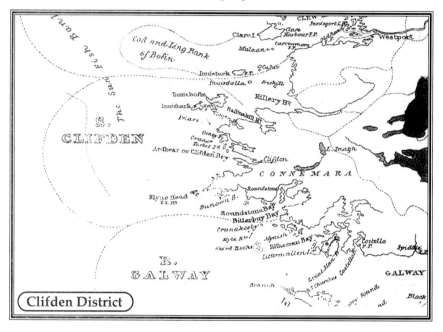

Clifden District

One of the many disadvantages for the fishermen of Connemara was the lack of proper equipment; they did not possess the large fishing vessels necessary to fish the lucrative fishing ground 30 to 40 miles off the coast. They fished instead from small *currachs*, wood and canvas rowboats, staying close to the shore and using nets or a line and hook. This left them highly vulnerable to the treacherous coastline, the boisterous Atlantic and the unpredictable Connemara weather. The lack of piers and safe harbours along the coast and the region's remoteness from the market place also hampered the development of the industry.

On the eve of the Famine, 1 January 1845, there were, according to the Commissioners of Public Works, 5,156 men and 1,287 vessels employed in fisheries in the Clifden District (see map). The 1845 season, the Commissioners reported, was 'less productive' than usual. In the months leading up to May very little fish had been taken. The state of vessels was said to have improved, there was no conflict among the fishermen and 'their general habits...orderly and peaceable.'[24]

When the fishing was good the fishermen, who sold their catch for cash, were in better circumstances than their neighbours. One government official reported in 1846 that the Connemara fishermen were

> a very different class of men...to any of the farmers or labourers: they keep themselves quite distinct, and are governed by laws and customs peculiar to themselves and are a very superior race to any of the other lower classes.[25]

However, when the fishing failed the fishermen were at the mercy of pawnbrokers, money lenders and middle men. An example of this was the control exercised by Henry Hildebrand over the fishermen of Boffin. In Boffin the fishermen sold their catch on the island. The sale of the fish was their only means of getting cash to pay the rent. The landlord was the Marquess of Sligo and Henry Hildebrand had acted as his agent for over 17 years. Hildebrand lived part of the year on Boffin and the remainder in Clifden.

Before the Devon Commission in 1844 he was accused by Father William Flannelly, the curate at Ballynakill, on behalf of the people of Boffin, of taking advantage of his situation on the island. The island people held no leases, they felt they were beholden to Hilderbrand and therefore in no position to seek redress of their grievances. Fr Flannelly accused Hilderbrand of monopolising the fish market on the island and of taking too high a profit on goods supplied to the fishermen, such as tar and fishing tackle:

> He has an exclusive monopoly of the fish and they dare not sell it to any other buyer in the neighbouring towns or parishes - if they do they know the consequences. They have told me repeatedly they would have come here; but holding no leases, they were afraid of exposing themselves to the consequences.[26]

Hilderbrand told the Commission that his goods were purchased in Liverpool and sold on credit to the people of Boffin, cheaper than they could be got in Clifden:

> The people give me their fish as a matter of course, to pay me for the means I gave them to fish with; they could not fish without those goods...If the men do not fish, I am not paid; it is the only means they have of paying me.

He charged ten to fifteen per cent on all goods purchased, which he considered to be the normal percentage. He had the pick of the catch for the first two or three days; after that it was left to outside buyers:

I have seen eighty purchasers of fish there on one day, from Westport, Galway, Cork, the Skerries and Dublin.

There were less than forty fishing boats on the island when he first went to live there. By 1844 that number had increased to nearly 200 and all were supplied by him. He built the boats, he claimed, at a cost of £6 and sold them on to the fishermen at £8; they paid £3 down and the rest over two years. He also built smaller boats from about £5.10s to £6.10s each, for these they paid £2 down and the remainder in two years:

I give them everything they want in the way of fishing on more reasonable terms than they would get them for here (Clifden), and in many cases for credit, and I am occasionally five years without my money.[27]

The uncertainty of the herring left the fishermen almost constantly in debt to men like Hildebrand. Repayments on loans and the payment of rent left little cash for improving tackle and boats. In times of scarcity, brought on by crop failure, the fishermen's almost instinctive reaction was to pawn their tackle and use the money to purchase food. It would prove to be the same in 1845.

Conditions Of The Tenants

Generally the diet of the people consisted of potatoes, milk, fish, oatmeal and eggs. For the poor it was only potatoes and milk, 'and they have but a little drop of that.' They were frequently forced to sell their milk, 'which would be a nourishment to the children and themselves'[28], to help pay back the £4 or £5 borrowed to purchase their cow:

The poor people will cling to the cow as the means of support for their family.[29]

Their clothing was locally produced 'frieze, and for the fishermen blue jackets and trousers; the females, flannel-cotton, but generally only a few of each family can make their appearance on Sundays.'[30] However, many, particularly the women and children, were often to be found nearly half naked.[31]

Their cottages were generally of stone and thatched with straw, furnished with a few

forms, chairs, and one feather-bed; but the greater number are cabins or hovels miserably furnished, the bedding and bed-clothing scanty and wretched.[32]

In the year before the Famine, Matthew Lewis Coneys, a farmer and shopkeeper residing in Clifden, told the Devon Commission:

the cottier tenantry and labouring population...(were) in the lowest and most abject condition in which it is possible for human beings to exist, often bordering on the verge of famine, as a necessary consequence of the low and precarious diet on which, with little exception, their subsistence depends - equally ill housed and clad, and are altogether destitute of the comforts so essential, not only to their physical wants, but to that contentment of mind, the best security for loyalty to the throne, and obedience to the laws.[33]

Tending their small holdings, cutting turf for fuel, harvesting the oats and potato crop and fishing for herring, were the chief occupations of the men, while the women knitted stockings, made flannel-yarn and nets, and drew seaweed from the shore to be used as manure on the potato plot.[34]

In the past there had been public works and the kelp industry, both of which had employed large numbers. But the public works had now ceased and, with the reduction of duty on barilla, the kelp trade had collapsed. The result was that for some months of the year, in the summer months 'before the harvest sets in, and after the cessation of potato-digging in November',[35] the poor had little to occupy them and little to sustain them.

However, despite their poor circumstances, Joseph Burke informed the Poor Law Commissioners that within the proposed Clifden union:

Destitution does not prevail to any great extent and the strolling beggar is seldom to be met with.[36]

Among the local population 'it was a boast, that there are no beggars in Connemara'[37], the region had a reputation as a hospitable place where 'no one would take money from a poor man for food'[38].

Periods Of Shortage And Famine

The lack of employment, and the possibility thereby of earning cash, was a serious drawback for the people and resulted in regular periods of distress for the very poor.

The summer months, between the end of the old harvest and before the digging up of the new, were always months of shortage, and were known as the *'hungry months'*. There was also frequent crop failure, usually due to bad weather. The crop failed in Connemara in 1817, 1822, in the 1830's and again in 1842.

When the crop failed the cost of food in the local shops immediately shot up, putting it beyond the reach of the poor. To help the people through this temporary distress local committees were set up, comprising of the landlords, the clergy and leading members of the community. These committees solicited funds from charities and individuals, at home and abroad, and with the funds received they purchased food and sold it to the

poor in small quantities in an attempt to keep the market price down.
The committees also contacted the Chief Secretary at Dublin Castle, who
was responsible for the allocation of relief funds in times of crisis, and
requested that public works be set up in the area. Public Works usually
consisted of road building, bridge building and the construction of piers.
They were a means of employing the able-bodied who would then be in a
position to purchase provisions at the inflated prices in the shops. The
works, financed by the government, were eagerly sought after by the
landlords and ratepayers of the Barony, as they offered employment to
large numbers of the population and did a lot to improve the area in
which they were carried out.

Many of the roads running through Connemara were built as a result of
public works schemes carried out by the government in times of crop failure. The main roads from Galway to Clifden and Clifden to Westport, and
those running through the Maam and Inagh valleys, were the result of
extensive public works carried out in response to the crop failure in 1822
and partial failures in the 1830's. Many of the piers along the coast were
also constructed at the same time.

Medical attention was almost non existent in the region. The county
infirmary and fever hospital were in Galway city. Efforts were made to
erect a fever hospital in Clifden and the foundations were put down, but
when funds ran out the plan had to be abandoned.

There was just one dispensary and one doctor serving the entire region.
The dispensary was established in 1819, half the cost of running it being
raised by voluntary subscriptions and the other half by assessment on the
county. In 1835 the medical officer in attendance was Martin A Evans M.D.
Surgeon, he was the only medical man in the whole Barony of Ballynahinch
and was paid £100 per annum. The doctor attended the dispensary three
days a week and was expected to respond to urgent cases at any time.

In the years 1830 and 1831 Dr Evans attended upwards of 3,000 patients
but, as was claimed since then there had been a

diminution, from a fear of the doctor and medicine, to whom the
peasantry attribute the propagation of cholera. The diseases treated
generally have been fever, dysentery, cholera, scarletina, small-pox,
diseases of skin dyspepsia.[39]

By 1842 Dr William Suffield was dispensary doctor and he lived in
Clifden. A partial failure of the potato crop in 1842 brought fever and
dysentery resulting in many deaths.[40]

Joseph Burke estimated that workhouse accommodation for 300 paupers
would be required in the union:

taking the usual average of one per cent for the rural population, and
a little more for Clifden.[41]

Two boys at Ballynahinch September 1842

W.B. Kerwan

Courtesy of the National Library of Ireland NLI 2085TX (2)

The expense of maintaining the workhouse was estimated at £1,960 per annum and would be raised by the Poor Rate levied on the occupiers of land over £4 in valuation:

> A rate of 7d per acre on one third the number of acres, exclusive of water within the union, will produce a sum amply sufficient to meet the probable annual expenditure of it, say 60,196 acres at 7 3/4d per acre = £1943.16.7.[42]

The Poor Law set up measures for dealing with relief of usual or 'normal' distress. However, time would show that indoor relief for 300 people in the Clifden union would be totally inadequate to meet the extraordinary distress caused by repeated crop failure.

Delaying Tactics

Shortly after the establishment of the union a valuation of the area for the Poor Rate began. The work took two years to complete, but the Board of Guardians refused to accept the report and the valuation team was forced to begin again. By February 1846 the valuation was still not completed. The Board was 'offering every possible opposition to the introduction of the Law', and the Poor Law Commission was unable to induce them to proceed:

> There is at Clifden no open hostility, but an avowed wish to carry out the Law, yet, practically, real hostility to every step when we attemp to advance.[43]

In 1842 a site for a workhouse was purchased from Hyacinth D'Arcy on the east side of Clifden. The cost of the site, including conveyance, was £23.7.9. The site was bound on the north by the 'intended new line of road from Clifden to Galway and on the south by the old road'.[44] It covered four acres, three roods and seventeen perches.

The building had already been contracted for on 7 January 1841, the contractor being William Brady[45], and it was estimated by the architect to cost £4,300, including fittings. The eventual figure was £3,600 for the building, £990.14.7d for fixtures, fittings and extra works not included in its contract, and £242.5.4d for ironmongery and incidental expenses. This brought the total cost of the building and site to £4,856.7.8[46].

The workhouse was declared fit for the reception of paupers on 22 December 1845 and, although the partial failure of the potato crop of that year was beginning to have its effect on the very poor of the union, the workhouse remained shut. Once the workhouse came into operation the Board of Guardians would be responsible for its upkeep and so they were delaying the opening:

> individual Guardians have said that they would never open the House, and that they would procrastinate at every step.

Because there was no 'open profession of hostility', the Poor Law Commission was not empowered to dissolve the Board but instead ordered a second election of Guardians. However, should the newly elected board 'follow the same course as the last'[47] the Commissioners planned to have it dissolved and to appoint paid Guardians.

The Chairman of the newly elected board was Hyacinth D'Arcy, Vice-Chairman Henry Blake, Deputy Vice-Chairman Major-General Thomson, Clerk John Griffin and the Treasurer was Bank of Ireland, Galway.[48]

It would be 8 March 1847 before the workhouse came into use and, as the Board of Guardians were forbidden by law to administer relief other than inside the workhouse, this left them free of responsibility to the poor and starving throughout the union during the early years of the Famine. They did write letters to the Poor Law Commission informing them of conditions in the union but they were required to do nothing more. Individual members did, however, play their part in other aspects of relief work.

CLIFDEN UNION,
TO
PROFESSIONAL VALUATORS.

THE Board of Guardians of the Clifden Union which comprises the Barony of Ballinahinch commonly known as Connemara, desire to receive Tenders from competent PROFESSIONAL Valuators, who are willing to undertake the valuation of all Rateable Property within the Union, upon which to found a rate for the relief of the Poor, according to the Act of Parliament. The Tenders must state the sum per thousand Irish Acres, including all rateable Property, as also a gross sum for the whole of the Union which contains about 118,176 Irish Acres.

The Valuator will be bound to attend all Appeals, and to make all necessary surveys at his own expense, and if the Ordnance Maps of the Barony are Published, he will be required to provide a set of them.

The lowest proposal will not necessarily be accepted, and the Valuator will be required to give security to the amount of his Tender for the due and proper performance of the work, to be finished on or before the time named by his Tender.

Tenders to be sent in addressed to the Clerk of the Board of Guardians, on or before twelve o'Clock on Tuesday, the 27th day of October 1840, at which hour on that day the attendance of persons proposing will be required at the meeting of the Board of Guardians, Clifden.

The Board of Guardians having decided on employing Professional persons to make the Valuation, none others need apply.

JOHN GRIFFIN,
Clerk to the Board of Guardians.
Sept. 30th, 1840.

Connaught Journal 1 October 1840

CHAPTER 2

BLIGHT IN 1845

The appearance of blight in 1845 resulted in a partial crop failure. For the poor of Connemara it meant yet another season of shortages and suffering. Throughout the winter of 1845 and 1846 the people survived on their own provisions and resources and it was Spring 1846 before reports of distress began reaching the authorities.

The government responded to reports of the 1845 crop failure with the usual relief measures. A Relief Commission was set up in Dublin with instructions to determine the extent of the crop failure and to keep a watch for the approach of famine. Indian corn, almost unknown as a food in Ireland, was imported and distributed to food depots throughout Ireland, to be released on to the market when food prices went out of control. Relief Works were set up by the Board of Works and by Grand Juries.

The Relief Commission, with Sir Randolph Routh as Chairman, established local Relief Committees to co-ordinate relief work in their own areas. The committees were instructed to investigate the conditions of every family in their parish; they were to be divided into categories and only the destitute were entitled to employment on the public works. They were also to raise subscriptions, the money to be lodged to their account, and a certificate of lodgement along with the list of subscribers to be sent to the Relief Commission in Dublin. The Lord Lieutenant had pledged to contribute half, and sometimes more, of the sum of all private donations received by the committees. The money raised would then be used to purchase food from the government depots and local merchants, to be sold in small quantities or, in very distressed cases, to be given away free to the very poor.

In Connemara Relief Committees were set up in Clifden, Ballynakill and Roundstone. Hyacinth D'Arcy was elected Chairman of the Clifden Committee, with Dr William Suffield as secretary and Rev Mark Foster, Church of Ireland curate at Clifden, as treasurer. Other members were: James D'Arcy, Clifden Castle, Henry Hilderbrand, John Lambert of Errislannan and J McCreight of Streamstown. Chairman of the Roundstone Committee was local priest Father Peter Curren and the secretary was James Ashe.

The price of food in the marketplace was steadily rising. The Clifden Relief Committee was given a store opposite the quay, free of charge, by James D'Arcy. They purchased potatoes in Mayo and sold them, below market price, in small portions to the very poor, but as soon as their supplies ran out prices in the shops reverted to their previous high level.

In March 1846 the priests of Ballynakill parish, John Griffin PP, James McManus CC and James McHale CC, wrote to Dublin Castle stating that half of the crop of '45 was diseased and that out of a population of 'eighteen hundred families, independent of Protestant and Descanters, two thirds...are in the state of destitution'.

Father Griffin had lived in the area for seventeen years and had experienced similar conditions in the past. The priests requested that

immediate employment aught to be given to the people who are able to work and immediate relief be given to those not able to work.[1]

Government Food Depots

Bringing food to the people of Connemara would prove to be too great a task for the local Relief Committees. Up until this the Connemara region supplied almost all of its own food. There were no major importers in the area, just small shopkeepers importing groceries and manufactured goods. However, by 1844 trade in the town of Clifden was on the decline and items imported were principally for the fishing trade; salt, iron, pitch and tar:[2]

Some of us used to bring in two vessels every year, and import a general cargo. Now nobody does any thing of the kind.[3]

In 1835, 800 tons of oats, the principal corn crop grown in the region, was exported to London and Liverpool,[4] but by 1843 corn exports were down to 450 tons, chiefly to Westport.[5]

The region simply did not possess men capable of importing large quantities of food and of distributing it to isolated districts. The road system had been improved over the years but it was still not suitable for transporting large cargoes of food and transportation by sea was dependent on the weather and on the availability of large boats: the lack of quays was also a hindrance. The Relief Committees looked to the government to supply food to the market.

However, it was April 1846 before the government food depots were in place in Galway and Westport and it was from these that the local committees were to obtain their supply. To facilitate the local committees, Sir James Dombrain, Inspector General of the Coastguard and a member of the Relief Commission, offered to set up small stores at each of the coastguard stations 'for the distressed localities on the coast'[6].

In the Clifden District, which covered the entire Connemara coast, stores were set up in the coastguard stations at Killary, Ballynakill, Tully, Cleggan, Clifden and Roundstone; temporary stores were later established at Inishbofin and Inishturk. The coastguard stations themselves were not always used but a store close by was taken for the purpose.

The main store in the district was at Clifden (often referred to in government reports as Mannin Bay). It was set up in James D'Arcy's store on the quay, part of which was still used by the Clifden Relief Commission, and opened on 4 May 1846.

Coastguard vessels were used to convey supplies from the government depots at Galway and Westport to the stations. The depot at Galway was under the charge of Assistant Commissary-General Wood and was responsible for supplying, as well as Galway and the Aran Islands, part of Connemara, included Oughterard and Clifden. The depot at Westport, under the charge of Captain Perceval, was responsible for supplying the northern coast of Connemara, from Ballynakill into Mayo and on up to Belmullet.[7] Captain Helpman was the officer in charge of the Clifden District and in the months that followed he kept an account of all food received and distributed by his officers.

By May reports from the area told of the rapidly deteriorating conditions of the poor. On 18 May Magistrates and ratepayers assembled at Clifden to agree measures for easing the distress of the people. The following day, Henry Blake of Renvyle, who had acted as Chairman of the meeting, wrote to the Lord Lieutenant at Dublin Castle requesting an advance of £802.4.0d to enable them to begin relief works in the area. He pointed out that it was essential that works begin within a fortnight to three weeks, as this was traditionally the time of real distress.[8]

On the same day, 19 May, Captain Helpman of the Coastguard was travelling along the coast delivering meal. He arrived at Cleggan to deliver his last supply and found the people, 'many from long distances', ready with their money to purchase. The supply, however, was not sufficient to meet the demand and many were left 'in tears for want of food'.[9]

Four days later Hyacinth D'Arcy wrote to Dublin Castle,

> Literally it is impossible to describe by letter the distress that exists, and what a very short time may witness...I have made the strictest enquiry and taken great pains to obtain the most accurate information as to the quantity of potatoes in the district.

Supplies, he discovered, were almost exhausted. Potatoes were selling at 6d per stone in the shops and the people were only able to have one scant meal a day. The normal cost of potatoes was between 2½d to 3d per stone. D'Arcy had just returned from visiting the Relief Commission in Dublin and had ordered five tons of Indian meal; but this was very little for distribution among so many. He requested that a steamer with a cargo of meal be sent into the area and that public works commence immediately. The area was peaceful and lawabiding: 'an isolated district not likely to be much affected by the example of other places'.[10] However, if relief was not sent, he warned, acts of violence might occur.

In response to this letter Thomas Redington, the Under-Secretary, wrote to the Board of Works advising them to move quickly on opening up works in this area.[11]

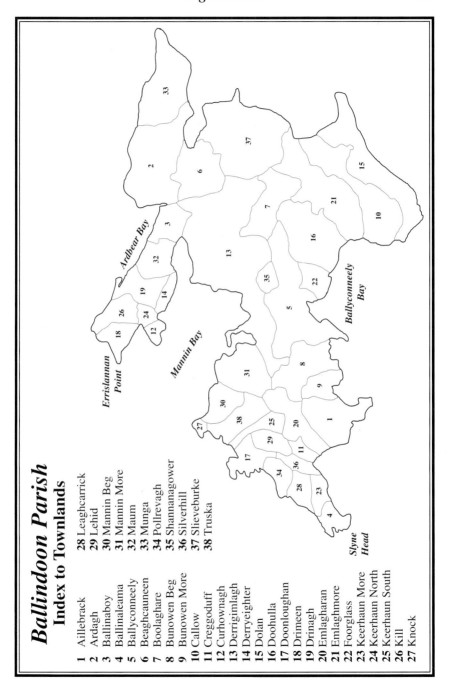

Ballindoon Parish
Index to Townlands

1 Aillebrack
2 Ardagh
3 Ballinaboy
4 Ballinaleama
5 Ballyconneely
6 Beaghcauneen
7 Boolaghare
8 Bunowen Beg
9 Bunowen More
10 Callow
11 Creggoduff
12 Curhownagh
13 Derrigimlagh
14 Derryeighter
15 Dolan
16 Doohulla
17 Doonloughan
18 Drimeen
19 Drinagh
20 Emlagharan
21 Emlaghmore
22 Foorglass
23 Keerhaun More
24 Keerhaun North
25 Keerhaun South
26 Kill
27 Knock

28 Leaghcarrick
29 Lehid
30 Mannin Beg
31 Mannin More
32 Maum
33 Munga
34 Pollrevagh
35 Shannanagower
36 Silverhill
37 Slieveburke
38 Truska

Conditions In Roundstone

The Roundstone Relief Committee had received two supplies of Indian corn from the Commission, which they put on sale. When the people gathered in the village to make their purchase the Committee members were horrified by their condition. The 'destitution and apparent starvation exhibited by the poor' was most painful to witness. From their appearance it was evident that 'distress has attained a most melancholy and fearful height'.

Many of the people had sold their livestock to purchase the meal and, when supplies quickly sold out, and they were told that there was nothing left:

> (they) retired to their cheerless homes with emotions of gloom and noisy clamour, having pawned and sold their effects to obtain the meal. The money thus obtained will be soon exhausted.

The committee requested another supply of Indian meal from the Relief Commission and suggested that public works be started immediately. There was, they informed the Commission, no likelihood of obtaining subscriptions because of the absence of respectable persons residing in the district. They called on the government to reduce the price of Indian meal to the minimum and requested that the meal be given grated to the extreme poor; to save them the extra expense of having it ground. They pointed out that the majority of those seeking food were unable to pay for it and if they did not receive food soon they would 'fall victims of disease and famine.'

In a reply, the committee was told that the action of the government was:

> merely auxiliary to local exertions, that a subscription should be forwarded together with a certificate of the lodgement of the money and government will then be prepared to add a donation immediately.[12]

The Commission also requested a list of proprietors or other 'opulent individuals'[13] in the locality who refused to subscribe. The Board of Works would be advised of the need for works in the area, but the Commission noted that there was a:

> total absence of local exertions on the part of the residence in the neighbourhood of Roundstone to provide means of relief.[14]

One of the many disadvantages in Connemara was the lack of wealthy landlords and individuals to contribute to the Relief Committees subscription lists. People did contribute; by 3 June 1846 the Clifden Relief Committee had raised £121.15.6 and received a £100 donations from the Lord Lieutenant; and Ballynakill Relief Committee raised £33 by 16 June to which was added a £30 donation[15], but the number of people with means was very few when compared with the number in need.

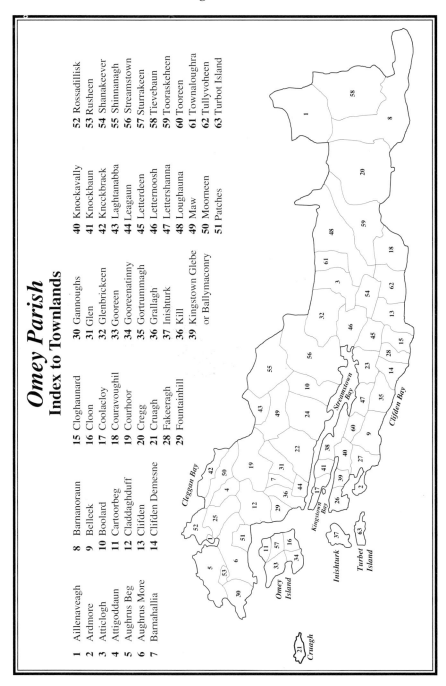

Omey Parish
Index to Townlands

1 Aillenaveagh
2 Ardmore
3 Atticlogh
4 Attigoddaun
5 Aughrus Beg
6 Aughrus More
7 Barnahallia

8 Barnanoraun
9 Belleek
10 Boolard
11 Cartoorbeg
12 Claddaghduff
13 Clifden
14 Clifden Demesne

15 Cloghaunard
16 Cloon
17 Coolacloy
18 Couravoughil
19 Courhoor
20 Cregg
21 Cruagh
28 Fakeeragh
29 Fountainhill

30 Gannoughs
31 Glen
32 Glenbrickeen
33 Gooreen
34 Gooreenatinny
35 Gortrummagh
36 Grallagh
37 Inishturk
38 Kill
39 Kingstown Glebe
       or Ballymaconry

40 Knockavally
41 Knockbaun
42 Kncckbrack
43 Laghtanabba
44 Leagaun
45 Letterdeen
46 Letternoosh
47 Lettershanna
48 Loughauna
49 Maw
50 Moorneen
51 Patches

52 Rossadillisk
53 Rusheen
54 Shanakeever
55 Shinnanagh
56 Streamstown
57 Sturrakeen
58 Tievebaun
59 Tooraskeheen
60 Tooreen
61 Townaloughra
62 Tullyvoheen
63 Turbot Island

Food Stocks Running Low

In June the local Committees were becoming alarmed at the shortage of food in the area but were told by the Relief Commission that the government depot would receive fresh supplies of Indian corn whenever the old supply was exhausted. The supplies would be sent by the coastguard and they would keep them in stock to meet the demand. This, however, would prove to be a false promise; the government was deliberately holding back supplies until the late summer, the 'hungry months', when the demand would be greater. This left the people at the mercy of small traders who were taking every advantage of the situation.

On 22 June Captain Perceval at the government depot in Westport wrote to Charles Trevelyan, Permanent Secretary at the Treasury in London; 'our issue is now very rapid', especially to the coastguard stations. Perceval had received instructions from Sir Randolph Routh, Chairman of the Relief Commission, not to send any more supplies to Clifden, 'as he feared my depot would be exhausted, and not able to meet the demands from the Relief Committees in the inland districts'. At the same time Sir Dombrain was demanding meal for Clifden. As soon as a vessel became available Perceval responded to Sir Dombrain's demands and 'shipped twenty tons on board the `Vulcan' steamer,' and she sailed for Clifden at 4am 22 June 1846.[16]

Mr Cuscade, the commander of the 'Eliza' revenue cutter, reported to Captain Perceval that, on his last trip to the Killaries, a boat pulled alongside and the men inside, from their 'emaciated countenance and prominent eye-balls', he judged to be in a state of starvation. They begged for some food for one of their companions 'who was stretched out half dead, and was unable to eat the bread' which Cuscade gave him. Seeing the destitution, Sir Dombrain ordered the free distribution of meal on the spot.[17]

Dombrain also used his influence and persuaded the captain of the `Rhadamanthus' to deliver his cargo of 100 tons of Indian meal to the Clifden store. His actions brought him into conflict with Sir Randolph Routh, who preferred to send just ten or twenty tons of meal to any station, as he was of the opinion that this was all they were capable of accommodating and administering effectively.[18]

Captain Helpman too preferred to send 'frequent small supplies, instead of a large quantity at once,' and on 14 July used a hooker to transport four tons meal each to Cleggan and Ballynakill.[19]

Public Works Under Way

Applications for public works, such as the extension of existing roads and the laying down of new ones, were proposed for the region by the Board of Works but these were rejected by the Treasury as being too 'extensive' and not 'consistent with the limited object of relieving distress'[20]. It was felt the works would not be completed before the distress caused by the present crop failure had passed. Instead the Board of Works was advised to select works which could be completed while the present distress lasted.

Eventually the sum of £5,150 was sanctioned for road works in the Ballynahinch Barony; the works to commence on 17 June 1846, and by week ending 1 August there were 7,237 men, women and boys employed on the public works in the Barony.[21]

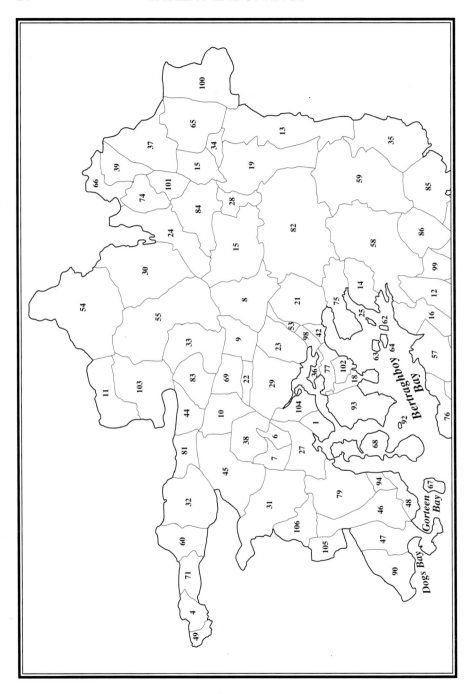

Moyrus Parish
Index to Townlands

1 Aillenacally
2 Ard East
3 Ard West
4 Ardbear
5 Ardmore
  (An Aird Mhóir)
6 Arkeen Beg
7 Arkeen More
8 Athry
9 Ballinafad
10 Ballynahinch
11 Barnanang
12 Beagha
  (Doire Iorrais)
13 Boheeshal
14 Bunnahown
  (Bun na hAbhann)
15 Caher
16 Callancruck
  (Caladh An Chnoic)
17 Callowfeenish
  (Caladh Mhaínse)
18 Canower
19 Cappaghoosh
20 Carna
21 Cashel
22 Cloonbeg
23 Cloonisle

24 Cloonacartan
25 Cruachnait Mhóir
26 Cuilleen *(An Coillín)*
27 Cushatrower
28 Derryadd East
29 Derryadd West
30 Derryclare
31 Derrycunlagh
32 Derrylea
33 Derrynaglaun
34 Derryneen
35 Derryrush
  (Doire Iorrais)
36 Derryvealawauma
37 Derryvealawauma
38 Derryvickrune
39 Derryvoreada
40 Dooletter East
  (Dúleitir Thoir)
41 Dooletter West
  (Dúleitir Thiar)
42 Doonreaghan
  (Dún Riachán)
43 Dooyeher
  (Dumhaigh Ithir)
44 Emlaghdauroe
45 Emlaghmore

46 Errisbeg East
47 Errisbeg West
48 Ervallagh
49 Faul
50 Finish Island *(Fínis)*
51 Garroman *(An Gharmain)*
52 Glendruid
53 Glencrees
54 Gleninagh
55 Glencoaghan
56 Glennaun
  (Gleannán)
57 Glinsk *(Glinsce)*
58 Gowla *(Gabhla)*
59 Gowlaun East
  (An Gabhlán Thaoir)
60 Gowlaun West

61 Halfmace
62 Illaunakrock
63 Illaungorm North
64 Illaungorm South
65 Illion East
66 Illion West
67 Inishlackan
68 Inishnee
69 Killeen
70 Kilkieran
  (Cill Chiaráin)
71 Killymongaun
72 Knockboy
  (An Cnoc Buí)
73 Kylesalia
  (Coill Sáile)
74 Lehanagh North
  (Léitheanach Thuaidh)

75 Lehanagh South
  (Léitheanach Theas)
76 Letterard
  (Leitreach)
77 Lettercaumus
78 Letterdeskert
79 Letterdyfe
80 Letterpibrum
  (Leitir Padhbram)
81 Lettershea
82 Lettershimna
83 Lettery
84 Lissoughter
85 Loughaconeera
  (Loch Canaortha)
86 Loughawee
  (Loch An Bhuí)
87 Mace *(An Más)*

88 Mason Island
  (Oileán Máisean)
89 Moyrus *(Maoras)*
90 Murvey
91 Mweenish Island
  (Maínis)
92 Oghly Island
93 Rosroe
94 Roundstone
95 Rusheenacholla
  (Roisín An Chalaidh)
96 Rusheennamanagh
  (Roisín Na Máiniach)
97 Rusheenyvulligan
  (Roisín An Bholgáin)
98 Scrahallia
99 Shannadonnell
  (Seanadh Mhac
  Dónail)
100 Shannakeela
101 Shannawirra
  (Seanadh Bhuíre)
103 Tawraghbawn
103 Tievebreen
104 Toombeola
105 Tullaghlumman Beg
106 Tullaghlumman More

CHAPTER 3

BLACKENED FIELDS IN 1846

By early August 1846 it was evident that blight had struck again and this time the entire crop would be lost. On 5 August Hyacinth D'Arcy told the Relief Commission that there was just four months supply of potatoes left in the area and the progress of the disease in the growing crop was so very great that no part of the county was expected to escape.

The rapid spread of the disease was alarming. On Friday the potatoes were 'looking quite green and luxuriant and on Saturday almost all the fields blackened and when dug were quite unsound', and 'the smell from the potato fields at night is quite offensive'[1].

Later in the same month D'Arcy requested money for public works for re-surfacing of roads in the barony. He was advised that all the money applicable to 'Extraordinary Presentment' had been used up before Galway's application was received and that there was nothing available until more money was granted by government.

The government was winding down relief operations, as these were the measures taken to deal with the '45 crop failure, and, although they were aware that the crop had failed yet again, measures for dealing with the '46 failure were not yet in place.

New Relief Measures

In the Summer the Conservative Government fell and a Whig/Liberal Government was formed, with Sir John Russell as Prime Minister. Under this new government the supply of food through government depots would be curtailed. All territory east of a line drawn from Derry to Skibereen was left 'to the exercise of private enterprise'.[2] No government food would be brought on to the market in that part of the country. It was the feeling of the government that the merchants in the east were capable of providing all food necessary for the maintenance of the people there.

In future the government would only supply food to those very distressed areas in the remote districts in the west and then only when private traders failed to keep up the supply. Captain Perceval in Westport, however, was confident that there would be little demand for government supplies in his region:

> If the merchants continue to introduce the Indian corn, as they are now doing, I consider that the agency of the Government may be limited to a very narrow field of action.

Westport, Newport and Clifden would be 'amply supplied by private enterprise', but, should government interference become necessary:

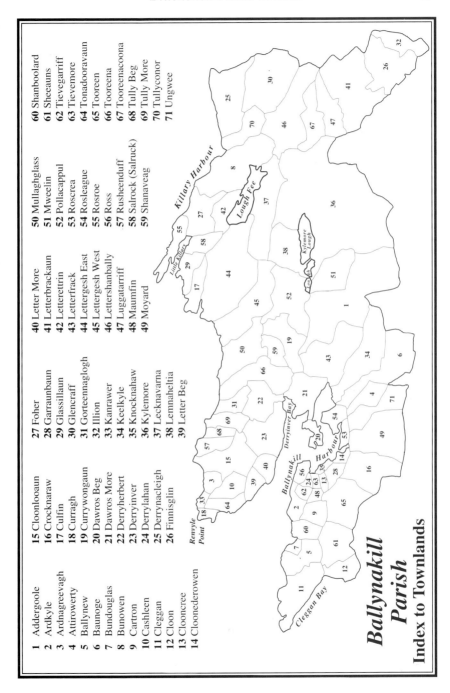

Ballynakill Parish
Index to Townlands

one...steamer of small burden which could come up to the quay to take in her cargo, would keep the whole of the district between Belmullet and Clifden constantly replenished.[3]

Public works would continue but these would now be financed by government loans on the rates.

Relying on private enterprise to supply the food needs of the population in the remote districts of the west was simply courting disaster. All over Europe the potato harvest was a total or partial failure and the high cost of food on the international market would, in the months that followed, be reflected in the price of food in the towns and villages of Ireland. The high prices demanded by merchants in Connemara would place food beyond the reach of the poor, leaving them dependent on government supply which would prove to be erratic.

However, in August some potatoes were coming on to the market and prices dropped. Assistant Commissary-General Amos Lister from the Westport depot was instructed by Routh to go and inspect the coastguard stores in Connemara and see if they should remain in place or their number be reduced.[4]

In Clifden potatoes were selling at 2d per stone and Lister found that the reduced demand for meal at the coastguard stations meant that supplies could be concentrated in Clifden. Any remaining Indian meal in the outlying stores was sold off or transferred to the Clifden store. The small depots could, Lister felt, be re-established in the future if necessary:

> This step will perhaps tend, in some measure, to dispel the somewhat too general illusion that the Government intend to feed the people, and may possibly stimulate individual exertion.[5]

The last of the meal in the Roundstone store was sold off on 22 August and the store closed. At the closure of the store Lister wrote to Routh: 'There will, I fear, be much distress in this locality.'[6]

With Clifden now being the only store in the region, it was decided to move the store to a new location; James D'Arcy's store next to the quay, which up until this had been guarded by the coastguard, was considered too vulnerable, and a building close to the police barracks was leased from A.J. Creighton. The Clifden Relief Committee objected to the move, stating that James D'Arcy, who had given his store free for many months, was now being denied the possibility of earning a rent from its use by the government.

In the event of more government stores being needed in the future, a schoolroom, about 300 yards from the quay in Roundstone, was noted as a possible site and also a stable close to the police barracks at Letterfrack.[7] Supplies for both stores would be issued from Clifden.

The depot at Clifden was to come under the control of the constabulary and Constable Robinson from Galway was put in charge. His instructions were, to sell meal 'only to poor people, and in small quantities' at 1s 3d per stone, or 7½d per half stone and sacks at 1s 8d each, and on no 'account or pretext whatever to issue meal gratuitously'. Money from daily sales was handed over to Sub-Inspector Ireland, head of the local constabulary, and all reports and accounts were sent weekly to Commissary-General Wood in Galway.

Gratuitous Issue Of Meal

Captain Helpman, of the coastguard, had asked to be relieved of his duties and Lister was instructed to examine and settle his accounts. On going through the accounts Lister discovered that:

> Gratuitous issues to a considerable extent have been made at several coast guard stations, on the authority it appears of Sir James Dombrain.[8]

The total quantity of meal sold at all the stations in the Clifden District came to 562,627 lbs. An extra 11,663.5 was given away free to the 'destitute sick in fever' on a certificate from Dr Suffield, signed by Sir Dombrain and countersigned by Captain Helpman. Lister forwarded a breakdown of the gratuitous issue and Captain Helpman's order to Sir Randolph Routh:

> **Statement of gratuitous issue of Indian Corn Meal made at Clifden and its Dependencies, under the command of Inspecting-Commander Helpman, R.N., between the 22nd June and 19 July 1846, to 'the destitute sick in fever,' on the authority of the annexed order, dated Clifden, June 22, 1846.**

Station.	Pounds of Indian Corn Meal
Mannin Bay (Clifden)	3,469.5
Cleggan	6,682
Ballynakill	105
Tully	42
Killaries	1,365
Roundstone	——
Total	11,663.5

Signed. Amos Lister, Assistant Commissary-General

Westport August 31, 1846.

Clifden June 22, 1846.

In pursuance of an order from Sir James Dombrain, Inspector General, you are to issue meal to the destitute sick in fever, on a certificate from Dr Suffield, M.D. after being countersigned by me, at the rate of 2 lbs for each member above 10 years, and 1 lb to each under, for the number of days specified in the certificate.

Signed. P.A. Helpman, Inspecting-Commander.[9]

KEILLINES, NEAR GENERAL THOMPSON'S PROPERTY.

Father and child near Killary

Sir Dombrain was called on by Charles Trevelyan of the Treasury, to explain his actions. He replied that he had been informed by his officers in the various stations that:

> sickness had become very prevalent, arising, as they were convinced, from a total absence of food, and without the means of purchasing it on the part of the sufferers...I told them they must not allow the people to starve...I was convinced Her Majesty's Government would justify the issuing of small quantities of food upon the certificate of the Dispensary Surgeon; but, I confess, I was quite unprepared for the quantity that had been issued.[10]

Sir Dombrain's explanation was considered 'not satisfactory' by the Treasury and his actions severely criticized. He should, they said, have called upon the leading people in the district to form a local committee to raise funds.[11] To which Dombrain replied that in the Killaries, 'where the first application was made to me,' the region was so poor that 'there was not a person within many miles who could have contributed one shilling'.

Dombrain pointed out that he had worked long and hard at the task set for him and he now felt

> deeply mortified and grieved at the censure their Lordships have passed upon me, for an act which I considered at the time to be one of pressing emergency.[12]

Low Wages On Public Works

On 18 September Henry Blake complained of the shortage of food in the Barony and of the difficulty in obtaining it. Public works were now in place but in order not to compete with the local labour market the wages were deliberately kept low.

On 21 September a large number of men come on to the lawn at Clifden Castle to complain of their distress. Hyacinth D'Arcy reported the incident to the Under-Secretary at Dublin Castle:

> I have for some time succeeded in preventing their assembling in such numbers...and have written to the Board of Works requesting an additional number of men might be employed on the works in the neighbourhood of the town, which they promptly attended to.

But still distress was on the increase daily and the cost of provisions had risen beyond the reach of the ordinary man. The people were beginning to panic.

D'Arcy requested that a supply of meal be sent urgently to Clifden, to be sold at a reasonable price, and that the rate of wages on the public works be raised from six to eight pence per day, which was the usual wage in the district:

Those who do succeed in getting employment suffer greatly from the high price of provisions and low wages. Six pence, the wages of one man out of a family of from six to eight, is insufficient for the day at the present price of food...Your urgent attention to these two points would afford considerable relief.[13]

Extraordinary Presentment Session

On 23 September there was an Extraordinary Presentment Session held in Clifden 'for the purpose of approving of public works to relieve the suffering poor.' These Presentment Sessions were called for under the new Labour Rate Act and were taking place all over the country; they were meetings of ratepayers where works were proposed and approved and then passed on to the Board of Works for sanctioning.

Under the Act the cost of the works would be advanced by the Treasury, all of it to be repaid in ten years by a rate levied on the Poor Ratepayers in the locality. What this meant was that the ratepayers were responsible for the relief of the distress in their own district. However, many of the landlords in Connemara were already in serious debt and would not be in possession of their estates in ten years and in no position to repay Treasury advances. But all of that was in the future, for now all that mattered was that any works sanctioned by the Board of Works would be financed by the Treasury and so these schemes were eagerly sought after by local ratepayers.

All over the country Presentment Sessions were taking place and angry scenes were witnessed, both inside and outside of the session-houses, as the people gathered to pressurise the ratepayers into doing their duty by providing works for the starving people.

On the morning of the sessions in Clifden, 23 September, farmers, smallholder and day labourers poured in from all directions. The press estimated the crowd to be between nine and ten thousand, and it was, they wrote, reminiscent of O'Connell's Monster Meeting held in the town three years before, almost to the day.

As the crowd gathered outside the courthouse, waiting for word of the proceedings within, one man, who spoke good English, called out:

We will not die of hunger: on this point we are all agreed - we will slaughter every beast in Connemara- we will not do the thing at night but openly in the light of day. The cattle belonging to the landlords must be first.

The crowd close to him murmured in agreement. Recounting the comment in a letter in a newspaper some days later, one observer wrote, 'I never heard a sentiment uttered with a more determined purpose of carrying it into effect.'

Inside the courthouse the following magistrates and ratepayers were in attendance: Thomas B Martin, M.P. Chairman, Hyacinth D'Arcy J.P., Henry Blake J.P., General Thompson J.P., J.A. O'Neill J.P., John Nolan J.P., F Graham J.P., and Messrs A Morris, W Coneys, J Flynn, P Glynn and W Lydon.

The courthouse was packed and all looked on in amazement as the magistrates and ratepayers unanimously voted £42,006 for the employment of the labouring poor in the Clifden union for the three months that followed. This amount, it was felt, would be necessary to sustain the population up until New Year's Day and it was hoped that by then the government would have set in place a fairer and more comprehensive measure of relief, one that would:

> enable landlords and tenants to borrow money from government for the improvement of the land, encouraging an improved system of culture, and instructing the small holders in the cultivation of crops that might be made a substitute for the potato.

The ratepayers allocated to each electoral division an amount in proportion to the destitution and extent of its population, then retired to another room to consider the numerous applications for roads and piers, etc. This went on until eight o'clock in the evening, when they adjourned, and continued the next day for a further nine hours before all works were allocated. The local newspaper commented:

> Too much praise cannot be given to them for their great patience and kindly feelings they manifested in the discharge of their arduous duties.[14]

Be Quiet, Be Peaceable, Be Patient

During the first day's proceedings the Rev Joseph Duncan from Kylemore brought news of the £40,000 granted by the ratepayers to the people outside, and advised the crowd to

> be quiet - be peaceable - be patient, and with God's blessing brighter and better days will yet dawn upon us. I am your friend and brother - (loud cheers). Believe me that in a christian country no man will be allowed to die of hunger.

Rev Duncan was then carried should-high around the town to the cheers of the crowd.[15]

One incident, which could have changed the atmosphere of the whole proceedings, arose when Mr Nolan proposed that a sum be sanctioned for 'the erection of the walls of a Catholic chapel in the electoral division of Moyrus.' John A O'Neill of Bunowen Castle seconded the proposal but Hyacinth D'Arcy opposed it 'on the ground that the act of parliament did not contemplate works of that description and also because he considered it a sectarian appropriation of public moneys.' A 'kindly and good humoured discussion,' followed and a show of hands was called for. Thomas Martin, Hyacinth D'Arcy and Francis Graham voted against the proposal while all the other magistrates voted in favour. 'Mr Nolan's proposition was therefore carried.'

The reporter, commenting on the above, added:

> Having mentioned Mr D'Arcy's name...I think it right to state that he has done more perhaps than any other gentleman towards relieving the distress which existed in the parishes of Ballindoon and Omey in consequence of the failure of the potato crop last year. The writer of this is no partizan of Mr D'Arcy's; he widely differs from him in politics and religion, but he cannot withhold from him the (words) of praise due to his truly Christian and philanthropic feelings.

This was strong praise indeed for a man who, because of his opposition to Daniel O'Connell and the holding of a 'Monster Meeting' in the town, was unpopular with certain members of the press and public.

At the close of the proceedings the following resolution was unanimously adopted:

> That having passed the presentments necessary for the immediate employment of a portion of the suffering population, we deem that we owe it to Government and to our country to declare that we consider the Government's plan for the relief of the distressed peasantry, which we have been called upon to carry out, exceedingly oppressive. That the loss of the potato crop is a national calamity, and of far too great a magnitude to be met by other than great understanding at the expense of the empire.[16]

Fever and Hunger All Around

In early September Fr Coyne, a Roman Catholic Curate, reported to the Clifden Relief Committee that fever was on the increase in the locality and that some deaths had already taken place. Fever among the poor was nothing new, it appeared regularly during times of food shortages. In a short period of time Fr Coyne had attended seventeen cases, the majority being destitute and without food. Proper treatment and attention was needed to prevent the spread of the disease.

The Clifden Workhouse, although declared fit for the reception of inmates on 22 December 1845, still remained closed. As yet there was still no fever hospital in the union even though, under the Poor Law, the Board of Guardians was responsible for providing relief for fever victims. The Board was empowered to rent a house as a Temporary Fever Hospital but it had made no move to do so.[17]

By early October 1846 Indian meal was in short supply everywhere and prices were rising daily. The local newspapers reported that starvation was not only staring the people in the face but greatly reducing their number. The presentment for public works was still not sanctioned by government and there was little employment to be had on the roads: on 3 October 1846 in the Barony of Ballynahinch there were 486 able-bodied, 93 infirm, 64 women and 20 boys employed on roads.[18]

Food prices were rising rapidly. The price of Indian meal in the government store at Clifden rose from 1s 6d to 1s 9d per stone, a rise of 3d per stone. As prices on the international market kept rising the government was having difficulty purchasing food to fulfil its promise of feeding the west.

On 3 October Dr Suffield, Secretary of the Clifden Relief Committee, wrote requesting a loan of £100 from the Relief Commission to purchase corn and have it ground into meal at Clifden, 'to supply the poor of this district,' many of whom 'are now in a state of actual starvation.'[19] He was informed that no loans would be granted: local subscriptions must be raised.

As food supplies ran low, suppliers in Westport and Galway began to panic and refused to sell. 'If the government do not keep up the supply of food in the district it is impossible to answer for the consequences,'[20] Hyacinth D'Arcy told the Lord Lieutenant.

Roundstone Pleas For Food

The Roundstone Committee wrote repeatedly to the Lord Lieutenant requesting a supply of Indian meal, 'for the relief of the starving poor of this remote and uncultivated district', but with little success. On 5 October they addressed their pleas to the Relief Commission, stressing 'the urgent and pressing necessity that exists for the transit of an immediate supply of meal to this locality.' The people had no food and unless they received some immediately 'the consequence will be awful indeed'.[21] In a reply, they were instructed to purchase supplies of corn, barley and wheat and to prepare them for use as meal in place of Indian corn.

The Roundstone Committee wrote back, yet again endeavouring to explain conditions in Connemara to men far removed from the district and, it would appear, totally oblivious to the circumstances of the people of every class.

On reading this letter one can imagine the Chairman of the Committee, Fr Peter Curren, circle the room, throwing up his arms in dismay, as he dictated to the Secretary James Ashe. 'We have no funds at our disposal', they told the Commission, 'nor is there any possibility of our procuring such.' And, even if they had, they could not make any purchases as this was not a corn growing country and the little that has been grown in the region would not supply the inhabitants for one week.

They drew the Commissioners' attention to the Chief Secretary's declaration of 7 September 1846:

In these districts to which the ordinary operations of the provisions trade cannot be expected adequately to extend, it will be absolutely necessary to provide a supply of food.

Fr Peter Curren pointed out:

Now here in a district in the wilds of Connemara far removed from the operations of any provision trade, utterly destitute of corn of any description and depending solely on the potato crop, which it has pleased the Almighty to render useless - we therefore earnestly implore of you, sir, as you value the peace of this district to lose no time in sending a supply of food for the people here, and should it be deemed necessary, a competent person to witness the destitution that prevails in this locality.[22]

The letter was passed to Routh, but his reply offered nothing but the official line on the operations of the Relief Commission.

The government reneged on their promise to supply food for the remote areas. Food stocks in the government depots were low and the commissariats were under instructions not to open up unless supplies locally were completely exhausted, and then to sell the food at market price and not lower.

Frederick Parker, who had replaced the constabulary and taken up the position as commissariat in charge of the Clifden depot, received word from Amos Lister, his superior at Westport, to close the depot down. He replied by demanding more supplies and was eventually given permission to offer small quantities of biscuits for sale twice a week.

The Board of Guardians of the Clifden union declared that the scarcity of food in the area was appalling and if supplies of food were not sent 'numbers must inevitably perish.'[23]

Hyacinth D'Arcy wrote to the Chief Secretary on the same day, 13 October, strongly corroborating the Guardian's statement. He pointed out that this was not a corn county, 'nor are there acres of wheat', and in many townlands there was no oats or grain of any kind grown. The mill at Clifden was capable of grinding about two tons a day. There were no large merchants in the area, the people were completely dependent on the government supplies for food.

Up to this point the people had shown remarkable patience:

but who can tell what hundreds of unemployed persons may be driven to by starvation. To my own knowledge many of them, accustomed to better things, and are at this moment living on what their neighbours share with them, hoping relief will shortly be given. I do all I can to encourage them, but I know they cannot hold on much longer and I (implore) of the government hasten some relief either in food or employment.[24]

In response to this letter the Chief Secretary requested that every exertion be used to expedite the works in the Barony of Ballynahinch, which had been approved of to the amount of £9,350.[25] This sum eventually went towards carrying out improvement works on one road and the construction of 24 new roads.[26]

Six days later, on 21 October, public works were in progress in the district but under the new system of taskwork; a system that had always been unpopular in the area. Under this system a number of people, such as the aged, the infirm, women and children, did not qualify for employment; the able-bodied objected to working alongside them because they were unable to keep pace.

The Clifden Relief Committee wrote to the Board of Work and to the Relief Commission requesting that some form of employment be offered to these weaker people as many of them had dependant families and, under the present regulations, they were unable to provide for them:

> Otherwise the works which were to support the destitute poor will only extend relief in a very limited degree.[27]

The old, feeble, women and very young were eventually employed for four pence per day filling wheelbarrows and breaking stones.

Other works were going ahead under the Piers and Harbour Act at Rosroe, Errislannan, Roundstone and Ballynakill.

Fish Curing Stations

The government, 'with a view to increasing the stock of food in the country and at the same time afford employment to some of the numerous fishermen on the western coast', decided to put aside £3,000 for the setting up of three fish curing stations; sited at Roundstone in Galway, Belmullet in Mayo and Killibegs in Donegal. Officers were sent to Roundstone to secure a suitable store, with an enclosed yard, where Board of Works employees could instruct the people in the curing of fish. Salt for the station was to be brought in from Liverpool and smaller quantities would be offered for sale for private use. Fishing tackle was also to be brought into the area and sold at cost price to the fishermen.[28]

CLIFDEN UNION.

THE Board of Guardians of the above Union are desirous of receiving TENDERS for the under-mentioned Articles, to be Delivered, Free of Expense, at the Workhouse :—

QUANTITY.

100 pair of Blankets		in 2 Sizes	at per pair.
100 " Coverlets		in 2 Sizes	do
200 " Sheets		in 2 Sizes	do
100 " Bed Ticks		in 2 Sizes	do
100 " Bolsters		in 2 Sizes	do
20 " Mens Jackets		in 2 Sizes	do
20 " Trousers		in 2 Sizes	do
20 " Boys Suits		in 2 Sizes	do
30 " Womens wrappers			do
30 " Petticoats		in 2 Sizes	do
20 Frocks for Girls		in 3 Sizes	do
20 Petticoats for do		in 3 Sizes	do
20 Mens worsted caps			at each.
20 Mens Shirts			do
30 Womens Shifts			do
20 Girls Shifts		in 2 Sizes	do
30 Womens Caps			do
20 " Mens Socks			per pair
30 " Womens Stockings			do
20 " Mens Shoes		in Sizes	do
30 " Womens do		in Sizes	do

Tenders (marked on the envelope as the case may be) will be received by me, up to MONDAY Morning, the 21st instant, on which day, at 12 o'Clock, the same will be taken into consideration.

Samples, where practicable, to accompany each Tender.

Security will be required for the due performance of each contract.

By Order,

JOHN GRIFFIN,
Clerk of Union.

Board Room, 1st December, 1846.

Galway Vindicator 16 December 1846

CHAPTER 4

THE ENLIGHTENED PRINCIPLES OF POLITICAL ECONOMY

Under new government regulations introduced in 1846 the relief committees were abolished and new committees set up in their place. Members of the new committees had to be nominated by the Lieutenant of the county. Their duties, however, remained the same; they would continue to raise subscriptions and administer relief in their areas.

In October a new committee was nominated for Clifden. The members were the same as the old, with just one addition, Captain Ward, the coastguard Inspector for the district. In the months that followed Captain Ward and members of his family gave generously to all the Relief Committees in Connemara.

Dr Suffield was asked to continue to act as secretary, a service he had provided for the previous committee, but one he now felt he could no longer maintain. He wrote to the Relief Commission informing them that he had acted as secretary in the past at 'much personal trouble and inconvenience' and while:

> it would afford me much gratification to be in any way instrumental to the relief of the destitute poor of this district, but my professional avocations (as dispensary surgeon) are sufficiently arduous.
> I am compelled to take this step as the duties of secretary to the Committee here are likely to be very onerous and to occupy much time. [1]

However, he was willing to act as secretary if the Commission felt his service worthy of enumeration. The funds in the hands of the committee did not allow for the employment of a secretary or a clerk, he informed them, and so it fell to the Commission to provide for his service.

In a reply, he was told there were no funds for payment of the expenses of Relief Committees except out of the subscriptions and donations in aid placed at their disposal. However, since the Clifden Committee had very little funds at its disposal and as Dr Suffield continued to act as Committee Secretary, it seems likely he did so without payment.

Ballynakill Relief Committee

On 12 October the Ballynakill Relief Committee was set up, with Henry Blake of Renvyle acting as Chairman and Treasurer, and Rev J Lees, Renvyle, as Secretary; other members were, Major-General A Thomson J.P., Salruck, Amerald Dancer, J Eastwood, F J Graham, J.P., and Rev Joseph Duncan, Kylemore.

In response to the Committee's request that a supply of food be brought into the area, Frederick Parker wrote to Henry Blake on 19 October:

> The government is under the impression that oats and barley are still
> in the country and that it is very desirable to convert it into food.

To assist in the grinding of these crops hand mills had been imported by
the Relief Commission and were offered for sale to the Committee at five
pounds each.

Four days later Henry Blake replied stating that he did not believe the
people were holding back food. The hand mills were too expensive for the
people and for the Committee, 'considering the multitude that are to be
fed', and he suggested they be put to use grinding the rye at the point of
entry.

The Committee was having difficulty raising subscriptions:

> No rents have been as yet collected, and the proprietors have before
> them the prospect of taxation very far beyond their means...I greatly
> fear that unless prompt assistance is afforded, many deaths from star-
> vation will occur within your district.

The *Galway Vindicator* published both letters and commented that there
seemed little chance of 'any effectual relief being afforded to the unfortunate poor of Connemara', unless officials discard 'the enlightened principles of political economy' and act with common sense and genuine feelings of humanity: 'If the people starve be the guilt upon the heads of their
rulers.'[2]

Later in the month the committee did succeed in raising £91 in subscriptions, to which a grant of £45 from the Lord Lieutenant was added.[3]

Rev Duncan Criticizes The Government

Rev Joseph Duncan of Kylemore, the man who declared outside the courthouse a month previous that, 'in a christian country no man will be
allowed to die of hunger', wrote to the Chief Secretary on 28 October:

> our fellow creatures are in the state of actual starvation. My residence
> is daily surrounded by persons entreating me with many tears to save
> them from dying from hunger.

The shortage of food in the region was causing untold hardship and suffering for the people. On Friday 23 October he sent a man with a cart to
Clifden to buy a hundred of meal. The man, a father of a family of eight,
had been unable to work for months and was

> in a weak and dying state , imagine my Lord that fellow creature and
> fellow countryman, already exhausted with hunger and on the verge
> of despair, travelling through wet cold and storm some ten or fifteen

miles to the government store at Clifden, is not this a state of actual want...and after losing two days, not to say anything about the expense, he returned home empty.

The family were forced to 'subsist on cabbage and turnips'. He warned of the consequences of the government's method of dealing with the present crisis:

> The people of Connemara are the most patient people in the world but their patience has its limits...Certainly, my Lord, this state of things cannot be continued, the landlords are discontented, the property has been heavily taxed, the poor man is starving, - at the expense of both, the trader is accumulating enormous wealth. My Lord, give your attention to our immediate singular calls. When the patient people of Connemara cry out for bread let not the paternal government give them a stone.
> I gravely and sorrowfully tell your excellency that our present state of starvation is laid at the door of the government.

If the government had not opened the food depot in Clifden, he argued, 'monied men' would have supplied the market with food. But they were put off when word got out that the government would supply the market through the depot, and now there was no food at the depot and no food to be had anywhere.[4]

Food Depots Almost Empty

The presence of the food depot, however, did little to interfere with local merchants. The government, not having enough food to fill the depots, held back their opening until all local supplies were exhausted. The merchants, on the other hand, were hoarding food and creating panic and this pushed up prices and the people were left hungry. The weekly statement of provisions in the depots for Saturday 31 October 1846, shows Clifden depot having just 4 ½ tons of Indian meal and a little more than 4 tons of biscuits.[5]

On 2 November Routh wrote to Trevelyan requesting a consignment of Indian meal to be sent direct to Clifden and Belmullet, 'the two worst parts on the western coast.'[6] The *'Cheshire Lass'* was already on route from London with 50 tons of wheat meal and 600 quarters of peas, and she arrived at Clifden on 6 November.

In the same month the Clifden Relief Committee complained that the district was again low on food and prices for the scant supply in the town were exorbitant. They had, they complained to the Commission, been lead to believe that 'an extensive depot' would be opened at Clifden, instead 'the issue of a few stones of bad biscuits twice a week only tantalizes the people.'[7]

The Committee was anxious to purchase thirty tons of wheat and other meal but were unable to obtain this at Galway. They asked the Relief Commission to purchase the food on their behalf in Cork, to be paid for on delivery. They were advised that the Commission was unable to 'make purchases for Relief Committees in the way proposed'. They were informed, however, that supplies had recently arrived in Galway and that they should make their purchases there.[8] Later in the month the Commission granted permission for the transport of thirteen tons of meal by steamer to Clifden.

Also in November Ballynakill Committee set up four sub-depots, to serve remote areas in their district; these were at the Killaries, Ballynakill, Tully and Kylemore. Major-General Thompson subscribed £60 to the setting up of the depot at the Killaries and Francis Graham gave £100 to the depot at Ballynakill. The depots at Tully and Kylemore came under the control of Henry Blake and Rev Duncan respectively.[9] On 2 December subscriptions of £50 were raised by the committee and this was matched by a grant of £25 from the Lord Lieutenant.[10]

Arrival Of Supplies

The Clifden Relief Committee, in an effort to cut cost, on 11 December attempted to borrow empty meal bags from the government depot but the request was refused, the bags were needed for use 'when the expected foreign supplies arrive'.[11]
A shipment of supplies arrived from Sligo on 21 December with 50 tons of wheat meal, 76 tons peas and 22 tons barley meal. However, two days later Routh complained to Trevelyan:

> We have the means of storing a larger quantity at Clifden and Belmullet than the two late shipments (supplied)...and it is very important in such poverty stricken spots to have a depot of some resistance. No picture of mine would do justice to the worst part of County Mayo...or of the Connemara district, which is proverbial. These are the two most pressing points and they will continue so throughout the season.[12]

The 'Rhadamanthus', which was then taking on a cargo at Portsmouth, was ordered to take on as much meal as she could stow and 'proceed immediately to Clifden and Belmullet and leave half her cargo at each place.'[13]

On 17 December subscriptions of £163.15 were lodged from Clifden and the list of subscribers passed to the Commission: the list was headed by a donation of £50 from Hyacinth D'Arcy, along with an anonymous donation of the same sum. A grant of £150 was added by the Lord Lieutenant and all funds were used for the relief of the distressed.[14]

That same day five tons of Indian meal were purchased in Galway by

1286.   RLFC 3/2/11/15

List of Subscriptions received towards
The funds of the Clifden Relief
Committee

Hyacinth D'Arcy, Esq.r	£50 " 0 " 0
In the hands of Capt. Ward.	
Lady Moore £48.	
Anonymous — 50.	100 " 0 " 0
Admiral Ward . 1 .	
Rev.d Mr Ward 1 £100	
Capt. Ward R.N .	3 " 0 " 0
Rev.d P Fitzmaurice —	2 " 0 " 0
Rev.d M C. Foster —	1 " 0 " 0
Doctor Suffield —	1 " 0 " 0
Rev.d Eugene Coyne	1 " 0 " 0
Rev.v P. Roche —	1 " 0 " 0
Henry Hildebrand	1 " 0 " 0
William Peirce —	1 " 0 " 0
Wm Arpell —	1 " 0 " 0
Mr Wade —	0 " 10 " 0
	£162 " 10 " 0

Amount Brought For.d	£162 " 10 " 0
Mr Rutledge —	1 " 0 " 0
Mr Anths Kearns —	0 " 5 " 0
total correct	£163 " 15 " 0

Clifden Relief Committee Subscription List 17 December 1846

the Clifden Committee and transported by a revenue cutter to Roundstone: the cost of transporting food into the area was cutting deep into committee funds and the services of the coastguard were frequently sought. The Committee was left to transport the cargo the remainder of the journey to Clifden at great expense, risk and inconvenience.[15]

The previous year all corn arriving in the country was ground at Cork. However, this year corn imported directly into Clifden had to be ground locally. On 19 December Parker reported to Routh that three mills were now working day and night in the area grinding corn. However, by New Year's Day he expected all stocks to be exhausted, 'and the people will have to look solely to Government, for there seems no effort making by the trade.' Parker was anxious that the number of people employed locally on Public Works schemes; 'though stated to be paid so badly and irregularly', would 'retard agriculture' in the future:

and so far from barren ground being brought to cultivation...cultivated ground will become barren.[16]

On 26 December the Clifden Committee wrote to the Commission telling them that twenty tons of Indian meal had been purchased in Galway and was awaiting transport to Clifden. Provisions of all kinds were again low in the town and prices were high: Flour was now selling at 4/6d per stone, wheaten meal 2/10d per stone, oatmeal 3/10d per stone and Indian meal 2/10d per stone.

The Commission suggested that, due to the expense of transporting meal to so remote a place, soup kitchens should be set up, where soup, made from barley, whole meal and whole peas, both cheap and nourishing, could be offered for sale.[17]

Local newspapers reported severe frost and heavy snow falls during December 1846. The Ballynakill Relief Committee noted in its Minute Book on 29 December:

Distress is dreadful, the condition of the poor manifestly deteriorating. The prices of provisions at the several markets have become so high that it is so difficult and in many cases impossible to procure meal.[18]

They requested that a government store be set up in the area and that some provision be made for the destitute poor who were unable to work on the public works. But the request was left unheeded.

Theft of Government Stores

In December searches by the police of homes in the Fakeeragh and Cloghaunard area outside Clifden uncovered sacks of food branded with government marks and numbers. On investigation it was discovered that these had been purchased from soldiers from the 49th Regiment, who were at the time acting as guards at the government depot. The food was confiscated, despite the protests of the families, and an investigation followed.

Frederick Parker, the commissariat in charge of the store, received information that the meal was being removed from the store through a trap-door leading to the guardroom below. In an attempt to gather evidence against the soldiers, he laid a trap one evening by placing two bags, weighing about a hundred weight, on top of the trap-door before locking the store.

On his arrival the next morning he found that the store had been robbed. Bags of meal and biscuits were pulled about and some had been slit open and their contents spilt on to the floor. The trap-door to the guardroom was open and it was obvious that the meal and biscuits could not have been got at without the guards knowledge. One of the guards was found to have meal on his trousers and there were tracks of flour under the guard's bed.

Arrests were made but it was later decided that there was insufficient evidence to convict. This decision by Dublin Castle greatly annoyed Hyacinth D'Arcy, the Magistrate for the area, but despite his protest the decision stood.

Must The People Starve

The *Galway Vindicator* brought the year to a close with a strongly worded editorial on 30 December 1846, criticising the government's inability to keep up food supplies in the west and its decision not to interfere with private enterprise in the market place. It also criticised local merchants for continuing to make huge profits out of the misery of the poor.

Galway Vindicator 30 December 1846
Must the People Starve

Never was the condition of the people so awful as at present -not merely the utterly destitute but every class of limited means. The prices of food have arrived at such a famine pitch that if not immediately lowered by the prompt interference of the Government, will most certainly either force the people to an outbreak for the preservation of their lives or doom them in hundreds upon hundreds to premature death. We see no other alternative. There is no use in thinking that the peace of the country can be maintained while the farmers, merchants, miller, meal monger, baker, and provision huxter, seem remorselessly determined with a cupidity, an avariciousness that puts to the blush every feeling of humanity and libels the very name of Christian, to wring fortunes, if they can, out of the vitals of the poor and reap a golden harvest in the plunder, shameful open plunder of the public.

Fair profits no one should or indeed would attempt to inveigh against; but surely the extortion of 50 or 70 per cent in the ordinary course of trade is not a profit but a plunder. To talk of inhuman, murderous extortion like this as legitimate profit is to compound every notion of right and wrong and sap the very principle of morality and religion. The people must get food or parish. They cannot exist without the necessaries of life. In this respect they labour under an inevitable necessity. It is not in their power to forego the purchase of food while they have a farthing to give for it. Whatever else they may endeavour to dispense without they cannot dispense without this, but at the sacrifice of their lives.

Who will dare pretend that under such circumstances the trade in food is morally authorised to exact any amount of profit he can extort? If such a principle as this could be established society would become a chaos where every one might be at liberty to regard the interest of self, as the only interest to be looked to. Yet, it is upon this principle that the existing trade in food is at present carried on.....It is, we repeat it, nothing else than murder of the people so to extort upon the cost price of food in order to realise profits to the enormous amount exacted at present, they are rendered unable,

even by the expenditure of every penny in their possession, and the sale of every article of clothing bedding and furniture to procure a sufficiency of provisions for themselves and their starving families. Food is at least double the price now that it was this time twelve months though the country was even then labouring under the effects of an extensive deficiency in food...If this were a calamity that could not have been provided against, however melancholy it might be regarded, the Government would not have been held responsible for its horrifying consequences. But what man in Ireland dare, with his hand on his hear, seeing the frightful condition of the people, assert that the Government in entering into a league with the private speculator not to interfere with the provision market, are not truly guilty of the murder of the people? Even now they seem as inhumanly apathetic to their awful situation as at the time they entered into this unholy league. The people are perishing unable to procure any food to sustain life and the Government permit the private speculator to hurry them to the grave without the least attempt at their rescue. Good God! was there ever such cruelty perpetrated before by any Government calling itself either civilised or Christian! Again we ask must the people starve.[19]

RLFC 3/2/11/19 D.336

9305
Reg N.ᵒ£

Co Galway.
B.g Ballynahinch.
Roundstone Relief Fund.

Slipbn Union
Workhouse not open.

Deposit £

Roundstone Relief
Committee
Office
Jan 19
1847

Sir

In reply to your letter the 14ᵗʰ inst
I send you a list of the subscribers to
the Roundstone Relief Committee for
the Parish of Moyrus. They are as follows

Revᵈ Robert Moore	£10 - 0 - 0
The Dean of Lincoln	5 - 0 - 0
Mr Charles Ward	1 - 10 - 0
Mr J F Ward	3 - 10 - 0
Captn J R Ward RN	1 - 0 - 0
	£21 - 0 - 0

The Committee humbly beg leave to thank
His Excellency for His Excellency's generous
donation and would feel gratified that
their sentiments be communicated to his
Excellency

Roundstone Relief Committee Subscription List 19 January 1847

CHAPTER 5

SEVERE HARDSHIP ENDURED BY THE PEOPLE

In the first week of January 1847 the Galway newspapers reported that doctors throughout the city and county were proclaiming death by starvation at a rate of seven to nine a week.

The Roundstone Relief Committee had at last succeeded in raising subscriptions and £21 was lodged to their account and the list of subscribers sent to the Relief Commission; the sum was then equalled with a grant of £22 from the Lord Lieutenant. Included with the subscription list was a letter informing the Commission of the:

> Extreme destitution which prevails in this remote and isolated locality...containing a distressed and starving population of six thousand souls. In the last two months no less than ten deaths have occurred in this parish from disease produced from want of food.[1]

The newly formed committee made up of 'clergymen of the Established, Presbyterian and Roman Catholic churches, but no gentlemen of note as chairman' was constantly squabbling. Their behaviour attracted the attention of the staff of the Board of Works who proclaimed them guilty of gross mismanagement. Their meetings were 'a scene of quarrelling amongst themselves,' a situation which the staff felt would 'lead to lamentable results.'[2]

The government store was closed yet again and the Clifden Relief Committee's supplies had run out. They purchased a supply of Indian corn in Galway but were having difficulty finding transport to bring it into the area. John Griffin, clerk of the Clifden union, wrote to the Chief Secretary on 7 January, stating that, with the government depot closed and the Relief Commission without supplies, the entire population was dependent on the market for food and was at the mercy of a few 'petty dealers'.

The Guardians estimated that one hundred and twenty tons of meal was required weekly to feed the district, but this was proving difficult to obtain. They called upon the government to increase the supply of food to the depot and to open the store for the sale of provisions.

Provisions on the open market were at famine prices with flour selling at 5/= per stone, wheaten meal 3/= per stone, oatmeal 1/8d per stone, barley meal 2/7d per stone, Indian corn 3/= per stone, and bakers were charging 4d for 15 ounces of bread.

The Relief Commission in reply told the Board of Guardians that:

> When the actual wants of the district are not sufficiently met from other sources the depot at Clifden will be opened...It is however to be borne in mind that the local prices cannot be altered by the commissariat supplies, but that their prices will vary with the import prices.[3]

In other words the government depot would remain closed as long as the district had sufficient food supplies from other sources, regardless of prices. And at no time would the government store open up in opposition to local merchants.

Two days later on 9 January supplies had arrived and the store was restocked with 81 tons of peas, 85 tons of Indian meal, 50 tons of wheaten meal and 20 tons of barley meal.[4]

Soup Kitchens for Ballynakill

The Ballynakill Committee decided, because of the extent of the area under their responsibility, to establish soup kitchens at Ballynakill and Killary. An existing soup kitchen at Renvyle was of little use to the people in these districts and relief there 'had been left to the exertions of the clergy of all denominations'[5]. Unfortunately the clergy were unable to maintain the soup kitchens and so the Committee felt it necessary to take up the responsibility. They wrote to the Relief Commission for funds to help set up the kitchen but were, once again, advised that government would only contribute to subscriptions raised locally.

On 18 January Dr Suffield wrote to the Commission informing them that twenty tons of provisions had been purchased in Galway and was now sitting in a store awaiting transportation to Clifden. Ballynakill Relief Committee also had twelve tons awaiting transport and both committees requested that the steamer 'Acheron', then anchored in Galway, be instructed to transport both into the area.

They were informed that the Commander of the 'Acheron' had received his orders from the admiralty which:

for the present precluded him for conveying supplies to your Committee, which is the only one apart from Ballynakill requesting the services of this vessel.[6]

The Commission recommended that the provisions be transported at the committees own expense. This again would simply reduce the funds available for purchasing food in the future.

No Seeds To Be Had

On 22 January the Clifden Relief Committee wrote to the Lord Lieutenant deploring the

inadequacy of the funds allocated by Government and the Board of Works for the maintenance of the many who are now in a state of utter want and whose sole dependence is on public employment.

The wages of one person from each family, should he be fortunate enough to be employed, was insufficient to support 'the inmates of each house...now that all provisions have reached famine prices.' The committee

> directed a strict scrutiny be made into the private means of each person in the locality...(and)remarked with the greatest anxiety and alarm the total absence of all preparation for sowing seed, or otherwise cultivating land for the approaching spring...(they) encouraged the people of the area to prepare the land but found them unwilling to do so saying, and rightly so, that they have no means to buy the seed,

And even if they had there was no seed to be had in the country. They went on to request aid and advised the Lord Lieutenant to encourage the sowing of the land without further delay, adding that they believed it was still within his power 'to convert the land from a state of starvation to one of plenty, for a trifling outlay of money for seed,' this to be issued at cost price or by loan. They proposed that the people be issued with instructions on the sowing of seeds other than the potato, 'which hitherto has so often caused misery and want in this and other districts of Ireland.'[7]

They suggested that simple farming books be distributed by the Relief Committee and that competent readers be employed to explain, in the Irish language, the several farming directions to the people who were most anxious for information. However, their advice was ignored, as the government believed all seed should be supplied by private industry.

Two days later, 24 January 1847, Hyacinth D'Arcy wrote to the Chief Secretary asking how long more public works would continue, as it was expected that works of a 'considerable magnitude' would be applied for at the forthcoming sessions, to be held in Clifden on 1 March. He was advised that no works of consequence should be presented as these would not be sanctioned.[8]

Employment On Public Works

Between October 1846 and January 1847, out of the £42,006 proposed, public works to the sum of £31,629 were sanctioned for the Barony of Ballynahinch, mostly for the construction of new roads. Where these roads lay and how many were completed is difficult to say. According to government policy, works approved and sanctioned would not necessarily be completed:

> it being always understood that the works, although they have been recommended and sanctioned, will be brought to an immediate close whenever, owing to any cause, they may no longer be required for the purposes of relief.[9]

Individual works frequently came to a close as funds ran out and the people were left unemployed until further works were opened, and then not always in the same district. Heavy falls of snow and hard frost were adding to the misery of the labourers, but still they showed 'patient endurance, under their severe privations'.[10]

In the Board of Works returns for the week ending 30 January 1847 there were 5,354 persons working on the roads in the Ballynahinch Barony: 4,488 able-bodied, 101 infirm, 453 women and 312 boys.[11]

Those fortunate enough to obtain employment appeared 'content and peaceable', but the Pay Inspector, William Pierce, found the labourers conduct 'subordinate in the extreme'.[12] Sickness was everywhere, principally dysentery, and deaths amongst the very young and the old were on the increase. Captain Hutchinson, R.N., the Board of Works Inspecting Officer for West Galway, reported on 23 January:

> The state of the country is remarkably quiet considering the very great distress the population are now labouring under...The high prices of food and the distance they have to bring it, chiefly done by the women on their backs, in many cases from 20 to 30 miles, add much to their privation, yet I have not heard of a single outrage on person or property in this remote part of the country.[13]

Such peaceful conditions, however, would not last for long in March, William Pierce reported that crimes, 'such as the killing of cattle and sheep and the result of absolute necessity', were becoming more frequent but were 'of a private nature' and did not appear to be organized.[14]

In February many works had to be closed as funds ran out:

> and many destitute persons thrown out of employment; those in operation are going on as well as the heavy fall of snow and subsequent hard frost, will admit.[15]

It was hoped that the food supply in the west would be improved by the operations of the curing station at Roundstone but this was not to be:

> The weather has been unfavourable, whilst the fishermen themselves, weakened in body from want of food, are still more reluctant from this cause to undergo the increased exertion which severe weather unavoidably requires, and which, from the wretched nature of their equipment, is inevitable.[16]

The Relief Committees in the region were not working well and were slow to provide the lists of those who qualified for employment, with the result that Captain Hutchinson felt

> obliged to sanction the employment of many who would otherwise have starved had I waited for lists from the Relief Committees.[17]

Relief Committees 'Indolent And Inactive'

Frederick Parker too was critical of the local committees. He was under instructions to issue food to the committees only. However, he found that the committees in Connemara were managed far differently from any he had previously worked with. He was of the opinion that while the members were:

> men of the nicest honour and character, perfectly incapable of either acting or conniving at wrong, but it should be born in mind that they are a very poor people, and cannot really devote that time which the service requires.

Many of them had appointed deputies in their place, men, Parker felt, who were not 'influenced by the same principles of rectitude.'[18]

Parker was receiving complaints that the Relief Committees were failing to reach all of the people and in many areas the job was left to private individuals. Meal and soup were distributed free by the local landlords, aided by their families, and by the clergy of all denominations. Routh agreed that the committees were 'indolent and inactive' and gave permission to Parker to open the Clifden depot on Saturdays to sell provisions direct to the people.[19]

However, the small amount offered to the heads of large families, usually no more than a quarter of a stone, was criticized by Rev Mark Foster, secretary of the Clifden Relief Committee, who pleaded lack of funds in defence of the criticism levelled at the Committee.[20]

They Are Dying Like Dogs

Between 18 and 26 January 1847, William Edward Forster, a member of the Central Relief Committee of the Society of Friends, accompanied his father and other members of the Committee touring the west of Ireland. They came to view for themselves the conditions of the people in the remote districts. Forster's reports to the Committee gave a clear assessment of conditions in the Barony, before and during the famine, and give a vivid description of the suffering endured by the people:

> This barony of Ballynahinch contains a population of at least 34,000, almost entirely composed of small tenant farmers or cottiers, and of squatters, of which last wretched class there is a considerable proportion. Hitherto these people have lived upon potatoes, of which they have generally grown good crops: potatoes have been their food. From the proceeds of their oats and live stock they have paid their rent; and with what little surplus there might be, bought their clothes and furniture. In some few of the coast villages there is a little fishing, but it is to so slight and partial an extent that it can hardly be looked upon as a resource.

Ballynakill Relief Committee Subscription List 10 March 1847

I now found their potatoes gone; what scanty crop they had gathered eaten up, together with the oats, including the seed-corn: the turnips also consumed: nothing left but the cattle, and they quickly going - the sheep, the pigs, even the poultry, almost all killed: eggs, were hardly to be bought; and I found on the Renvyle estate, containing some 850 families, where almost every tenant had owned two or three pigs, there were now scarcely a dozen left. In a short time, the population of this barony, hitherto accustomed to live entirely upon their own produce, must die, or be kept alive by either public or private relief. And yet, in some respect, from its number of cattle, and somewhat better crop, both of oats and potatoes, this has been till now a favoured district; but the spread of famine plague is rapidly levelling all localities to an equality of destitution.

Their first night in Connemara was spent at a lodge at the head of Killary harbour where Forster found, 'the magnificence and repose of nature forming a sad contrast to the misery of man'. In the village of Leenane they came across a large body of men employed in making a pier. Their overseer was old Jack Joyce: 'whose name will be recognised by all tourists in Connemara.'

Public works had been in operation in the village for some weeks and, as wages at pier making were higher than those earned on the roads, the village was in better shape than most. Yet, even here they found that the men were weak and showed evidence of wasting away from lack of sufficient food.

Across the harbour in the village of Bundorragha, they found that, out of a population of two hundred and forty, thirteen had already died 'from want', and the rest were walking skeletons. The men looked gaunt and haggard, stamped with the vivid mark of hunger, the children cried with pain and the women in the cabins were too weak to stand.

In the past each cabin in this village had kept a cow and many of the villagers owned sheep and pigs. But now only one pig remained, all the rest having been killed for food. Some of the men had worked on the Public Works for three and five weeks before receiving any pay, the cause of the delay was put down to negligence or mistake by the overseer, but Forster poses the question, 'Would this have been acceptable to starving Englishmen?'

On their way to Clifden they stopped at Kylemore and found one hundred men making a new road. The wages were 4/6d per week, and for this many of the men walked five to seven miles.

Out of this 4/6d a week the head of a family was forced to purchase Indian meal at 2/10d to 4/= per stone. Foster declared:

what is this but slow death - a mere enabling the patient to endure for a little longer time the disease of hunger?

They found that in some districts there were no public works in operation and in those fortunate enough to have them, insufficient numbers were employed.

In Clifden they were told of 'four cases of death from want, within the last three or four days'. They asked the waiter in their hotel what condition the people were in and were told:

> they are dying like dogs...One woman who had crawled the previous night into the outhouse had been found the next morning, partly eaten by dogs. Another corpse had been carried up the street in a wheelbarrow, and had it not been that a gentleman accidentally passing by had given money for a coffin, it would have been thrown into the ground, merely covered with a sheet.

Many were not being buried without coffins and church services, the surviving family members too weak to do more than cover the dead with earth.

Ballynakill Relief Committee were holding a meeting at Renvyle when the Forsters and their companions arrived. The building was crowded with people applying for a ticket to get on to the public works. Work on one road had recently stopped and the people were desperately trying to get back on to the payroll, some even went on to the works and began working free in the hope of getting a ticket.

They found extreme poverty on the islands of Inishbofin and Inishshark and two recent deaths were attributed to starvation. Inishbofin in 1841 had a population of 1,612, and while distress was bad it was not thought to be as bad as on the mainland. Forster declared that if the fishing season was good the people would get through, but if it failed the island could be depopulated in a few weeks. The Society set up a soup kitchen there and at Cleggan and Salruck.[21]

Appalling Conditions in Cleggan

Of Cleggan, Forster declared:

> The distress was appalling far beyond my powers of description. I was quickly surrounded by a mob of men and women, more like famished dogs than fellow creatures, whose figures, looks and cries, all showed that they were suffering the ravening agony of hunger.

They went inside many of the cabins and were shocked by what they saw:

> In one, there were two emaciated men, lying at full length, on the damp floor, in their ragged clothes, too weak to move, actually worn down to skin and bone. In another a young man was dying of dysentery; his mother had pawned everything, even his shoes, to keep him alive; and I never shall forget the resigned, uncomplaining tone with which he told me that all the medicine he wanted was food.

They were told of a girl of eight years of age who was left alone, uncared for in her cabin because she had fever. They went to find her. After a long walk they found the child

> in a most miserable cabin by the sea-side, into which we could scarcely crawl, we found this poor child yet alive, but lying on the damp clay, in the dark, unable to get up, no clothes on or covering but a ragged cloth, the roof over her open to the rain. Since her mother's death she had lived on meal and water brought to the cabin door.

Those who brought it were too frightened to enter. She crawled to the entrance each day to eat, but that day she was too weak to do so. After examining the girl they discovered she was not suffering from fever but starvation. They gave her water and Foster reproached the crowd who had followed them for their neglect of the child. They in reply cried out 'We are all of us dying of the hunger'. Forster was forced to agree that 'their excuse was but too true.'

On the road from Clifden to Galway they noticed that some of the women and children 'were abject cases of poverty and almost naked.' The few rags that they had on would fall apart in a few weeks and as they were in no position to provide themselves with fresh clothes 'they must become absolutely naked.'

Up until this the people had provided their own clothing, they wove the fabric out of their own wool, or from wool bought from their neighbours. However, because of the crop failure the small sheep farmers were forced to sell their wool for food, and the people were in no position to buy wool or clothing, and so were reduced to rags.

Female members of the Society of Friends were at the time planning to set up work projects employing women in their own homes. This, Forster believed:

> will not only help to clothe the naked, but probably save the lives of many women by enabling them to earn food by labour to which they have been accustomed.[22]

Forster recommended the setting up of small depots and provisions stores throughout Connemara to cater for the population.

CHAPTER 6

THE SUMMER OF THE SOUP KITCHEN

In February 1847 the Temporary Relief Act came into operation. This allowed for the setting up of soup kitchens by the Relief Commission, for the free distribution of cooked food or soup: it was also made available for sale at 1d per quart. At the same time public works would be wound down and eventually brought to a close, leaving the people free to attend to their own plots of ground and prepare for future harvests.

The Temporary Relief Act, commonly referred to as the Soup Kitchen Act, was to be financed by the Poor Rate. However, initially, government loans would be issued on the security of the rates and in some cases grants would be given to poorer unions, such as Clifden. The soup kitchens were to be set up and administered by the local Relief Committees and were to open on

Clifden Workhouse

15 March and continue to operate until 15 August. However, for several reasons their opening was delayed and it was May before they were fully operational in the Clifden union. In the meantime the local Relief Committees continued to solicit subscriptions from individuals and charities to enable them to purchase food to feed the starving people. On 18 February Trevelyan ordered 'the first ship which can be ready to be sent to Clifden,'[1] with a cargo of barley meal and biscuits.

Large quantities of food were now coming on to the market and prices were falling, but the depressed circumstances of the people meant that they were in no position to purchase food at any price. The Roundstone Relief Committee required an eighty gallon soup boiler as it prepared to open a soup kitchen[2].

On 3 March the Clifden Committee lodged £94.16.6d in subscriptions, including a donation of £25 from Archbishop J McHale of Tuam. The list of subscribers was attached to a letter informing the Commission of the extent of misery and disease existing in the area and of the great difficulty being experienced in raising local subscriptions.[3]

Fever was on the increase and the Galway newspapers reported famine and disease running through the county, and still the Clifden Workhouse remained closed.

Opening The Workhouse

The Board of Guardians had hoped to open the workhouse on the 18 January but was having difficulty in obtaining supplies. They advertised on several occasions for tenders for the supply of provisions but received none. They asked the Commission to instruct Frederick Parker to allow them to purchase food from the government depot, but this was refused: food from the government depot was not to be sold for consumption in the workhouse.

The workhouse, with accommodation for 300 inmates, was eventually opened on 8 March 1847. A separate Fever Hospital, which accommodated 46, was opened nine days later.

Although the workhouse could accommodate 300, for the first two months it was rarely ever half full. This was because of the harsh regime that existed inside the workhouse and the fact that fever was prevalent among the inmates.

Number Of Inmates In Workhouse And Hospital from 20 March to 1 May 1847.

DATE. 1847. Week Ending	NO OF INMATES.	IN HOSPITAL	FEVER CASES	OTHER CASES	NO OF DEATHS.
March 20	132	34		34	6
March 27.	182	56		56	8
April 3.	166	82			8
April 10.	168	76	11	65	11
April 17.	151	93	16	77	15
April 24.	146	73	-	-	8
May 1.	148	89	89		3

Under the Poor Law the workhouse was financed by the Poor Rate levied on the inhabitants of the union. However, collecting rates in the Clifden union was proving difficult; between 25 March and 30 April 1847 just £25 had been collected, and now the added expense of the workhouse meant the striking of an additional rate.

Estimated Expenditure Of The Clifden Board Of Guardians Covering The Period From 27 February to 1 November 1847.

Maintenance & clothing of paupers in the Clifden union . . . . .£700.

Establishment expenses . . . .£417.

. . . . .Total: £1,117.

Amount in hands of treasurer February 27 . . . . .Nil.

Amount of rates uncollected in February 27 . . . .£653.

Deficit after rate collected (if collected) . . . .£464.

To be raised by additional rate. . . . .**£464.**[4]

Barcley Fox's Visit To The West

In March and April 1847 the west was again visited by members of the Society of Friends. Among them was R Barcley Fox who reported the group's findings to the Central Committee. The Society had made generous donations to the local Relief Committees which helped to finance soup kitchens in the area, and a store was set up at Clifden.

They found soup kitchens already established at Spiddle, Lettermore, Roundstone and Clifden. As more and more public works closed down the people's condition deteriorated. After seeing conditions in Clifden the Society agreed to contribute a quarter of the committee's needs for the following fortnight: another quarter would be raised by the committee and the remainder contributed by the government.

A meeting of the Relief Committee was taking place inside the courthouse at Clifden when they visited the town. Fox told the Society:

a crowd of emaciated and cadaverous beings followed us through the streets, crying for food. A widow, crouched at the door of the courthouse, lifted an old piece of sacking, which surrounded her group, and said, pointing at them with a wild look: 'There's my family, gentlemen!' Two young children were lying on each other, shrunk almost to skeletons, and apparently unconscious. A girl of seven or eight was huddled over a piece of smouldering turf, endeavouring to supply with warmth the absence of food.

There was also a boy of 10 or 11 dying of hunger; he died an hour or two later.

At the soup kitchen they found a one hundred gallon boiler containing just eighty gallons of half-boiled meal-porridge:

> Whilst another boiler, landed at Clifden by Edmund Richards [a member of the Society] three weeks before, was lying in the warehouse. There were large supplies of meal in the town, considerable funds remaining in the hands of the Committee, and yet the place remained thus famine-stricken. To prompt them to immediate and efficient measures of relief, we made the offer [of funds to supplement their subscriptions]. Meanwhile we ordered the erection of the second boiler without a day's delay.5

They also distributed a bag of biscuits amongst the starving crowd.

Fever On The Increases

The *Galway Vindicator* reported that fever was making rapid progress in Galway and not just among the poor:

> even among the comfortable and affluent and with fatal results...In fact the rich and poor, the priesthood and the people are rapidly falling under its desolating sway.6

On 23 April 1847, Thomas Martin of Ballynahinch Castle, after many days of illness, died of fever contacted while visiting his tenants at the Clifden Workhouse. His final words are said to have been, 'My God, what will become of my poor people!' The people of Connemara had lost a benefactor and friend.

All Martin's adult life had been lived in Connemara, except for a brief spell in the army. He was the largest property owner in Connemara, his estate covered 196,540 acres. However, earlier in the same year he had mortgaged the entire estate to pay off family debts, while at the same time the family were said to have spent very large sums of money on clothing and meal for their 'pauper stricken people, giving at the same time continuous employment to hundreds of labourers.'7

His daughter and heir Mary, along with her husband Arthur Gonne Bell, would, five years later, be forced to sell the estate to the mortgagees the Law Life Insurance Company for £180,000, a sum well below its value, a fate that would be shared with many Connemara property owners in the years that followed.

Hyacinth D'Arcy too was ill, and under the heading, 'Protestant Liberation', the *Galway Vindicator* reported that his position as Chairman of the Clifden Relief Committee was taken up by Rev Peter Fitzmaurice P.P., for Clifden. Rev Fitzmaurice was proposed and seconded as

Chairman by two 'Protestant Gentlemen'. The proposal was carried unanimously and the report continued:

> The Protestant clergyman having been present, the fact speaks volumes for the truly liberal principles of the gentlemen concerned, as well as for the kindly feelings towards one another which actuate the Protestant and Catholic clergy of this district.[8]

Dealing with the extraordinary circumstances presented to them at this time did bring the community closer together. However, the 'kindly feelings' would be severely tested in the coming years with the arrival of the Irish Church Mission and their proselytizing activities throughout the region.

Ballynakill Soup Boiler now at St Thomas' Church Moyard

Large Numbers Attend Soup Kitchens

Under the Temporary Relief Act each person over the age of nine had to collect his/her own ration at the soup kitchen, excluding the sick and infirm. They stood in line with their bowl or pot, waiting their turn. The people found the system degrading and resented it greatly, and yet, in the summer months of 1847, between two and three million people lined up daily throughout the country to receive their soup or stirabout. Connemara was no exception.

In the Clifden union, 8,846 free rations were issued on 8 May.[9] This figure had almost doubled one month later to 16,549 on 5 June[10]; just under half the population of the union was receiving free rations. One month later, on 3 July, the figure had jumped to 24,403.[11] However, by 31 July the number was beginning to fall, at 18,793[12] and by 28 August it was down to 7,972.[13]

However, despite the large numbers receiving free rations, deaths from starvation continued to increase. On 17 June, the Magistrates of the area wrote to the Lord Lieutenant:

Deaths amongst the peasantry are fearfully numerous, caused from absolute present want or long spells without sufficient food.[14]

The bringing together of large numbers at the soup kitchens was also facilitating the spread of fever. A temporary hospital, with accommodation for 25 patients, was opened in Ballindoon on 22 July 1847; it employed two nurses and one ward maid, and on 12 August a dispensary was opened in Roundstone.[15]

Because of the severe distress in the union the Relief Committees were instructed that the closing date for the soup kitchens was to be extended to 12 September.[16] It was hoped that by then the potato crop would be ready for harvesting and that conditions would have eased in the country.

However, reports coming in from all districts in the union told a different story. The potato crop that year showed no sign of blight, but the small quantity sown would be insufficient to feed the people.

Land Left Untilled

As early as February reports were reaching the authorities of the lack of preparation being carried out on the land throughout the union. Working on the roads was keeping the people from their farms and the land was left unattended. Many were too weak to till the land, while others had thrown up their lands but remained on in their houses, believing that public works or government food would support them in the future.[17]

The farmers and landlords were without cash and in no position to hire labourers, with the result that large sections of land were left untilled. Henry Blake of Renvyle put the problem to the Chief Secretary, Henry Labouchere:

There is no rent to be expected from our lands and no labour instead of rent is permitted; when therefore there are no other funds...the lands occupied by the landowners will remain insufficiently tilled and it will become problematical whether they will ever reap their harvest.[18]

In April Thomas Scully, the Receiver appointed to the D'Arcy Estates, purchased barley and oats seed to the sum of £278.17.2d for distribution among the tenants of the Clifden Estate on the basis of an 'IOU' from the tenants. The seed, however, was 'foreign' and appeared to be unsuitable for the soil and 'generally produced a bad crop' leaving the tenants in even more difficulty and debt.

On the recommendation of the Receiver a portion of the rent arrears due by the tenants on the estate was struck off[a]. It was felt that this move would encourage many tenants to set about improving their holdings, while many others could be induced to give up their holdings. These could then be amalgamated and larger divisions given to a 'better class' of tenant.[19]

Employment on the roads was also keeping the fishermen from the sea. The Commissioners of Public Works reported in April that the fishermen in Roundstone were reluctent to leave the public works and the certanty of pay and return to the 'more laborious business of the fisheries'. To force the fishermen back on the sea the Board 'obtained a list of such boat owners as had boats fit to go to sea,' and directed that those should not receive employment on the public works. Following this the supply of fish to the station improved but would remain irregular.[20]

The Relief Committee had done all it could to encourage the people to cultivate the land but seeds were expensive and difficult to obtain, and so little had been sown. The result was that in Connemara, out of an area of 191,426 acres, only 5,500 were under seed.

In June the Magistrates from the locality warned the Lord Lieutenant that the growing crop of potatoes would not be sufficient to feed the population for more than four months. Rents were falling due, but the landlords did not feel they could take part of this crop as payment. For many, payment of part rates was also due and the people did not have the money to pay, 'such was the extent of the distress of the area.'[21]

However, despite the efforts of the Magistrates and the Committee to acquaint the authorities with conditions on the ground, the government was insistent that every effort be made to collect the Poor Rate throughout the union.

[a] A schedule of tenants, townlands and arrears struck off was drawn up on 30 May 1847, see Appendix 1.

CHAPTER 7

COLLECTING THE POOR RATE

Once again new measures for dealing with relief of the distressed were introduced in 1847 with the passing of the Irish Poor Law Extension Act and the Amendment Act in June and July of that year. Under these Acts food depots and soup kitchens were to close and the burden of relieving the distress was to shift to the ratepayers. From now on the Board of Guardians, aided by the Poor Law Commission, would be responsible for the distress in their own area and all relief measures would be financed entirely by the Poor Rate.

Under the Amendment Act, relief, outside of the workhouse, was to be issued to the aged, infirm, the sick, orphans and destitute widows. Strict control was to be kept on the administration of outdoor relief as it was felt that in the past, under the Labour Rate Act and the Temporary Relief Act, relief had been given to some not utterly destitute.

Outdoor relief was to be in food, preferably cooked, and only issued when the workhouse was full. Destitute able-bodied were to be accommodated in the workhouse; it was considered that the harsh regime practised there would be a test of their destitution. The able-bodied qualified for outdoor relief only when the workhouse was full and no other accommodation could be found for them. They had to be unemployed, with no member of their family employed, and they were set to work for eight hours of each day.

Under the Quarter Acre Clause in the Amendment Act, any person occupying more than a quarter of an acre of land was not entitled to relief. This clause had the effect of forcing people to throw up their holdings in order to qualify for relief. Much of this land given back to the landlord was left to waste, so as not to be liable for rates in the future.

Another clause in the Act left the landlord, and not the occupier, liable for the poor rate on all holdings valued at under £4. Subdivision had left the Clifden union with many holdings under £4 valuation and rates due on these holdings now became the responsibility of the already financially embarrassed landlords.

Along with the cost of the day to day expense of relieving the distress within the union, repayments due on loans received for previous relief measures and for the construction and furnishing of the workhouse, were also expected to be paid out of the rates. This placed a huge burden on the ratepayers of the union, and in Clifden, as in many other unions in the west, rates were proving difficult to collect: in the three months leading up to the end of May '47, out of an annual net value of £22,426, only £129 rates had been collected. The union was being maintained by government loans: Clifden, up to 14 August, had been granted loans totalling £7,352.[1]

The landlords declared that they were unable to collect rent and therefore in no position to pay rates. Many were already in severe financial difficulty and the two largest in the district, the D'Arcy and Martin estates, were bankrupt.

Recognizing that some unions in the west were unable to function without external financial assistance, the government declared twenty-two unions as 'distressed'. Clifden was recognized as one of the 'distressed' unions.

As the rate was to be the source of finance for the union, and aid would not be extended to the 'distressed' unions until every effort to collect had been made, its collection was vital if the union was to function effectively. Therefore any opposition to its collection was quickly brought to the attention of Dublin Castle and the Poor Law Commission by the guardians and Resident Magistrate. At the same time the small farmers were close to despair and many resorted to violence as they watched their few remaining livestock and crops being seized for rates.

Attacks on Poor Rate Collectors

The Poor Rate Collectors for the four Electoral Divisions in the union were: Joseph McDonnell for Renvyle, John Flynn for Ballindoon, John Lydon for Roundstone and Francis Mullin for Clifden.

In May Joseph McDonnell seized cattle in lieu of poor rate in the Renvyle district, only to have them forcibly retrieved by their owners; John Turny, John Cosgrave, Terence Sweeney and Pat Flaherty. Forced to leave the area empty-handed, McDonnell had the four men brought before the Magistrates at the next Quarter Sessions. However, at the trial the men were told to return home and pay their rates before the next Quarter Sessions in October.[2]

After this lenient decision by the Bench, most of whom were themselves in debt for rates, the collectors met opposition and in many cases violent resistance when they attempted to collect rates in the months that followed.

On 15 June John Lydon made a seizure of cattle on the property of Robert Barry in the district of Carna. Barry, aided by his wife, son and neighbours, rescued the cattle and forced Lydon to abandon his efforts. Lydon continued to another townland but once again was forced to retreat when threatened: he was told by the people that they were prepared to lose their own lives and 'take the life of any collector who would attempt to distrain them.'

As a result of this threat Lydon applied to John Dopping, the Resident Magistrate, for police protection, which he felt was needed if he was to carry out his duty successfully:

> I therefore believe that my life would be in danger if I were to go there again and have no doubt but that I should not only be unable to impound any of the cattle in that neighbourhood but that I and my

assistant would be attacked and perhaps killed if we endeavoured to do so without a strong police or military force...no less than 70 to 80 armed men could with safety collect the rates in that remote district.[3]

Also meeting considerable resistance was John Flynn who admitted, 'I am forced to carry arms whilst executing my duty and should not be safe without them.'

On 10 September Flynn and his five bailiffs came under attack when trying to seize a horse, the property of Eoin O'Connell, in the townland of Doonloughan[b]. He called to Michael O'Malley, a native of the area, who had in the past acted as his bailiff, to come to his rescue. O'Malley helped to get him out of the area but both he and his wife, Margaret, were later attacked and beaten by his neighbours for coming to the aid of the collector. O'Malley was left with a large cut on his nose and Margaret's left arm was fractured and her hand bruised and discoloured, her left hip was also injured.[4]

As a result of these attacks John Dopping R.M., was instructed by Dublin Castle to provide police protection for the collectors when he felt it justified. But Dopping, it would seem, had little regard for the rate collectors and drew the Lord Lieutenant's attention to the extra high charges demanded by the rate collectors in the Clifden union, 'in cases in which it had been necessary to enforce payment of the Rate'.[5]

He appears to have been reluctant to supply police protection until the collector had first made an attempt to collect the rate accompanied only by his bailiffs. The collectors complained to Dublin Castle of Dopping's slowness to comply with government guidelines. Joseph McDonnell, who had been threatened by several people in the presence of Dopping when it was openly stated that unless he had police protection 'they would break his skull',[6] complained when he was refused protection in collecting rates in Renvyle. Dopping told him he must first make an attempt at collection.

McDonnell made the attempt two to three days later, accompanied by six men provided by Henry Blake of Renvyle, some of whom were armed. They were attacked and pelted with stones, receiving cuts to the face and blows to the body. McDonnell went back to Dopping who issued summonses against the assailants to appear at the next Petty Sessions.

Following this incident the Board of Guardians requested that the company of military about to be removed from the district be replaced by another company to assist in the collection of the Poor Rate. But the Poor Law Inspector, Joseph Burke, was of the opinion that the assistance of the police would be sufficient.[7]

John Lydon went to Innishnee on 30 November and seized some cows of Michael Conneely. But Conneely and his wife Mary, with the help of two women, 'got before the cows with sticks and forcibly rescued the cattle from me'.

[b]The following residence of Doonloughan are listed in John Flynn's sworn statement: Eoin O'Connelly , his wife Mary, daughters Margaret and Honor, his son and wife Michael and Mary, Pat Reilly Snr and his wife Mary and daughter Mary, and Pat Reilly Jnr, Richard Reilly, Michael Reilly, Michael Folan, Ellen Maley wife of Pat Maley, her son Val Connolly and daughter Ann Cahill. John Gahan of Pollrevagh and his wife Bridget.

On 3 December, Lydon intended to seize a cow on lands at Murvey but was prevented by Bryan McDonagh who 'brought a hatchet out of his house and went before the cow and said he would not let any cow be taken by me.'[8]

Resistance at Leitheanach Mór, Moyrus

On Monday 10 January 1848 the Head Constable at Roundstone, William Wilks, with four sub-constables, proceeded to the townland of Leitheanach Mór to protect John Lydon and his bailiffs. Lydon and his men seized three cows. However, immediately the people assembled and 'endeavoured to rescue them by force and violence.' Constable Wilks ordered his men to load and fix bayonets and cautioned the people 'against attempting to persist in resisting', but without effect.

Wilks succeeded in moving Lydon, his party and the cattle a little further along the road, but they met with resistance again with the arrival of more supporters. The crowd made a rush at the collectors and began throwing stones; Constable Wilks was struck on the hand which held his sword and Sub-Constable Bennett was struck in the leg.

In the confusion that followed Wilks was also struck in the hand by the point of a bayonet belonging to one of his own men. One of the drivers, Michael King, was 'dangerously wounded in the head by two stones.' Bennett had his bayonet taken from him by one of the crowd, Michael Mulkerrin; it was pointing directly at him at the time, but he returned it almost immediately.

As the crowd continued in their attempt to rescue the cattle, Constable Wilks then ordered the two men next to him, Constables Hanly and Corkern, to fire. Still the people persisted, declaring that they 'would sooner die than allow their cattle to be taken away.'[9] They eventually succeeded in retrieving the cattle and lead them away. Wilks then recommended to Lydon to retire.

When reports of the incident reached Dublin Castle Lieut-Colonel William Miller, Deputy Inspector-General of the Irish Constabulary, regarded the matter as 'a very serious outrage'. He criticized John Dopping for not sending adequate protection with Lydon and for not being present himself:

> If the two policemen who were ordered to fire had done their duty, wounds must have been inflicted upon some of the assailants who were pressing upon the party.

This would have brought the matter to a more satisfactory conclusion, in the opinion of Lieut-Colonel Miller.

Dopping in reply stated that he had ordered a head constable and eight policemen to attend, double the number eventually used, and, had he anticipated the resistance, he would have attended himself. However, from his experience:

> of the easily-subdued disposition of the population of this district, I considered that force, acting with judgment, determination...quite sufficient to protect the poor rate collector under the circumstances detailed in the sworn information.[10]

Dopping received the following curt reply:

> I am directed by the Lord Lieutenant to state that you should give your attendance with the constabulary when employed in aiding the collection of poor rates.[11]

Dopping felt he was unjustly reprimanded and tried to justify his decision with the following comment:

> The duties of the police in this district have of late become so extremely arduous that I have felt unwilling to impose on them any labour which I might have thought unnecessary - I shall however in future take care that a large force shall attend on all similar occasions and shall myself act in accordance to the instructions I have had the honour to receive.[12]

Later that month the case came before the Roundstone Petty Sessions. J B Kernan, Resident Magistrate for Galway, was requested to attend. The evidence of the police was taken and the accused: Michael Mulkerrin, John Hart, John Faherty, Thady McDonagh, John O'Loughlin, John King, Mary O'Loughlin, Patrick McDonagh and Honor Faherty, were instructed to appear at the next sessions.

During the hearing the police seemed anxious to minimise the damage resulting from the incident. Head Constable William Wilks stated that in his five years as Head Constable of the Roundstone police station he was never previously been obstructed in the discharge of his duties. He stressed that the crowd carried no weapons, just sticks and stones.

Constable Bennett seemed to be justifying Michael Mulkerrin's behaviour in taking his bayonet when he stated that the bayonet was pointing directly at him at the time:

> I think it was fear of being stabbed that made Mulkerrin take my bayonet.[13]

The opposition given to the police and collectors on this occasion was due to some confusion among the tenants as to whether they were liable for rates. However, the tenants had now paid the rates and so John Lydon declined to prosecute.

J B Kernan R.M., stated, in his report on the Petty Sessions, that he did not anticipate any further interference with the rate collector in the discharge of his duty in that part of Connemara and felt that locating a police force at Leitheanach Mór, which was under consideration by Dublin Castle, would be unnecessary.

After receiving Kernan's report, which vindicated John Dopping, it was decided that Sub-Inspector Ireland, and not Dopping, was responsible for the small number of constabulary present on the day.

Collecting Rent

Collecting rent too was met with resistance. Thomas Davis, a driver and deputy agent for Lord Ffrench, accompanied by six men went to the townland of Tooreen, in the parish of Ballynakill, on 16 November 1847 to seize six head of cattle in lieu of rent. The men were on the way to the pound with the cattle when they were stopped by a group of about forty. A stone was throne which struck Davis on the head and cut him above the eyes and the crowd called to him that:

> if I or any of my assistants took a beast to the pound, they would have our lives - I was then obliged to give up the cattle.

He went next to Sheeauns and seized two head of cattle there, but a crowd of about sixty, carrying sticks and stones, immediately surrounded them and took the cattle by force. They threatened to take the lives of Davis and his men if they should again attempt to distrain.

Davis was armed with a gun and one of the group, John Toole, tried to take it from him. In the struggle the ram rod was pulled out of the gun and some of the crowd tried to wrench it free from his grip.

Davis, in his sworn statement before John Dopping, which was later passed on to the under-secretary at Dublin Castle, stated that he was a native of the area:

> well acquainted with the habits and feelings of the people, and I firm-ly believe that my life or that of any other person would not be safe if we proceeded to enforce the payment of rents without being under protection.[14]

Francis Graham, a neighbouring landlord, was worried that:

> the example will be most injurious in this neighbourhood unless some strong and prompt measures are adopted...I hope something can be done at once to assist Davis to collect the rents on Lord Ffrenche's estate, as if not every tenant in this county will...refuse to pay any rents.[15]

The offenders were summoned to appear at the next Petty Sessions. Dopping was informed by Dublin Castle that protection was to be given to Davis and other similar cases when he felt the circumstances warranted protection.

Clifden Union:—Ballindoon Electoral Division.

RETURN of POOR RATE uncollected, made by Mr. FRANCIS MULLIN, Collector for the above Division, this 29th day of January, 1848.

No. in Rate Book.	Street or Place, or Name of Property rated.	Persons from whom the Rate is due.	Amount of Rate due.			Observations as to cause of Non-Collection, &c.
			Due for last Rate made.	Arrears of previous Rate due.	Total.	
			£. s. d.	£. s. d.	£. s. d.	
	Bunnowen and Errismore.	John A. O'Neill, Esq., ex-officio Guardian.	..	Due.	189 11 7	Proceedings taken already for 40l. of this amount.
	Errislanen . .	Anthony Morris . . .	..	Due.	11 4 4	Noticed fifteen days; not expired.
	Errismore . .	Martin O'Maley , . .	..	Due.	20 3 4	Application made; will be paid.
	Manin Errismore	Michael P. Browne . .	..	Due.	26 14 8	Application made; will be paid.
	Derrigiarla . .	A. B. Martin, Esq., ex-officio Guardian.	..	Due.	27 7 5	Noticed fifteen days; not expired.
	Errislanen . .	John Lambert . . .	..	..	35 0 0	Property in Chancery. Board have ordered proceedings.
		Total . . .	..	..	310 1 4	

(Signed) FRANCIS MULLIN, *P. R. Collector.*

Clifden Union:—Clifden Electoral Division.

RETURN of POOR RATE uncollected, made by Mr. FRANCIS MULLIN, Collector for the above Division, this 29th day of January, 1848.

No. in Rate Book.	Street or Place, or Name of Property rated.	Persons from whom the Rate is due.	Amount of Rate due.			Observations as to cause of Non-Collection, &c.
			Due for last Rate made.	Arrears of previous Rate due.	Total.	
			£. s. d.	£. s. d.	£. s. d.	
	Clifden . . .	Hyacinth D'Arcy, Esq. .	..	..	73 11 8	This property is in Chancery. Application made to agent of receiver. Reported by me to Board of Guardians. No order made.
	Coolacly . .	John D'Arcy, P.L.G. .	..	..	6 1 8½	Noticed fifteen days; not expired.
	Kingstown Glebe	Rev. Mr. Thomas . .	..	..	7 17 6	Application made; will soon be paid.
	Cliflen . . .	Mr. Wm. Corbett, P.L.G.	..	..	4 11 8	Noticed six days.
	Clifden tolls and customs . .	John Mullin, and John Corbett.	..	..	8 1 6	Noticed six days.
	Cushatrough .	John Davis	..	..	3 12 5	Noticed six days.
	Cruckbrack . .	Mr. Kearns	..	..	2 2 0	
	Clifden . . .	James D'Arcy, Esq. .	..	..	5 16 9	Application made; promised that he would pay.
	Clifden . . .	Henry Kearney . . .	..	..	2 0 10	
		Total	..	..	113 16 0½	

(Signed). FRANCIS MULLIN, *P. R. Collector.*

Poor Rate Uncollected 29 January 1848
Relief of distress fifth series, 1848 [919] lv

RETURN of POOR RATE uncollected, made by Mr. JOSEPH M'DONNELL, Collector for the above Division, this 29th day of January, 1848.

No. in Rate Book.	Street or Place, or Name of Property rated.	Persons from whom the Rate is due.	Amount of Rate due.			Observations as to cause of Non-Collection, &c.
			Due for last Rate made.	Arrears of previous Rate due.	Total.	
			£. s. d.	£. s. d.	£. s. d.	
	Renvyle . . .	Henry Blake, Esq., ex-officio.	..	..	48 14 2	Noticed fifteen days 25th.
	Salruck . . .	General Alex. Thomson, ex-officio.	..	..	42 1 10	Promised to pay me on this day, 29th January, 1848.
	Kylemore . .	Sir George Beresford .	..	..	13 1 0	Made no application.
	Ballinakill . .	Hon. Martin French .	..	..	8 14 7	Reported to Board.
	Cluggan . .	A. B. Martin, Esq., ex-officio.	..	..	6 7 2	Application made. To be served with fifteen days' notice.
	Ballinakill . .	Lady French . . .	..	..	12 7 8	Reported to Board.
	Ballinakill . .	Thomas Coneys . .	..	..	3 10 6	Noticed fifteen days, 28th.
	Davris . . .	Pat Gorham, P.L.G. .	..	..	4 17 2	Noticed fifteen days.
	Cluggan . .	Walter Coneys, P.L.G.	..	..	2 14 0	Promised to pay this day, 29th January, 1848.
	Ballinakill . .	Robert Graham, Esq., ex-officio.	..	..	10 3 4	Application made.
	Ballinakill . .	Matthias Burke, P.L.G.	..	..	3 6 0	Promised to pay this day, 29th January.
		Total . . .	..	..	155 17 7	

(Signed)   JOSEPH M'DONNELL, *P. R. Collector.*

Clifden Union :—Roundstone Electoral Division.

RETURN of POOR RATE uncollected, made by Mr. LYDEN, Collector for the above Division, this 29th day of January, 1848.

No. in Rate Book.	Street or Place, or Name of Property rated.	Persons from whom the Rate is due.	Amount of Rate due.			Observations as to cause of Non-Collection, &c.
			Due for last Rate made.	Arrears of previous Rate due.	Total.	
			£. s. d.	£. s. d.	£. s. d.	
	Ballinahinch .	Miss Martin. Husband an ex-officio Guardian.	..	..	194 1 6	Noticed ; fifteen days' notice served on 20th.
	Bunnowen . .	John A. O'Neill, Esq., ex-officio Guardian	..	Due.	9 16 4	No application made.
	Clifden Castle .	Hyacinth D'Arcy, Esq., ex-officio Guardian.	..	Due.	23 8 11	No written application.
	Faul . . .	J. D'Arcy, Esq., solicitor	..	Due,	1 13 4	No written application.
	Killewongaul .	Patrick D'Arcy, Esq. .	..	Due.	3 4 0	Application made. To be paid on Monday.
	Inisnee . .	Pat Blake, Esq. . .	..	Due.	38 0 10	No written application.
	Gowlane . .	Edward Lynch . .	..	..	6 16 9	Application made.
	Cool-park . .	Gregory of Coole . .	..	Due.	3 0 0	No application.
	Errisanagh .	Waste Land Company .	..	..	32 15 9	Application made; will be paid.
	Glendalough .	David Lucas, Esq. . .	..	..	10 19 0	Application made a week since.
	Innistrover .	Martin O'Maley, Esq. .	..	Due.	6 16 9	} Application made.
	Croonecorra	Ditto . . .	..	Due.	2 2 7	
		Michael Browne, Esq. .	..	Due.	4 5 2	Never inquired who he is.
	Carna . . .	John Barry . . .	..	Due.	6 12 0	
	Ditto . . .	Robert Barry . . .	..	..	5 14 7	} Served with fifteen days' notice, but never proceeded further.
	Ditto . . .	Thomas Barry . . .	..	Due.	10 3 7	
	Ditto . . .	Anthony Barry . . .	..	Due.	6 4 8	
	Moyrus . .	John and Wm. Lyden .	..	..	21 1 6	Noticed fifteen days; not expired.
	Meenish . .	John Nolan, Esq. . .	..	Due.	47 6 1	19th made application to agent.
	Lettuard . .	Bidelia M'Donough .	..	..	24 8 4	Noticed fifteen days on 20th inst.
	Ervillagh . .	Matt. Duane. . . .	..	Due.	4 10 8	Fifteen days' notice not expired.
	Roundstone .	John King Stephen . .	..	..	3 16 10	Noticed fifteen days on the 21st.
	Errisbeg .	James Ogle, Esq. . .	..	..	8 15 10	Returned name to Board.
		Total . . .	..	..	500 1 6	

(Signed)   JOHN LYDEN, *Collector.*

CHAPTER 8

UNION IN DEBT

By Autumn 1847 the Board of Guardians was in financial difficulty, the small sums raised through the Poor Rate along with the loans received from the Treasury not being sufficient to cover the cost of supplying indoor and outdoor relief. The British Relief Association, a charitable organization set up in England, issued funds through the Poor Law Commissioner to assist Clifden, along with twenty-one other 'distressed' unions along the west coast. A Temporary Inspector, John C. Deane, was appointed to the union on 25 October to assist in the distribution of the funds and to ensure that strenuous efforts to collect rates would continue.

On 1 November Deane attended his first meeting of the Board of Guardians. The venue for the weekly Board meetings had been moved to the courthouse. The members refused to meet at the workhouse because of the prevalence of fever among the inmates there. The Chairman of the Board, Hyacinth D'Arcy, was absent, being again unwell.

Deane tried to 'impress on the members present the absolute importance and necessity of proceeding to the immediate collection of the rates.' Part of the old rate was still outstanding and the new rate was now due for collection. The Board was under pressure from local dealers and tradesmen to pay the monies owing to them for goods supplied to the workhouse, but the union treasurer had just £19.9.2d at his disposal:

> The debts due by the Guardians in the immediate neighbourhood, and in the town of Clifden, are about £260; this sum is due among forty creditors, who are taking every advantage of the necessities of the Board, and are charging at an exorbitant rate for the goods they supply.[1]

Under John Deane's direction the Board solicitor started legal proceedings against defaulting ratepayers and most responded shortly after receiving his first demand. By the end of November the rate collection for the month amounted to £300, a sizable improvement on the £37 collected in the previous month,[2] and the Guardians were 'gradually paying off their liabilities.'

Because of the high prices charged by the suppliers, Deane suggested that, to encourage keener pricing among the suppliers, purchases should be made with ready cash. The Poor Law Commission disagreed, pointing out to Deane that under the 17th article of the General Regulations of the Commissioners all 'supplies of provisions and necessaries for the workhouse should be procured by contract'.[3]

Up until this the Bank of Ireland branch in Galway had acted as the union's treasurer. However, the distance of fifty miles between it and the Board was proving inconvenient. The Board was anxious to appoint a local treasurer and Dr William Suffield was appointed to the post on 22 November[4] at a salary of £30 per annum.

Three Relieving Officers were also appointed: Pat Joyce, Thomas Cooke and Henry Kearney. These officers were to assess the conditions of the people and list the names of those who qualified for relief. They had the power to issue 'immediate and temporary relief in cases of sudden and urgent necessity, either by admission to the workhouse or fever hospital, or out of the workhouse in food, lodgings, medicine and medical attendance.'[5] Given the conditions of the country at the time it was a powerful position to hold, and one open to abuse. It carried a salary of £35 per annum plus rations.

To acquaint himself with the union, Deane toured the region and found that in parts 'the most abject poverty and distress appear to exist'. A very small amount of agricultural produce and live stock was to be seen on the farms of the small farmers. It was his belief that the cows and sheep were still at the mountain pastures and would remain there until brought to market. This seems unlikely, however, given the lateness in the year. Still, Deane told the Commission that:

> the apparent poverty of a man (whose house may, perhaps, contain nothing but a few miserable articles of furniture) is by no means a safe criterion to judge of his available resources to meet legitimate demands.

And although he anticipated future difficulties in collecting rates from these small farmers, he felt that with the full use of the law 'all difficulties can be overcome'.

There were, however, other sections of the union, particularly in the Renvyle electoral division, where some farmers' 'untiring and zealous exertions, turned the piece of the wild district where they have located themselves, into cultivation.' Messrs. Eastwood, Butler, Pim and Dancer, 'with some others who held leases for ever under a Mr Graham,' were endeavouring to improve their holdings and give employment under the Land Improvement Act.

Francis Graham had received, to within £10, his entire rent of £1,025 which fell due in May: 'His tenantry have interests in their farms, and are contented and industrious.'[6]

Along the coast Dean found that fishing was all but abandoned:

> Boats are lying useless and unemployed, and in vain can one seek for a satisfactory explanation for the indolence and apathy of the fishermen, who, indeed, can scarcely be called such, applying themselves but periodically to this pursuit, and only at a time when the fish absolutely swarm their bays. Half fishermen, half agriculturist, they neglect both occupations.[7]

Later in the month this scene had changed and Deane reported:

> the supply of fish is most abundant on the coast...I myself witnessed some men bringing down their nets from the mountains to the sea coast, to catch the swarms of herrings in the bay. This is a step in the right direction, and holds out some hope for the future.[8]

Workhouse Conditions

Deane next turned his attention to the workhouse, which he found to be in

> a very unsatisfactory condition. Fever is raging among the inmates, and, I fear, until accommodation be supplied for fever patients apart from the workhouse, neither cleanliness, order, or regularity can be insured.

The master and matron were incapable of taking charge and running the house properly. The fact that the Guardians no longer met at the workhouse meant that it did not receive regular inspection, 'so necessary for its proper management.' They refused to appoint a visiting committee until the fever and dysentery was brought under control.

The workhouse was full to capacity with 300 inmates and 45 patients in the hospital. Deane's report to the commissioners was backed up by a letter from Francis Bodkin, Apothecary and medical officer for the workhouse, stressing the need for a temporary fever hospital to contain contagious diseases and prevent them spreading among the inmates, whose 'vital energies and spirits (were) so much depressed, by starvation and wretchedness.'[9] A week later Deane reported to the Commission that there were 45 cases of fever in the workhouse and fever was on the increase in the union. He feared 'a fatal spread of it during the approaching winter.'[10]

A permanent fever hospital was planned for construction in the spring and a sum of £600 allocated for the job. In the meantime the Guardians requested permission to establish a temporary hospital; a vacant National schoolhouse in the town was recommended by Deane, but it would take some months and a good deal of correspondence between the Board and the Commission before the hospital came into use.

There was already a fever hospital in operation in the Ballindoon electoral division, but the Board of Guardians was trying to shut it down. The medical officer there, however, was refusing to comply. Dr Robert John Morgan reported the Board's actions to the Central Board of Health and, supported by John Deane, he forced the Guardians to extend sufficient funds to retain it.

As predicted by Deane, the number of fever cases began to increase and conditions inside the workhouse continued to deteriorate. On Christmas day 1847 he reported to the Commissioners the terrible conditions endured by the inmates:

The inmates of the house are crowded together in a day-room, breathing a tainted atmosphere; there is an insufficient supply of bedding and clothing. The rain pours down through the ventilating turrets into the rooms, and the paupers are thus subjected to increased liability of infection...Directions have been given to provide increased accommodation, such as can be obtained. The contractor has been directed to supply additional bedding. A minute appears on the proceedings of the Guardians directing advertisements to be issued for tenders for the keeping in repair the house according to the printed specifications furnished to me. All this has been formally done, and yet I can tell the Commissioners from the experience I have obtained since my residence here, that it will be no easy matter to determine when these orders shall be completed. The contractor for clothing must be paid a portion of his debt before he gives any additional credit. The slatier, carpenter, mason etc., will urge the state of the weather as being against their respective operations; and while this delay is being experienced, pestilence rages among the wretched inmates...On visiting the house a few days ago, I was disgusted at learning that the dormitories (particularly those appropriated for children) are not supplied with night buckets. I forbear to describe the abominations consequent to this. The buckets had been long since ordered by the Guardians; but the idle laziness of the tradesmen occasioned a delay in the execution of the order, and the result was as I have stated. Now setting aside that the Guardians have no visiting committee, and bearing in mind that they had actually ordered these articles, and had also directed their contractor to supply bedding, and had issued advertisements for tenders, I cannot attach blame to them, since my official connection with their Board. And the Commissioners will, I trust, agree with me, that the difficulties I have to meet are associated with, and almost inseparable from, the locality in which the workhouse is placed in the Union; so distant as it is from towns where the Guardians could supply themselves with materials, and contractors for executing necessary works.

I regret to state that Dr Bodkin's brother, who accompanied him to the workhouse hospital about a week since, for the purpose of assisting him in his medical duties, died to-day, of malignant typhus fever. I mention this fact, with the view of assuring the Commissioners that I shall now find it still more difficult to induce the Guardians to visit the house.

Within the last week the weather has been most inclement, and has brought with it a vast increase of disease and misery.[11]

As conditions worsened, and the numbers of able-bodied seeking entry to the workhouse increased, two thatched cottages close to the workhouse were rented as temporary accommodation. Outdoor relief was offered to the permanently disabled and widows with two or more children and under this provision 200 inmates were removed from the workhouse but these places were quickly taken up by the able-bodied.[12]

Many of the old and the infirm had already abandoned their homes and thrown up their lands in order to qualify for entry into the workhouse. This left them with nothing to return to, and so many were forced to exchange a portion of their food rations for a space in the already crowd-ed tenements in the town, or to move into caves in the hills nearby.

In the Autumn of 1847 James A Tuke, a member of the Society of Friends, toured Connemara and reported that the Clifden union was bankrupt and 'a few days previous to my visit the wretched inmates of the poor-house had been expelled and the doors closed.'[13] This was not entirely correct; the union was in serious financial difficulty but it was still functioning.

He was, perhaps, referring to 15 persons discharged from the workhouse on 20 December; disqualified under the quarter-acre clause on 'information received from the relieving officers',[14] or maybe the 200 inmates mentioned above, when he describes inmates being forced to take 'up their abode in holes or cavities in a hill side' outside the town: 'Their sunken faces and wasted forms told too clearly the tale of hunger and privation.'

Tuke had been told that:

one inspector of roads had caused no less than 140 bodies to be buried, which he found scattered along the highway. In some cases, it is well known, that where all other members of a family have perished, the last survivor has earthed up the door of his miserable cabin, to prevent the ingress of pigs and dogs, and then laid himself down to die in this fearful family vault.

He criticized the poverty and ignorance of those elected to the office of guardians in Connaught which added to the difficulties in 'carrying out the provisions of the new Poor-Law' in the province.[15]

Relief For Children

A grant from the British Relief Association was issued to each of the `distressed' unions to finance relief for children. The relief was to be distributed to the children through the schools. Count Strzelecki, who acted as agent for the Association in Ireland, requested information from John Deane on the number of schools and pupils in the Clifden union. There were, however, very few schools in operation in the Clifden union.

Church leaders of all denominations seemed to prefer denominational schools and so were reluctant to participate in the National School system. Archbishop John MacHale, the Catholic Archbishop of Tuam, an advocate of denominational education, objected to the system set up under the National Education Board, established in 1831, of educating Catholics and Protestants together. The result was that the state National School system was virtually ignored in his diocese. Some private schools were available but for the most part there existed 'the most lamentable and culpable neglect of education in this extensive district.'

As a result, it would be difficult to extend this relief to the children in the Clifden union although their need was obvious:

> The condition of the children of the peasantry is very lamentable; their haggard looks painfully tell what insufficiency of food and want of clothing have brought them to.

In response to the Count's request, Deane investigated the schools in the union and reported his findings to the Count and to the Commissioners:

> In the electoral division of Renvyle, containing a population of over 7000, I found but two schools; in one there were 47 scholars, male and female, in another, none on that day, and, as I was informed, the aver-age attendance 12! In Clifden electoral division, two of the schools are unoccupied, and the houses are in wretched repair.

The schoolmaster of the Cleggan school was receiving a full salary, although there were no scholars to teach.

In Ballinafad the schoolhouse was empty. The only school in the entire union with a regular attendance of pupils was at Roundstone, where the monks, with the support of the Society of Friends, were feeding the children.

John Deane immediately set about organising the relief, which was to be given in food to the children attending the schools and to adults employed 'in manufacturing frieze and flannel for the children.'[16]

In early December two schools in the neighbourhood of Clifden began distributing the food. In these 400 children were being fed daily. Once it became known that food would be issued to all children attending schools the number of attendants increased dramatically. On 28 January 1848 Deane was able to report to Count Strzelecki that he was feeding about 2,000 children throughout the union. Some children left the work-house to attend the schools, easing the pressure on numbers there.[17]

The rations for each child consisted of '10 ounces of bread (a mixture of three parts rye and one part Indian meal), with a half pint of meat soup, and fish soup on fast days.' The older children prepared the soup themselves. 'The female children are employed in making shirts...At one school, at the head of the little Killaries Bay (Salruck), which is under the guidance of Major-General Thomson, the boys are employed in making nets'. With the funds at his disposal Deane was able to employ 160 women, spinning wool for flannel, and others as weavers and tailors and the clothes were distributed among the people.

The effects of regular feeding were soon visible on the children and in January Deane wrote to Count Strzelecki:

> Since the food has been given to the children their appearance has been wonderfully changed - on my arrival here I found the greater part of them emaciated and wretched, they are now showing the effects, in improved health, of the wholesome food so benevolently provided for them.[18]

Between November 1847 and 30 April 1848 the number of children receiving relief under the British Relief Association scheme amounted to 4,698, with 527,723 rations issued through the schools. The denominations of the schools and the number of children attending were as follows: National 516, Established Church 1,174, Dissenter 440, Catholic 2,568.[19]

However, this source of relief ceased on 20 August 1848 when the British Relief Association wound down their operation in Ireland.[20]

Guardians Declared Incompetent

Fever was everywhere in the workhouse, in the general wards as well as in the fever wards. It was also to be found in every part of the union and the number of deaths was rising. The Board was having difficulty administering the union and was relying more and more on John Deane taking up that responsibility.

On 30 December Deane offered to travel to Dublin to lay before the Commission the conditions of the union but was advised by the Commissioners not to leave the district, where his presence was 'so much required.' The Commissioners felt that 'they could only impress upon' Deane and the Guardians to continue with their efforts 'for affording relief to the destitute poor of the Clifden union, and for the collection of sufficient rates for that purpose.' However, the Commissioners suggested that, if in his opinion the Board members were not carrying out their responsibilities under the 'Act for Relief of the destitute Poor in Ireland,' they would be prepared to dissolve the Board and replace it with paid officials.[21]

The following day the Board was issued with orders to extend outdoor relief to the able-bodied. John Deane communicated to the Commissioners his belief that the Guardians were 'totally unfit to meet an emergency of this kind...The members of the Board are, for the most part, men of the more humble (indeed I may say of the lower class of life),' and were 'unable, from their want of business-habits and experience', to carry out the task of extending outdoor relief to the able-bodied.

The extension of outdoor relief to the able-bodied required 'so much vigilance' that it was his feeling 'that the present Board of Guardians is unequal' to the job. As it was, 'there appeared to be an impression on the minds of the Guardians (generally) that all responsibility should be thrown on me'. On conclusion of the weekly meetings he never saw the members again for the rest of the week; with the exception of 'Mr D'Arcy, the chairman, to whose indefatigable exertions and ready co-operation at all times I wish to bear testimony.'[22]

Deane, however, was advised that his remarks

> would not form a ground for the dissolution of the Board, unless accompanied by the enumeration of special instances in which they had neglected their duty.[23]

Distress was 'becoming daily and hourly more alarming throughout the union.' On 3 January, while the Guardians were holding their weekly meeting, 'crowds of the most wretched and miserable objects surrounded the Court-house' and the police had to be called on to 'preserve order'.

Previous to the meeting, John Deane discussed with Hyacinth D'Arcy his recommendation to the Commission that the Board of Guardians be dissolved. D'Arcy agreed with Deane's assessment of the Board's inability 'to meet the difficulties of the present crisis.' D'Arcy was himself 'willing and anxious to devote a certain portion of his time' to his duties as an ex-officio Guardian, but Deane could not expect 'regular attendance from the other members of the Board.'

On hearing of Deane's recommendation to the Commission that the Board be dissolved the Guardians grew alarmed and resolved to meet two days a week for the future, in order to get through all the business of the week. Deane, however, felt the resolution would 'not be practically put into effect'.[24]

Number Of Fever Hospitals Increased

In early January 1848 the increase in the number of fever patients was putting pressure on hospital accommodation:

> The relieving officers cannot send in patients to the present hospitals, either at Clifden or Ballindoon, as both are crowded to excess, and unable to accommodate more. Several wretched beings have died by the road-side and in their huts.[25]

The Board of Health authorized the setting up of temporary fever hospitals in Ballynakill and Roundstone, under the attention of Dr Suffield and Dr Gannon respectively. Alterations to the Clifden schoolhouse were held up by lack of finance and bad weather. However, on completion the fever hospital there would come under the direction of Dr Bodkin and his salary was increased to £60 per annum.

The poor were no longer able to provide coffins for their dead and the Guardians were prevented by instructions from the Poor Law

Commission from doing so. Coffins were to be provided 'by the church-wardens, and the expense assessed on the parish'. However, a meeting of the vestry in Clifden had not been held for some time, 'and the church-wardens are unable to meet the demands which are daily made on them for the supply of coffins.'

Deane sought directions from the Commissioners citing a case brought to his attention by the relieving officer for Ballindoon of a man:

> lying dead on the road-side, with his widow and children around him, and that they had no means to bury him...It is lamentable that public decency should be thus outraged.

Clifden was, he informed the Commissioners, 'infested with beggars, several of whom' he 'had committed as vagrants.' His house was 'constantly surrounded by a crowd of wretched beings seeking relief.' They were under the apprehension that he alone could relieve them and were so insistent that he was

> unable frequently to sit down to my meals with that quiet necessary for one whose whole time is devotedly and anxiously directed to the faithful discharge of the duties entrusted to him.[26]

Deane found Hyacinth D'Arcy to be the only member of the Board on whom he could depend. The two men formed themselves into a visiting committee and, for a time, took over the supervision of the workhouse, the other members of the board still refusing to set foot inside the building.

An inspection of the house was authorized and carried out by Dr Bodkin and Dr Suffield. They 'classified the inmates', separating the healthy from the sick, agreed a diet and 'made other arrangements as to cleanliness and order'. They found that there was a 'total disregard to discipline, order, or regularity.' Contrary to Poor Law regulations, 'the men, women, and children, are allowed to mix one with another, and even to pass and mix with the hospital patients.'

The yards were filthy and the 'privies' were 'all in a most filthy and dilapidated state, the roofs and slates are broken, and in wet weather cannot be used by the paupers.' The interior of the building required white-washing but the Guardians were having difficulty obtaining lime. In the dormitories 'three or four lie in the same bed.' More beds and blankets were needed. The contractor was refusing to supply clothes and bedding because of the large sums, over £200, already due to him. As a result, many of the inmates retained their own clothing; these had to be washed on arrival in an effort to keep down the spread of disease.

It was the opinion of the doctors that:

> If order and regularity were kept, the house whitewashed, cleansed, and fumigated, the yards properly cleaned, and kept so, the roof and other matters repaired, a sufficient supply of bedclothes and wearing

apparel obtained, and a little more hospital accommodation, I do think (if the officers do their duty) in a little time you would have the poorhouse all you could desire.[27]

Bad weather delayed the arrival of a consignment of hammers, necessary to set the able-bodied to work breaking stones. The Board employed the local smiths to make them up but the delay was leaving the able-bodied idle. Following the doctors' report the able-bodied were put to work whitewashing the interior, levelling the yards and covering them with gravel.

Pressure on workhouse accommodation was not helped by the actions of Arthur Gonne Bell Martin of Ballynahinch Castle, husband of Mary Martin and now the largest landlord in the union. On 23 January 1848, Deane informed the Commission that Martin was taking advantage of the Quarter-Acre Clause to clear his land of tenants. Martin issued certificates, through his agent or bailiff, to any tenant willing to give up his home and land. This would entitle him to relief. His agents then pulled down the cabin, leaving the tenant without shelter and forcing him and his family into the workhouse.

Deane complained to Martin 'very decidedly on the inhumanity of putting so many families as an additional charge on the rates of the union'. Martin himself had paid only part of his rate and there was still over £200 outstanding.[28]

Board of Guardians Dissolved

In order to comply with the order to extend relief to the able-bodied, food depots were set up in each electoral division for the distribution of food to all who qualified. On the first day the system was to come into operation, 24 January, the suppliers failed to deliver. Some debts were still outstanding and food stocks in the area were depleted due to bad weather and so the merchants were holding fast. John Deane intervened and eventually persuaded a Clifden merchant to supply the necessary food. Deane called for the government store to be re-opened and a supply of food for sale be made available in the town. He complained to the Commission:

> The state of misery and destitution in the Union is most alarming at the present moment. Several deaths have taken place by the road-side from starvation.
>
> While sitting at breakfast this morning my servant informed me that there was a woman at the door with a dead child in her arms, which I found upon inquiry to be too true. I directed the relieving officer to offer the poor woman provisional relief.[29]

The Commission wanted to know if any of those who died at the road side had requested relief and been refused. In reply Deane informed them that Joyce, the relieving officer for Ballindoon, named two individuals who had died from want, but these had not applied to him for relief. However, he was now relieving their families:

> The same officer informed me that a man of the name of Flaherty, of Ballyconneely, in Ballindoon electoral division, made application to him for relief, that he visited his place of residence, and found that he was in the occupation of more than a quarter of an acre of land. This relieving officer refused the applicant relief, and he died by the road-side from actual starvation.[30]

Over the next fortnight forty one people died of fever and dysentery inside the workhouse.[31] Food supplies eventually reached the region but the Board was having difficulty agreeing contracts with the suppliers. The Commission sent Richard Burke, Poor Law Inspector, to investigate and report back on the ability of the Board of Guardians of Clifden union to administer relief in the union.

Burke arrived in Clifden on 27 January. He began his investigation immediately and reported back his findings to the Commission on 31 January. In Burke's opinion the entire operation of the Board had fallen to just one member, the Chairman Hyacinth D'Arcy. The rest of the Board, unwilling as they were to properly supervise the workhouse, the relieving officers and the rate collectors, left too much on the shoulders of the Chairman and John Deane:

> the irregular mode in which the Guardians transact their affairs, and the confusion into which they have allowed their finances to fall, have deterred merchants of respectability and capital from entering into contracts with them.

Any successes achieved in the collection of the rates could 'be attributed to the personal exertions of Mr Deane'. The Guardians took no interest in the work of the collectors and made no effort to prosecute defaulting ratepayers through the courts. This was hardly surprising, given that many of the Guardians were themselves among those ratepayers in arrears.
Burke felt that:

> this Board of Guardians have failed in using due activity and diligence in carrying out their duties in this Union; and I cannot hope, from what I have seen of them, that they will meet their difficulties with the energy necessary to surmount them. With the exception of the chairman, who has shown great anxiety to perform his part with zeal and efficiency, little is to be expected from the Board...Under all these circumstances I beg leave to recommend that the Board be dissolved, and paid officers be appointed.[32]

Burke's report was followed by letters to the Commission from Hyacinth D'Arcy and Major-General Thomson, both referring to the inability of the Board to continue its work. D'Arcy declared that the Board was 'not equal to the present emergency.' The recent deaths from starvation weighed heavily on him, it was his feeling that the Board were; 'morally responsible, although I cannot say legally, as it appears no application had been made to them'.[33]

Thomson lived some distance from Clifden and was unable to regularly attend the weekly meetings:

> I have with much difficulty paid my own rate, and having done my duty, have nothing to reproach myself.
>
> I consider the elected Guardians, from their class in life incapable of managing the affairs of the Union, and...I do not desire to hold myself responsible for their acts. I need not say that in any observation made I mean (not) to include Mr D'Arcy, whose entire time has been devoted to his duty as a Guardian.[34]

Hyacinth D'Arcy's estate was at this time under the management of the receiver and he therefore had more time than most to devote to his duties as Guardian.

The Poor Law Commission, on receipt of Burke's report, and giving due recognition to the efforts made by Hyacinth D'Arcy:

> arrived at the conclusion, that the Board of Guardians have failed to administer relief duly and effectually either in the workhouse or out of it, and have especially failed to provide themselves with a sufficient amount of funds at this season of distress, by a timely and vigorous collection of the poor-rates...The Commission are convinced, however, that the debts of the Union are too heavy, and the amount of destitution is too great...(and) they have determined to issue a formal order dissolving the Clifden Board of Guardians.[35]

The Board was to transact business as usual until 7 February when the arrival of paid officials would see them take over its duties.

CHAPTER 9

VICE-GUARDIANS TAKE CONTROL

There were in all, thirty-two Board of Guardians, mostly along the western seaboard, dissolved by the Poor Law Commission and replaced by paid officials.

The Commission felt that paid officials would have the time to administer these unions more efficiently, would be impartial in making a rate and more effective in its collection. They would pay close attention to the relieving officer's lists of applicants for relief and examine the circumstances of each individual case. They would also be more 'amenable to the close observation of the statutes, and the regulations issued by the Commissioners'.[1]

On 7 February 1848 Denis V. O'Leary took up his appointment as vice-guardians to the Clifden union and Hamilton Smith was appointed Secretary. O'Leary was joined on 14 February by Lee McKinstry. One month later, on 15 March, McKinstry was replaced by Joseph Jackson.[2]

Once in position the vice-guardians set about re-organising the union. Their priorities were the collection of outstanding rates and the reduction in the numbers receiving outdoor relief. They were instructed daily by circular from the Poor Law Commission covering the Law and the correct procedures for the day to day administration of the union; sanitary conditions in the workhouse and hospitals, instructions on how to deal with fever and cholera, and request for statistical data on those receiving indoor and outdoor relief.

Weekly accounts and reports were returned to them, along with details of expenditure for the past week, food requirements for the following week, rates collected and rates outstanding. Any irregularities or errors were picked out by the Commission and queried. Reports of fraud by depot managers, relieving officers, carriers and others were investigated and those proven guilty were sacked.

Relieving officer's books with lists of individuals receiving outdoor relief were regularly examined and investigated by the vice-guardians. Rate collectors were constantly queried on the slow remittance received and urged to be more efficient in their duty. Defaulting ratepayers were prosecuted in the courts, but still for many weeks of the year there was simply no rates coming in.

In the months that followed grants of £300 and £500 were regularly given by the government and the British Relief Association through the Commission, which still retained the services of their inspector, John Deane, to report on the work of the rate collectors, relieving officers and vice-guardians, and on the correct use of all funds received.

Advertisements were placed in local newspapers for tenders for supplies to the workhouse and food depots, and the carriage of some. With the promise of prompt payment the vice-guardians were in a position to stimulate local trade by encouraging the small traders to keep up the supply of meal in the local market.

Large supplies were purchased and the weekly accounts showed large sums of money paid out for Indian meal, barley, rice and oatmeal to suppliers in Clifden, Westport and Galway. Relieving officers, suppliers, the workhouse master and matron and their assistants, in fact, any person in a position to defraud the union, had to give sureties before being appointed.

When the vice-guardians took over, the union was £564 in debt, rates of £2,035 were still uncollected, the number receiving relief, both indoor and outdoor, came to 10,760, and the mortality rate inside and outside of the workhouse was rising daily.[3]

On 9 February Deane wrote to the Commission: 'I think the time has arrived when relief should be given to this Union in aid of rates.'[4] The Commission pressed for more effort in collecting the rate. Deane's reply, coming after four months of living in the union, seems a lot more realistic than his 'all difficulties can be overcome' synopsis of the previous October:

> taking into consideration the circumstances of the landed proprietors of this Union...the collection has not been at all deficient. Several of the rate-payers who have contributed to the rate are themselves fit objects for out-door relief, and will shortly have to be relieved.[5]

Two weeks later, 23 February, the Commission applied to the Treasury for £205.17.9d to cover the cost of outdoor relief to the able-bodied in the Clifden union for one week.

Administering Outdoor Relief

In February and early March the number of food depots was increased to facilitate the daily distribution of cooked food and the weekly distribution of dry food:

> Boilers are in course of being placed in localities where they have been deemed necessary...The Vice-Guardians propose to give cooked food not only to the able-bodied, but also to the widows with two or more children. The permanently disabled must in some instances be served with dry meal.[6]

Efforts were made to offer the able-bodied work near the feeding stations so 'that they shall not suffer inconvenience in coming for their rations': in Roundstone the able-bodied paupers were employed sweeping the streets and cleaning sewers.[7]

To control the administration of outdoor relief the union increased its number of relieving officers to ten, each receiving a salary of £20 per annum. Because of the extent of the union the electoral divisions were divided up as follows: Roundstone divided into North, East and South Roundstone, Ballindoon into North and South Ballindoon, Renvyle into North and South Renvyle and Clifden into North and South Clifden.

Mathias Maley and A.G Kearns covered Clifden, John Corbett, East Roundstone, M.L. Coneys, North Roundstone, Thomas Cooke, South Roundstone, Patrick Evans, South Renvyle, John Joyce, James Dooner, Richard Burke and Peter Joyce covered the remaining districts.

The distribution of cooked food began in the Clifden Electoral Division on 7 March and it was expected to extend to all divisions within a few days. Rations to the aged and the infirm were issued in the morning at 11 o'clock and to the able-bodied at 4p.m.[8]

The cost of outdoor relief was estimated at 1 ½d a ration.[9] Cooked food was cheaper than dry food to produce and could not be easily sold on by the recipient; it was the aim of the vice-guardians to issue all rations in cooked food in the future.

The large numbers applying for relief led Deane and the vice-guardians to suspect that abuses were taking place; many who were not entitled were applying for relief and others were receiving double rations. It was hoped that:

> the rigorous imposition of the workhouse test, the use of cooked food, and the exacting of labour in return for rations, will soon materially decrease the numbers on the lists.[10]

The vice-guardians were aware that, because of the extent of each relieving district, the officers were having difficulty reaching the extremes of their district and of familiarizing themselves with each applicant on the relief books. Still the vice-guardians urged them to keep a check on applicants, reminding them that their first duty was to ensure that 'no one wanted relief who was a fit object to receive it...(and) to be diligent in detecting imposition.'[11]
While at the same time telling the Commissioners that:

> the utter confusion of the system hitherto pursued precludes the possibility of any immediate check on them (the relieving officers), or on their orders to the distributors. We, as public officers, the rate-payers, and the destitute, are totally at their discretion.[12]

On a personal examination of the union the vice-guardians concluded that:

> the feeding of the destitute is not provided for as fully as it may be, and that thousands are receiving rations who are not entitled to them. Thus the poor famish, and the rate-payers are plundered.

They proposed that a ticket system be introduced whereby each applicant entitled to relief be given a ticket, made of parchment or some durable material, showing their entitlement and the electoral division: 'so that the holder of such ticket in any one district cannot get relief under its permit in any other'.[13] The vice-guardians were informed that any improvements to the administration of relief deemed necessary by them would be sanctioned by the Poor Law Commission.

When the Board received instructions to suspend outdoor relief to the able-bodied on the 18 March, John Deane listed the following reasons for not carrying it through:

1st. The amount of distress is so considerable that relief will be absolutely essential to prevent the population from starving.

2nd. There is little if any employment provided under the Land Improvement Act in this union.

3rd. From the circumstances of the majority of the landed proprietors, they are unable to employ the labouring population on their respective properties.[14]

The vice-guardians, feeling that applicants for outdoor relief should not have to walk further than two miles to the distribution point and two miles back, brought in extra boilers to the areas were they were most needed and placed them four miles apart. They also increased the rations for all persons above nine years of age from three-quarters of a pound of dry meal, which produced 'an imperial quart of Indian-meal stirabout', to a pound of dry meal, 'no matter how its bulk may expand'. Rice was introduced into the cooked food whenever possible, to try and keep down the instances of dysentery among the people.[15]

In March, as the collectors were again experiencing difficulty in collecting rates, funds as well as provisions were sent from the Poor Law Commission 'for the maintenance of the destitute poor in the Union,'[16] and the vice-guardians were urged to keep a tighter control on the relieving officers.

Union Doctors

On 28 February 1848 John Deane reported that fever was on the decline in the workhouse, there being 'but eight cases of fever in the hospital. The mortality has greatly decreased.' Dysentery was still a problem; the children were the principal sufferers. Dr Bodkin was reported to be ill and within a few days had 'died of fever, contracted in the discharge of his duties,'[17]: Dr Suffield took over his duties.

Fever may have been on the decline in the workhouse but in other parts of the union it was on the increase. In a region almost devoid of substantial

buildings finding suitable accommodation for hospitals was difficult.
Converting these into functional buildings took time and the delay cost
lives. The conversion of the schoolhouse into a temporary hospital to accommodate 50 patients in Clifden was slow to complete and the building was
not opened until 18 March. In Ballynakill the vice-guardians were having
difficulty securing a building, although on a visit to Cleggan they found:

> the misery and destitution there exceed any other district we have as
> yet visited...Disease in that locality is very prevalent, measles, dysen-
> tery, and fever, abound.[18]

A house was taken at Roundstone, which would, when alterations were
complete, hopefully accommodate up to 40 patients; it was expected to be
in operation in April. Reports from Roundstone were causing alarm. On 8
March Deane reported to the Commission:

> Fever is rife in every house; there is no medical man in the whole divi-
> sion. The population is in utter want, without any resource, and
> unless some remedial steps are promptly taken, a plague will carry
> them off in hundreds. We would ask the instructions of your Board on
> this matter.[19]

Because of the extent of the disease in the area, Deane recommended that
a further hospital be opened at Carna. In response, the Commission send
Dr Phelan, Poor Law Inspector, to investigate the extent of the disease.

After Dr Phelan 'carefully inspected' the workhouse, which he found to
be in a 'vastly better' state than when he last visited, he toured the union
and reported conditions to the Commission. The doctor was critical of the
standard of medical service offered in most parts of the union but particularly so in the South Roundstone division, which was under the direction
of Dr Gannon.

All three doctors working in the union, Dr Suffield, Dr Morgan and Dr
Gannon, were away attending the Galway Assizes during Phelan's visit.
He took over Dr Suffield's duties as workhouse doctor and dispensary
doctor to Clifden during his absence, believing that it was:

> these domiciliary visits that bring us to have a perfect view of the
> wretchedness, and of the extremely depressed physical and mental
> state of the people; hospitals or workhouses afford nothing like it.

While attending patients in the town he found:

> a considerable number chiefly in fever, dysentery, and diarrhoea: sev-
> eral were in a hopeless state...I am unable to describe the extreme
> wretchedness of several families whom I visited on this occasion.
> They were literally without bed-clothing, except a ragged rug or old
> blanket, and, without straw to lie on. Filth and every circumstance
> that tend to create or to extend disease existed in the highest degree,

and the crowding in some places was awful. In one house designated the 'hulk', there were 58 persons; in another, called the 'rookery', there were 42; not one of them, except one family, was in good health; not one but was half naked. The apartments of some were so foul that I could not remain in them for many minutes.

The 'hulk' and the 'rookery' were perhaps the two houses taken as additional accommodation for the workhouse, or perhaps two of tenements occupied by the aged and infirm discharged from the workhouse. Dr Phelan hinted in his report that Dr Suffield was perhaps `stretched', holding as he did three appointments in the union: workhouse doctor, dispensary doctor and union treasurer. He suggested that a letter be written to him reminding him of his duties: 'he is fairly called upon in an emergency like this to give every aid in his power, and probably will do so' on receipt of such a letter.[20]

Roundstone Electoral Division Neglected

In Roundstone he again found:

> fever, others with dysentery and diarrhoea...The misery and the extent of disease here were as great, perhaps more so, than in Clifden.

Medical attention here was 'merely nominal.' Dr Gannon rarely attended the sick and Dr Phelan could find no-one 'that gave a favourable account of him.' While visiting houses in the area he came across the Keough (sic) family. One member of this family became ill with fever on 1 January and in the weeks that followed the entire family of eight children, as well as the mother and father, contacted the disease. Between 1 January and 21 March Dr Gannon paid just one visit to the family, although they lived 'within a few perches of his (Dr Gannon's) residence.' When Dr Phelan visited on 21 March he found:

> six of the family in bed, four in the only bed they had, two lying on the floor. The father had been buried that morning; the mother and two children were barely convalescent. Until attacked by this illness, although in humble circumstance, they were decent, and comparatively respectable; even in the abject state of misery in which I saw them, they commanded more respect and excited more commiseration that any I have seen. Fever...has completely pauperized them.

The Roundstone dispensary catered for a population of 11,969, large numbers of whom lived long distances, over 20 miles, to the south and west of the village and separated from it by a large bay. Dr Gannon was expected, in his capacity as dispensary doctor, to cover this extensive area which Dr Phelan was forced to admit 'even a well managed dispensary there could afford little or no medical relief to those who are so remote.' The doctor was said to visit the district 'once in a fortnight or three weeks'.

One example of Dr Gannon's neglect of his duty was the case of Peter Joyce, 'the son-in-law of one of Mrs Bell Martin's drivers'. Joyce contacted fever and his wife went to Mary Bell Martin who supplied her with a note for Dr Gannon, and recommended that he visit the sick man. When Joyce's daughter took the note to Gannon he refused to visit the man, declaring that the note was a forgery.

Mrs Joyce returned to Mrs Bell Martin and acquired another note, which she herself took to Dr Gannon. The doctor told her to bring a horse or car for him and that he would then make the visit. She brought him a horse, but the doctor 'said it was then too late, and he would not go that day, but if the horse were sent next day he would.' When Mrs Joyce got home she found one of her children dead and 'finding so much difficulty in inducing Dr Gannon to visit her family, she took no further step in the matter.'

When Dr Phelan visited the family 'Peter Joyce and three children were still ill of fever, but convalescent.' He was of the opinion that 'some medical attention might have been useful; but although written to by the proprietor of this immense but very wretched estate, the medical officer withheld that attention.' When prepared to ignore a request from Mrs Bell Martin, it seems unlikely that Gannon would respond to a request from 'less influential persons,' or from the poor on whom it was his duty 'to attend when time would permit.'

In Carna and Kilkieran there was fever,

> dysentery and dropsy, evidently caused by want of food...No description could give an idea of the extreme wretchedness of these people...In some houses every member of the family was ill.
> The same state of wretchedness and of disease is said to prevail in the islands and in the coast part of the   district, which for want of roads I did not visit.

The Ballindoon fever hospital was well managed and Dr Phelan noted that in the period between 21 August 1847 and 15 March 1848 there were 192 patients admitted to the hospital and just four deaths.

Wretched Assembly At Cleggan

The doctor arrived at the Cleggan food depot when 'about 500 or 600 persons were assembled, waiting for the day's rations; many of them appeared to be literally starving - some to be nearly moribund from starvation and disease.' He was quickly surrounded by the people 'and although they were in the open air' the putrid odour rising from them was intolerable, and would:

produce fever in most persons that had not been seasoned to it. Even I, myself, who can bear any amount of stench in an hospital, was soon nauseated by it, and was compelled several times to retire from amongst them-certainly not from any disgust of their persons, which only excite my commiseration, but from the unbearable foetor emanating not only from their clothes, but perceptively from their persons; but as many of the applicants for relief were sick, some very feeble, I returned again and again amongst them, and had again and again to retire.

This was the most appalling sight I have yet beheld. There is no medical relief through any part of this division. I went into several houses in which I found whole families in fever, dysentery, diarrhoea, and in that state of marasmus or wasting, which is caused by gradual inanition, and by living on food of a very inferior description.

He was critical of the issue of cooked food only as this left the people waiting for many hours to be fed and suggested that some dry food be issued when numbers were so great. He also recommended that rice, oatmeal, sugar and cocoa be issued to the sick as many were 'unable to use Indian meal.'

The district of Ballynakill did not appear to be as bad as Cleggan, 'but [was] still an extremely destitute one.' A house had at last been found for use as a fever hospital and was in the process of being fitted out. However, in Dr Phelan's opinion the house was 'quite unfit for the purpose' and 'its accommodation is totally inadequate to the number of sick in the district, comprising Cleggan, Ballynakill, and Renvyle.' It was situated half a mile from the road:

> the approach is on a bye-road so rocky and stony, and so difficult to be traversed, that I do not see how any car or wheeled vehicle, with or without springs, can bring sick persons along it...I think the sick would be more injured by bringing them to it than served by being in it'.

On concluding his report Dr Phelan gave the opinion that it would be impossible to 'afford medical relief to one in twenty of those who are in need of it' in the South Roundstone district. The district was so large and the people so far removed from centres such as Roundstone and Carna that fever hospitals in both place would serve very few. He suggested that a doctor be appointed to the area to attend the sick, 'give medicines to those that require it,' and make out a suitable diet which should then be provided by the relieving officer.

He recommended that the same be done at Cleggan, Ballynakill, Renvyle, West Roundstone and Ballindoon. The doctors and the relieving officers should work together and, whenever possible, the patient treated in his own home. The hospitals in the union would benefit some, 'but hundreds will die in the district who cannot be sent to it, or if sent, cannot be admitted into it for want of room.'[21]

The vice-guardians took up Dr Phelan's advice regarding the diet of the sick and lighter foods such as rice, cocoa and sugar were included in their rations; Indian meal, which was 'sound and suitable for those who can use it', was totally useless to the sick.[22] But such foods were not easily obtained in Connemara, and expensive to purchase. With the passing of each day more and more people were removed from the able-body list and placed on the list of infirm and the vice-guardians grew anxious that they would not be able to keep up a supply of suitable food for the sick. In response to requests from the vice-guardians commissariat supplies of corn and rice were sent into the area in March and April.

CHAPTER 10

BLIGHT RETURNS 1848

Since the arrival of the vice-guardians the master and matron of the work-house had been sacked and a new master, Patrick Joyce, a former reliev-ing officer, appointed. Joyce was highly regarded by the vice-guardians and by John Deane, who within a week of his appointment was able to report that 'there is a visible improvement in the state of the workhouse.'[1] It was expected that, in time, all necessary alterations and improvements would be carried out under Joyce's management. The vice-guardians were, how-ever, having difficulty finding a suitable person to act as matron.

Five acres of land 'immediately fronting the house, at each side of which are the two roads leading into the town of Clifden', was leased from Hyacinth D'Arcy for cultivation by the inmates of the house. Land to the rear of the house was under consideration as a site for a permanent fever hospital and graveyard.

Many bills were still outstanding in the town and towards the end of March traders were again withholding supplies. Since their appointment relations between the vice-guardians and the suppliers had been good. The suppliers had 'honoured every order; and they now look to us for payment.' Over £1,000 was due and the vice-guardians warned the Commission that 'to depend on the rates outstanding to meet this sum would be hopeless.'[2]

On that particular week, 27 March 1848, just £4.19s was collected in rates and there was £1,168.12.8d outstanding. Summonses were issued against the immediate lessors, who accounted for most of the arrears, but many of these had closed their houses and left the area to avoid 'the levying of the rate or the serving of the notice'.[3]

The remainder was due from those who were now so poor that many were themselves availing of relief and this portion of the rate was there-fore considered uncollectible. An example of the reduced circumstances of the retepayers was the condition in which the collector found J Corbett. Corbett, a member of the previous board, owed £4 rates in the Clifden Division but when the collector went to serve the warrant he found only 'a bed and a few miserable articles of furniture,' in the house. However, every effort to collect the arrears would be made and 'every legal means to compel payment shall be used.' But Deane was of the opinion that it would be impossible to collect the new rate until the next harvest.[4]

Anticipating A Successful Crop

Encouraged by the success of the crop of 1847 and the low cost of seed potatoes, selling at six to seven pence per stone, the people returned to the cultivation of the land with determination and enthusiasm. In April, J B

Kernan, the Resident Magistrate for Galway, reported that the people along the coast were anxious to purchase seed at all cost and had been 'led to pawn[c] every movable article they possess to obtain money wherewith to purchase seed.'[5]

In the same month John Deane reported that a large quantity of potatoes had been planted and the people were confident of a successful crop: 'The confidence in the success of the potato crop has induced the people to rely upon it almost exclusively.'

Less oats and barley were sown than in previous years and the people were reluctant to sow green crops: 'The lives of thousands depend upon the experiment.' Many people had sold their cattle and furniture to purchase seed, many others 'having saved seed since last year witnessed their family in want of food rather than use it.'

The Society of Friends offered to advance £400 to two parishes in the union to purchase seed. Security was required for the repayment of the sum, and although a committee was appointed to make the necessary arrangements, the offer was not taken up as no landlord could be induced to go guarantor; 'Mr Hyacinth D'Arcy was the honourable exception.'[6]

'The experiment', however, failed and by early August John Deane was able to confirm that blight had struck again. Following a ten day inspection of the union Deane reported that:

> every field of potatoes I saw was black. The disease is spreading rapidly to the potato itself, specimens of which are brought daily to my house from all parts of the union. I consider the late crop to be entirely destroyed, the early crop will not suffer so seriously.
>
> I have made particular inquiries in reference to the appearance and prospect of the corn crop, and have received encouraging reports as to their success, but I regret to state, that there is fully a fourth less of oats, barley and rye than in three previous years. With respect to green crops, the amount is so small, that it is scarcely worth noticing, the sowing of turnips has been almost entirely confined to land in occupation by the few gentlemen farmers in the district.[7]

Four days later on 15 August, Denis O'Leary, vice-guardian for the union, reported to the Commission: 'For several weeks I was confident that the rumour of the spread of the disease was a groundless alarm', but on investigation he confirmed that the blight was 'universal throughout the union.' Some districts with sandy soil, which were exempt from blight in 1846 and 1847, were this year hit. There was, he estimated, only four months supply of food of any kind in Connemara.

Opinion was divided as to whether those potatoes not yet showing signs of disease should be left in the ground or quickly dug up:

[c] This is illustrated in the Pawnbroker's Returns, Appendix 2, which shows the number of pledges received in January and February of 1847 to be greated than for the same months in any previous year.

In some places the poor people are digging them in despair, and bringing them to market at any price they can obtain for them. I regard this anxiety of the people to get rid of the crop they suffered every privation to secure, as conclusive of the general despair of their being able to preserve them either for food or for seed.[8]

The failure of yet another potato crop threw the already desperate people into even further distress. During the summer months the number receiving outdoor relief had continued to rise. The average number on outdoor relief during April 1848 was 10,360, by June this had risen to 18,325. Once it became obvious the crop had failed yet again panic gripped the people and in the coming months thousands would turn to the vice-guardians demanding relief.

Preparing For Further Distress

It was also becoming increasingly evident that, even under the control of the vice-guardians, it was proving impossible to cover the cost of administering the union out of the poor rate alone and continued Treasury support was necessary to save the people from starvation. Although the government was committed to assisting the distressed unions, demands for aid were not met until the Treasury was satisfied that their need was absolutely justified. This slowness on the part of the Treasury to release funds resulted in severe hardship, and sometimes death, for the recipients of both indoor and outdoor relief in the months that followed, particularly during the winter of 1848/49.

The Clifden union was now surviving almost entirely on Treasury grants. The expenses for the union in the twelve months leading up to 29 September 1848 came to £23,405. The rate collected over the same period was £2,529. The amount advanced in aid by the Treasury on the recommendation of the Poor Law Commission was £17,666.

The union was £5,237 in debt on 29 September 1848 and it was estimated, given a similar level of expenditure for the next year, that a sum of £28,642 would be needed to cover union expenses up to September 1849.[9] On 19 September a new rate was made, amounting to £2,997 or 3s in the pound of valuation. However, taking into account the conditions in the union at the time, this would be difficult to collect, forcing the vice-guardians to look to the Treasury, through the Poor Law Commission, for the shortfall.[d]

The Poor Law Commissioners were still not satisfied with the relieving officers in the union. They constantly complained of their inefficiency and lack of attention in making up their books. The vice-guardians explained that they were having difficulty procuring persons fit for the situation.

[d] see Appendix 3, One Week In The Workhouse.

In September the officers were ordered to hand in their books to the secretary, Hamilton Smith, for inspection. The books of Peter Joyce, John Joyce, Richard Burke, James Dooner and Patrick Evans were said to be satisfactory and were returned to the officers with instructions to 'preform their duties promptly and effectively.' M L Coneys was given until the next board day to have his books in order.

Some books, however, were found to be in a 'very imperfect state'[10] and eventually clerks had to be appointed to assist in bringing them up to date. The clerk's wages, 12/6d per week, was paid for by the Reliving Officer. The books of Thomas Cooke, John Corbett and Mathias Maley, were found to be in arrears and all three were suspended. Corbett was replaced by Edward Joyce and Mathias Maley was later re-installed in South Roundstone.

Richard Burke was called on to resign because of physical inability. However, 'taking full account of his integrity,'[11]he was given the position of distributor at a food depot. Patrick Evans came under investigation for issuing 'illegal relief'[12] and was forced to resign.

In the months that followed the officers were moved from one district to another. They were frequently sent to cover for officers absent due to illness or removed from their post while under investigation for fraud. Complaints of corruption made against the officers were quickly investigated by the vice-guardians, yet still these men, along with the rate collectors, were viewed with suspicion by the poor and the authorities alike. The relieving officer John Joyce[e] was immortalised in the song `Johnny Seoighe' written by a local poet to flatter Joyce in the hope of obtaining relief.[13] Lieutenant-Colonel Edward Archer[f], agent for the Law Life Assurance Company on the Martin estate, declared that:

> they are not of that class of people in whom I have the slightest confidence, knowing full well that they are very deficient in those principles which would induce them to perform their duty conscientiously and well...Collector and the Relieving Officer...have obtained land and have purchased cattle at their own prices, and put persons on or off the list, just as they pleased.[14]

In October the number of persons on the relief list was on the decline; averaging between 9,000 to 9,500 per week, compared to 18,145 on week ending 15 July. It was decided that this was a good time to carry out a further revision of the list 'and make personal enquiries into the cases.'[15]

[e] In May 1849 John Joyce, South Roundstone, was discharged following a full investigation into charges made against him by Harrison Briscoe and he was replaced by Mathias Maley.

[f] Lieutenant-Colonel Edward Archer was Inspecting Officer of the Relief Committee in the counties of Westmeath and Meath in 1846-47. His was the brother-in-law of A O'Flaherty M.P. for Galway town and employed as agent by the Law Life Assurance Company who foreclosed their mortgage on the Martin estate in November 1848.

Applicants for relief in the Ballindoon Division were ordered to attend, with all the members of their families, at their local depot on Thursday 2 November at 10 o'clock for assessment. The same was demanded of those in the North Roundstone district on Wednesday 15 November. The families, half-starved and often half-naked, travelled many miles in harsh weather to be included in the list.

Auxiliary Workhouses

Anticipating the increased demand for workhouse accommodation and outdoor relief which would follow the failure of the 1848 crop, the Clifden workhouse was again cleared of the aged and the sick to make way for the able-bodied. The number of food depots was increased and extra houses were rented, at a rent of £6 per annum, from Richard Hynes at Carna, F W Culla at Roundstone and Robert Caine at Cashel. The district served by the Cashel depot was later found to be too extensive and a further depot had to be opened at Cloonacartan.

Ever watchful of expenditure, in October the Poor Law Commission complained that 'the average cost of maintenance of the workhouse inmates is higher than usual in all departments'.[16] A statement showing the cost of maintenance in other unions was forwarded for comparison. In order to comply with the request to reduce costs changes were made in the diet of workhouse inmates. Bread, composed of half Indian meal and half barley flour, was substituted for wheaten bread, oatmeal gruel was substituted for milk for four days of the week, (the Commission later recommended that the words 'farinaceous soup' be substituted for 'gruel' when written into the minutes). Meat was withdrawn from the diet, except for inmates of the hospital and official's rations, rice was discontinued, and later,in December, fish soup was introduced for three days of the week.

The medical officers working in the union were instructed 'to limit their orders for relief in food to cases of urgent necessity and of utter destitution.'[17] Rice, milk and cocoa were withdrawn from recipients of outdoor relief to enable the relieving officers 'to administer Relief in money to...urgent cases among the sick',[18] but only when considered absolutely necessary by the medical officers.

Ovens were set up at the Clifden food depot and at the workhouse and a baker named Lysaght was hired at 3/= per week to provide bread for the workhouse.

As the number of applicants for indoor relief began to rise it was becoming imperative that workhouse accommodation be increased. All available space in the workhouse was quickly converted into accommodation and auxiliary houses were established at Kylemore, Roundstone and Clifden.

In Clifden the workhouse tailors were moved to a shed in the front yard and their workroom, along with a day room, was made into a dormitory for women with infants. At the same time tin plates were erected to prevent clothes being passed through the windows.

William Creighton's store at the bottom of Beach Hill was leased as a school and the loft was converted into a dormitory for girls. Henry Hildebrand's store, also in the town, was rented at £70 per annum and made into a dormitory for boys.

At Kylemore, Rev Duncan proposed:

> to erect a range of buildings enclosing a quadrangle...to extend 120 feet long by 100 feet, to be 10 feet high...thatched, provided with the requisite number of windows, doors, ventilators, and to give 10 acres of this adjoining land at £30 per annum with a lease of 31 years. Containing clause to surrender every third year - the premises to be fit for occupation in 8 weeks.

Clifden.

1 Twelve Bens. 2 Road to Galway. 3 Workhouse. 4 Jail. 5 Mr. Griffith's 6 Waterfall.
7-8 Church. 9 Parochial school. 10 Carr's Inn, all public conveyances stop here.
11 Hart's Hotel. 12 Road to Clifden Castle. 13 Road to school and church.
14 Mitchell's shop. 15 National school temporary fever hospital. 16 Road to quay.
17 Children's auxilary workhouse. 18 The sea. 19 Infant's school.

In Roundstone, Joseph Revill proposed his houses and outoffices as a possible site for an auxiliary workhouse, these to be extended by 100 feet, along with 10 acres of land at £37 per annum and 'clause of surrender every third year'.[19]

Both proposals were accepted and work began immediately. Before long a section of Roundstone house was fit for habitation and seventy two boys were sent on 31 October, accompanied by two tailors and Patrick Kearns as overseer.

In keeping with Poor Law policy all workhouse inmates were set to work. The men were employed:

> in construction of auxiliary workhouses, some breaking and bearing limestone, some making floors in the new day room, the rest employed in works around the house.

However, finding employment for the women was more difficult. Due to the crowded state of the female side of the house, 'using day rooms and infirm wards as sleeping apartments' and the lack of supervision, the master felt the women were 'not as industrious'[20] as he would have liked. Six spinning wheels had been recently purchased and eighteen women were employed carting and spinning wool in a room which at night was used as a dormitory. More spinning wheels were later purchased and a shed in the female yard was boarded up and used as a temporary workroom. The insurance cover on the building was extended to cover the introduction of flax and wool into the workhouse. The women also made bed ticking for the auxiliary workhouses.[21]

Credit Refused To Vice-Guardians

By November the Guardians were again complaining that there was still a 'deficiency between the amount of rates received and the sum of the unavoidable expenditure'. Because of their lack of ready cash the small traders were unable to keep up supplies and the larger merchants were refusing credit and pushing up prices:

> Mr Robertson, the contractor for supplying the depots of the Roundstone electoral division, refused to give meal without cash; since then the agent of Mr Livingston, Mr Lydon, Mr Griffin and others have also declined to supply without prompt payment.[22]

John Deane and the vice-guardians became anxious: they had 758 inmates in the workhouse and auxiliary workhouses and 8,831 applicants for outdoor relief. Deane, accompanied by James Copeland, who had recently replaced Joseph Jackson as vice-guardian, went to Galway to arrange for supplies.

Copeland had lived in Galway for some years, and was therefore known to the merchants, and it was hoped he would be able to persuade the suppliers to issue meal on credit to the union. However, in Galway the men were told by all the main suppliers that meal would only be supplied if a guarantee of payment on delivery could be given by the Guardians. Copeland was not in a position to give this guarantee as he held 'no hope of the collection for the week being at all equivalent to the estimated expenditure of the week.'[23]

Eventually, 'with some difficulty', Copeland persuaded Messrs Rush and Palmer to send twenty tons of meal to Clifden: 'The vessel was to be loaded and despatched immediately.'[24]

Along with food, the suppliers were also refusing to supply clothing and supplies for the auxiliary workhouses. Lack of clothing meant that new inmates were obliged to retain their own cloths which it was felt would only aid the spread of disease.

The crisis was compounded by McDonnell, the rate collector for Renvyle, being sick in bed and so the amount expected from that division was not available. John Deane felt that progress in the collection of the rate was good and that, apart from those being pursued through the courts, the collection would be completed within the specified time. But some financial assistance was needed in the meantime.

The following week the circumstances were the same. This time the people were fed when Mr Livingston:

> only by a special favour to Mr Deane...advanced seven tons of Indian meal, which being far below the quantity required, we directed the relieving officers to distribute amongst the most destitute in their several districts.

The vice-guardians, watching the deterioration of the people, predicted that if relief was not made available immediately:

> innumerable deaths from starvation must take place. During the past two weeks numerous applicants...have come, with their families, three or four times to the workhouse, from a distance of ten, fifteen, and thirty miles; and, in consequence of the house being full, were unable to gain admission. Many of these cases have now become 'urgent', yet the relieving officer is without the means of giving the provisional relief which the law authorizes...We are doing all we can to provide increased in-door accommodation; but even in this our every step is impeded by want of ready money to pay for labour and materials.

It was feared that the people would revert to the condition 'from which the administration of relief...rescued so many thousands last year in this Union.'[25]

James Dooner, relieving officer for Roundstone, wrote to the vice-guardians on 25 November 1848:

> the people of this district are in a most wretched condition, in consequence of their not getting their weekly allowance. I know them to be perishing for want of both covering and food, and the able-bodied that were some time ago, are now perfectly disabled from want; so that if there be not an immediate supply sent here, the lives of numbers of the people are in the utmost danger...I am striving to keep the starving poor up with promises that we will have a supply by Monday next.[26]

That same week Henry Harrison Briscoe attended his first board meeting as Poor Law Inspector for the Clifden union, replacing John Deane, and he brought with him a cheque for £500 from the British Relief Association. The money, to be used 'not in payment of past debts, but in the actual relief of urgent cases of destitution.'[27]

Still More Accommodation Needed

In December the Master reported to the vice-guardians that due to the

> increased numbers in the workhouse, the great many applicants, with auxiliary houses under his charge, and with the insecure state of the house, he feels himself unable to discharge his duty efficiently.

He needed an assistant to keep accounts, otherwise his 'whole and undivided time would be required at office business.'[28] John Winter was appointed Assistant Master at the end of the month at a salary of £12 per annum, plus rations.

Officially the workhouse could then accommodate 480, with auxiliary workhouses in Clifden taking a further 80, and Roundstone 175; Kylemore was not yet in operation, and hospital accommodation came to 46, bringing the total accommodation available in the union to 781.

However, on week-ending 9 December 1848 the number of inmates in the workhouse and auxiliary houses stood at 925. There were 72 patients in the two hospitals; 41 fever cases, 31 other cases. The number admitted during the week came to 225: 61 males, 76 females, 50 boys, 36 girls and 2 infants. Two deaths had taken place in that week.

The cost of provisions and necessaries consumed during the week was £65.17.5½d: the average cost of an inmate for the week was 1/4¼d, average cost in the infirmary 2/1d, average cost in fever hospital 2/2½d. The expenditure on outdoor relief was £131.7.6d. Rates collected for the week came to £102.5.11d, with £2,090.14.1½d still outstanding.

The Master's estimate of provisions and necessaries required for the ensuing week was as follows:

500lbs	bread.	33lbs	sugar.
4 doz	fish	170lbs	meat.
392lbs	oatmeal.	2lbs	pepper.
280lbs	salt.	10ston	onions.
49 lbs	soap.	3 ½ lbs	tea.
1 ton	barley meal.	2 lbs	starch.
18 lbs	dipped candles.	6 lbs	mould candles.
2half tons	Ind. meal.		

The number receiving outdoor relief in the previous week came to 7,875: relief was almost entirely of Indian meal at this time. However, the Minutes for that week recorded, yet again: 'The Vice-Guardians were unable to provide supplies for relief officers' for the coming week. The Commission issued £500 on 16 December which covered the cost of providing meal for outdoor relief up to 30 December 1848 and on that date a further £300 was issued.

The Poor Law Commission, concerned about the financial state of the union, wrote to the Home Secretary advising him that some monetary assistance would be needed for the union in the months leading up to the next harvest:

it will be impossible, during the next eight months, to relieve the destitution in the Clifden Union from the poor rates alone.[29]

It was the feeling of the Commission that the best assistance that could be offered to the union would be a grant of £1,500, by government, to enable them to erect a temporary workhouse to accommodate a further 1,000 paupers. The Commission advised that accommodation for 2,700 persons was needed

to meet the increasing destitution in the Union, and if possible to prevent the necessity of that demoralizing system; outdoor relief to the able-bodied.[30]

There was, in their opinion, no existing building suitable for conversion into an auxiliary workhouse and so the erection of a temporary building was necessary.

When questioned by the Home Secretary as to how these extra 1000 workhouse inmates would be maintained, the Commission was forced to admit that the union would not be able 'from its own resources to maintain those 1,000 paupers.'[31]

The Home Secretary in reply voiced the concern that, should the government provide the sum requested to fund the erection of the work-house, they would later be called on to finance the maintenance of the inmates. And, 'as no funds have been placed by Parliament at the dispos-al of the Government for this purpose, they do not feel that they should be justified,' in sanctioning the expenditure without putting the issue before Parliament. Furthermore the government felt that:

> under present circumstances, the aid to be afforded from the public treasury ought to be limited to the relief of urgent cases of distress in Unions in which every exertion is made to enforce the collection of rates, and that the relief given by any funds advanced by the Government should be given in food.[32]

The Commission, concerned that the delay in awaiting the Parliamentary sanction would cause administrative difficulties for the union, withdrew the proposal.

At a board meeting held on 26 December, the vice-guardians decided to take up the offer of a lease on Bunowen Castle, to be used as an auxiliary work-house. The Castle, situated southwest of Clifden, was the property of John Augustus O'Neill. O'Neill had moved to London some years before and was then on the brink of ruin and, like so many other landlords in Connemara, was being pursued through the Courts for non-payment of rates.

The Castle, with offices, yards and two acres of land, was leased at £80 per annum. It would accommodate 500 persons, bringing workhouse accommodation in the union up to 1,700, still 1,000 below the Commission's desired number.

A good deal of work was needed to convert the Castle into a workhouse for women. No children were to be included for the present, but it was hoped that the Commissioners would finance the conversion of the farm buildings into a girls' school in the near future.

Kylemore auxiliary workhouse was expected to come into operation in January; Patrick Pye was appointed overseer at 10/= per week, and the house at Roundstone was extended.

The cost of clothing and bedding for the auxiliary workhouses, advanced by the Commission from funds issued by the British Relief Association, was estimated as follows:

Clothing -	960 persons at 8/=	.£384
Bedding -	320 children, 80 blankets at 6/= }	
do	640 adults, 320 blankets at 6/=...}	. . .£120
do	400 rugs at 2/=	.£40
do	400 bed-ticks at 4/=	.£80
do	400 sheets at 1/6d	.£30

$$\overline{}$$

£654

The following diet for inmates of the workhouse and auxiliary workhouses was adopted by the Board and written into the minutes on 2 January 1849:

Suggested Diet For Workhouse Inmates

Classes.	Breakfast.	Dinner.
Able-bodied men & women	8oz Indian meal made into 'stirabout' and one pint farinaceous or fish soup.	8oz Indian meal made into 'stirabout' or 12oz coarse bread and one pint of farinaceous or fish soup.
9 to 15 years	6oz Indian meal made into 'stirabout' and a pint farinaceous or fish soup	6oz Indian meal made into 'Stirabout' or 10oz coarse bread and. three quarters pint farinaceous or fish soup.
2 to 9 years	4oz Indian meal made into 'stirabout' and half pint of milk.	8oz coarse bread and half pint farinaceous or fish soup.
Infant under 2.	half pound of bread and one pint of milk in the 24 hours.[33]	

Inspection of Temporary Fever Hospitals

In December, Dr Suffield, on the request of the vice-guardians, carried out an inspection of the fever hospitals in the union, these were situated in Kilkieran, Daily Hill (Ballyconneely), Roundstone and Ballynakill. Three months earlier Doctors Asken, Smyth and Morgan, already working in the union, were offered appointments under the Temporary Fever Act to attend to the temporary fever hospitals in their districts; Dr Asken to Kilkieran, Dr Smyth to Ballinakill and Dr Morgan to Ballindoon. The salary offered was 5/= per day, as recommended by the Board of Health.

The following month Dr Smyth resigned, stating 'that the salary which the vice-guardians offered was insufficient for his support'. The vice-guardians responded with the regret that they were unable to retain Dr Smyth's

valuable service, as his time and most zealous exertions were constantly devoted to the laborious duties of his very extensive district.[34]

Dr Morgan and Dr Asken took a similar stand and offered their resignations. Still the vice-guardians declared that, given the present state of this union (they) cannot propose a higher rate of salary for those gentlemen, and which, they admit is quite disproportionate to the services performed.[35]

The previous year the Physicians and Surgeons of the town of Galway protested at the 'paltry sum of five shillings per diem offered by the Board of Health to a medical man for his services in a Temporary Fever Hospital', and anyone who would lower himself to accept such conditions of employment 'forfeited his right to be considered a medical gentleman and that consequently we decline to meet him in consultation.'[36]

All three doctors agreed to continue working until replacements could be found and advertisements were placed in the Galway papers for medical officers to fill the three divisions, at 5/= per day. Dr Suffield, however, did accept his appointment as medical officer to Clifden Fever Hospital at a salary of 5/= per day.

On his inspection of the Fever Hospitals in the union, Dr Suffield was accompanied by Harrison Briscoe, the Poor Law Inspector. The Doctor was also to enquire into the sanitary conditions of the districts in which the hospitals were situated. The inspection took four days to complete and the doctor was paid one guinea a day, plus expenses.

In his report Dr Suffield stated that sickness was on the decline over the previous two months and that any new cases of fever which had appeared were of a 'mild character'. At the Clifden hospital there were twenty patients, the majority of whom were convalescents and would be discharged in a few days. In Roundstone there were two cases, also convalescents. In Kilkieran there were nine cases, three ready to be discharged and the rest, with the exception of one old man, were expected to be discharged in a week. In Ballinakill there were four cases, three soon to be discharged; but the other, 'one of inflammation of the lungs', was to be removed to the Clifden Infirmary.

The doctor ended his report with the warning:

In conclusion I think it right to state that it is very doubtful how long this satisfactory state of the health of this district will continue as at present distress and poverty are vastly on the increase.[37]

However, despite the warning the vice-guardians closed down the fever hospitals, declaring that they were 'unable to keep up such establishments having neither money nor credit, nor any prospect of obtaining either'. The Relieving Officers were instructed to provide transport to Clifden fever hospital for 'such destitute poor persons as may be afflicted with fever in the district'.[38] Considering the extent of the union this journey must surely have been an arduous one for many a fever sufferer in the months that followed. Two houses were rented in the town to accommodate convalescents from the fever hospital, to free beds for the new arrivals.

CHAPTER 11

FEVER AND CHOLERA

January 1849 brought the same reports of destitution and want from the Clifden union as in previous January. The vice-guardians wrote to the Commissioners on 22 January:

> It is a source of regret to us that we are not enabled to report any permanent improvement in the condition of the bulk of the population since last year...the same causes which then operated still continue, and the same aid to mitigate the privations of the people will be again required.[1]

Harrison Briscoe, the Poor Law Inspector, felt that 'the destitution this year is greater' than last, the cause being, 'failure of the potato crop, and of the herring fishery, and want of employment.'[2] There were no mills or factories and no 'export trade from any part of the union,' and the seaweed,

> which in former years was most profitable both as manure and in the manufacture of kelp, is now almost valueless...The successive failure of the potato crop have completed the ruin of the majority of the population. As a consequence, payment of rents has been suspended, and immense tracts of land left untilled.[3]

The few people who had given employment in the past no longer did, either because of their reduced circumstances or out of fear that any improvements made to their property might cause an increase in taxation. The large number of the fishermen's boats were in need of repair, and many good boats were without nets. Fuel was also in short supply. The previous season was so wet, that, 'although the whole of this union is a mass of bog, all classes are suffering from a want of fuel.'

The clothing of the people had deteriorated to the extent that many no longer attended fairs, markets or chapel:[g]

> There are few cattle, and scarcely a stack of corn to be seen. The people are fast selling their furniture. The few potatoes that came to perfection have nearly disappeared.

Some farmers were holding potatoes for seed, but the poorer classes had none. Indian meal was the main food of the people.

The union finances made sorry reading. Debts to the sum of £6,535.6.3d were hampering the administration of the union:

> Among the creditors are all the officers, small traders, mechanics, distributors, carriers, nurses; in fact, every description of occupation within the union, independent of large sums to meal contractors.[4]

[g] see Appendix 2.

Added to that, the total estimated expense for relief and establishment for the month of February, was £2,088.4.4d. The Treasurer had just £194.7.8.½d in hand and it was expected that out of an outstanding rate of £1,455.2.11.½d, only £455.2.11.½d could be collected. 'The collectors are excellent officers, and have done their duty', they now met with almost no opposition to the collection of rates. However, many who payed rates the previous year were now in the workhouse. It was agreed by the vice-guardians and Briscoe that the balance of £1,000:

> will be impossible to collect until harvest next.
>
> All classes of proprietors and occupiers are in such a destitute state that any attempt to collect another rate until next harvest would be useless, and be the means of sending numbers into the workhouse; consequently it is necessary for the Government to provide means for the current and future expenses of the Union.[5]

For some months now the Commission accepted that it was impossible for the union to maintain its destitute poor on the poor rate alone. The estimates for the coming year showed clearly the necessity for government aid.

Liabilities and Assets For 1849

Liabilities for 1849:

Debts due 27 January 1849.	£6,535.
Relief advanced due 1849.	£3,228.
Expenditure, if the same as in 1848:	£23,405.
Total liabilities	£33,168.

Assets for 1849:

Outstanding Rate on 27 January 1849	£1,442.
Rates as collected in 1848.	£2,529.
Total supposed assets	£3,971.

Leaving a deficit of	**£29,197.** [6]

RETURN of Immediate Lessors, Defaulters for Poor-Rate.

E. Division.	No.	Name.	Amount. £. s. d.	Proceedings taken.	Observations.
CLIFDEN	1	Edward Coneys	2 15 3½	Collector states this will be paid.	
	2	Thomas Bodkin	7 19 7½	" "	Lives 80 miles from Clifden; has been written to; if no satisfactory answer, will be sued.
	3	John Hart	1 5 7		Lives in Galway, do. do.
	4	Basil Madden	4 17 6	Owes now 1l. 16s.—will be paid.	
	5	John Davey	3 8 6	"15 Days' Notice" served	Promised to be arranged immediately.
	6	A. Bell Martin	46 0 0½	Col. Arthur wrote to Inspector that rates on this property will be arranged without delay.	Same.
	7	Hyacinth D'Arcy	60 0 0	Mr. D'Arcy has not been at home. Collector states this will be settled in a week.	Same.
	8	Mathias Duane	11 8 0	"15 Days' Notice" served.	
BALLINDOON	9	John A. O'Neill	366 6 4	In Superior Courts.	In Superior Courts.
	10	Martin O'Malley	26 0 0	" "	Dead. No personal representative.
	11	A. Bell Martin	55 13 8	"15 Days' Notice" served. Summons issued.	Promised to be arranged immediately.
	12	John Lambert	59 16 3	"15 Days' Notice" served.	
ROUNDSTONE	13	A. Bell Martin	44 5 9	"15 Days' Notice" served	Promised to be arranged immediately.
	14	Martin O'Malley	21 19 10	" "	Dead. No personal representative at present.
	15	General Thomson	25 14 7	"15 Days' Notice" served	Promised to be arranged immediately.
	16	James Ogle	21 1 1	"15 Days' Notice" served.	
	17	Mathias Duane	6 18 8½	Summons issued.	
	18	John A. O'Neill	15 15 1	See No. 9.	
	19	Dr. Gray	1 7 10	"15 Days' Notice" served.	
	20	Hyacinth D'Arcy	13 8 4	"15 Days' Notice" served	Promised to be arranged immediately.
	21	John King	6 17 3½	Collector states this will be paid.	Same.
	22	Michael J. Browne	16 5 9	"15 Days' Notice" served.	
	23	Henry Blake	85 16 3½	"15 Days' Notice" served	Promised to be arranged immediately.
RENVYLE	24	General Thomson	42 14 11½	"15 Days' Notice" served	Same.
	25	A. Bell Martin	54 10 11	"15 Days' Notice" served	Same.
	26	Lord Ffrench	51 16 4	Mr. Barlow, the agent, promises to settle.	Same.
	27	Sir George Beresford	13 5 9½	"15 Days' Notice" served.	
	28	John Robertson	7 10 0	This will be paid.	
	29	John D'Arcy	6 8 1½	This will be paid	Promised to be arranged immediately.
	30	Anthony Gorham	6 1 8½	Summoned to Petty Sessions	
			£. 1490 9 2		

HAMILTON SMITH, *Clerk of Union.*
December 21, 1848.

Return of immediate Lessors, Defaulters for Poor Rate[7]

Fr Fitzmaurice Attacks The Poor Law

On Saturday 20 January the *Galway Vindicator* published a letter from Father Fitzmaurice P.P. for Clifden, attacking the inadequacies of the Poor Law and the harsh effect its implementation was having on the people:

> The quarter-acre clause, exterminating and inhuman as it is, has ceased to be a test here. Nine-tenths of our population have no land, no houses (for I will not so designate their wretched hovels), no beds or bed clothing, save their tattered rags - not even fuel. The workhouse is filled to suffocation...Cold and comfortless as there abodes of misery are, yet every day hundreds are crowding to them enfeebled and emaciated, carrying their almost naked skeletons of children on their backs, craving admission, and denied it, until other receptacles are prepared, and in the meantime no food given to them! Of the nine-thousand receiving out-door relief last August in these parishes, there are only three thousand three hundred at present on the lists.
>
> From the woeful experience of last year, we know what will be the result of a repetition of that cold, calculating and heartless system.
>
> A few facts will suffice. In the district of Kingstown, containing a population of only 100 there were, from February 1st to May 14th last year, 201 deaths from starvation!!! The names of the deceased and the dates of their deaths I have...The other districts in these parishes are almost as destitute. I challenge the government officials or relieving officers to deny these facts...if substantial and timely relief be not afforded to these creatures in the way of gratuitous food, they will inevitably perish? Let then, the cruel system be abandoned by order of the government, of undertaking to support the greatest number of human beings upon the smallest quantity of food.[8]

In the three months between 29 September and 30 December 1848, 5 deaths were recorded inside the workhouse. Between 6 January and 7 April 1849 the number jumped to 123, and the number of patients in the hospitals doubled. Fever, diarrhoea and dysentery were again attacking the inmates. Whooping cough was also prevalent among the children. Dr Suffield's duties were extended to include the auxiliary workhouses and his salary increased to £100 per annum. Workhouse accommodation had increased to 1,190 and the number receiving outdoor relief was daily increasing.

Given the overcrowded state of the workhouse, the stench that accompanied fever; and the obvious threat to the health of the staff, it seems little wonder that two attempts were made during January to move the boardroom and the clerk's offices outside of the house. At the board meeting on Tuesday 9 January it was proposed that:

in consequence of the great necessity which exists for extra accommodation in the workhouse the apartment at present used as a boardroom be fitted up for the reception of paupers, and that accommodation be provided elsewhere for the boardroom and clerks offices.[9]

This proposal was, however, rejected by the Commissioners. Still, two
weeks later the vice-guardians tried again; on this occasion they suggestion that the boardroom and clerks offices be moved out of the workhouse
for a short time, while alterations inside the building were being carried
out. They believed that the change was 'most desirable as the room lately
held as a boardroom was over large - not floored and exceedingly cold.'[10]
This time, not waiting for a reply from the Commissioners, William
D'Arcy's house in the town was rented until 25 March. When the
Commissioners did voice their disapproval, the vice-guardians agreed to
hold the weekly board meetings in the workhouse, but the offices
remained in the town.

The numbers receiving outdoor relief averaged about 7,000 a week and
the Commissioners again recommended 'a personal examination of all the
persons in receipt of relief in the union.'[11]

Restructuring Of Relief Districts

In February a restructuring of the relief districts and workhouse accommodation was proposed by the vice-guardians and sanctioned by the
Poor Law Commission. The number of relief districts was reduced from
nine to six, each under the control of a relieving officer with a central food
depot for the administration of outdoor relief.

At the suggestion of Harrison Briscoe the number of Relieving Officers
was reduced and their salaries increased so as to attract 'a better description of officer'.[12] The officers were allocated the following districts: A.G.
Kearns, Clifden; Peter Joyce, Ballindoon; Edmond Joyce, North
Roundstone; John Joyce, South Roundstone; J Dooner, Renvyle; and W
Coneys, West Roundstone. The salaries of the relieving officers for
Clifden, Ballindoon and Renvyle were increased from £45 to £50. The
salaries of the officers for the North, South and West Roundstone districts
were increased from £35 to £45 per annum.

The new districts were made up as follows:

1st: Clifden District, to comprise the whole of the Clifden Electoral
Division, with the depot at Streamstown, (William McDermott's
house).

2nd: Renvyle District, to comprise the whole of the Renvyle Electoral
Division, with the depot at Letterfrack, (Bryan Powell's house).

3rd: Ballindoon District, to comprise the whole of the Ballindoon Electoral Division, with the depot at Daily Hill (Ballyconneely).

4th: North Roundstone District, to comprise that part of the Roundstone Electoral Division bounded as follows: on the West by the road leading from the marble quarry in the townland of Barnanoraun, this townland to be included, to the lake of Ballynahinch - the lake, Toombeola river (Abhainn Mhór), the fisheries, Cloonisle Bay to the sea- North by Renvyle electoral division, East by the Galway union, South by the following townlands; which were not included: Gowla (Gabhla), Gowlaun East (An Gabhlán Thoir) and Derryrush (Doire Iorrais). The depot at Garroman (An Gharmain).

5th: South Roundstone District, to comprise all that part of the Roundstone Electoral Division south, and including, the following townlands; Gowla (Gabhla), Gowlaun East (An Gabhlán Thoir) and Derryrush (Doire Iorrais) with all the islands lying south and east. The depot at Carna.

6th West Roundstone District, to comprise all that part of the Roundstone Electoral Division lying west of the road leading from the marble quarry on the townland of Barnanoraun; not including this townland, to the lake of Ballynahinch - the lake, Toombeola river (Abhainn Mhór), the fisheries, Cloonisle Bay to the sea, with all the islands lying south and east. The depot at Roundstone.[13]

Once the above depots were in place the remaining food depots would close. The Clifden depot was also to close when the oven at the workhouse became fully operational.

In keeping with the Poor Law policy of segregation, the following plan was drawn up for the full utilization of the union's workhouse accommodation:-

Clifden workhouse and the auxiliaries at Roundstone and Kylemore would in future accommodate adult males: these houses had land attached which would be cultivated by the inmates.

Bunowen Castle, when alterations were completed, to accommodate adult females - and in time girls also. Hilderbrand's store to accommodate boys, with a school attached. Creighton's store, then housing children, would, when Bunowen was fully functional, be attached to the fever hospital.

The house formerly occupied as a fever hospital in Roundstone was taken from John King, at a weekly rent of 5/=, as an infirmary for that district.

Assistant masters were appointed at Kylemore and Roundstone, at £15 per annum, plus rations: William Clesham at Kylemore and Mathias Maley (former relieving officer) at Roundstone. Peter Kneafsy was appointed

Assistant Master at Bunowen Castle, at £10 per annum and John Freston (Preston) took over the position vacated by him of Labour Master at Clifden workhouse. Superintendents of labourers, at a salary of £10 per annum, plus rations, were also appointed at Kylemore and Roundstone.

The Matron would take over the running of Bunowen Castle. Mary King, a former schoolmistress, was appointed Assistant Matron at a salary of £10 per annum, plus rations. Once the above arrangements were complete, schoolmasters and mistresses would be appointed to instruct the children according to the National System of Education.[14]

The minutes of the board meeting held on Tuesday 13 March 1849 recorded that Dr Gannon, medical officer of Roundstone auxiliary workhouse and the man who had attracted Dr Phelan's criticism, was sick with fever: he died later in the month. Dr Morgan was appointed in his place temporarily, at a salary of £2.5s per week. The minutes also recorded that 20 deaths had taken place in the workhouses in the previous week; in which houses these occurred it is not stated. Between the workhouse and auxiliary workhouses there were on that date, 1,295 inmates, 168 patients in the hospitals: 78 fever cases, 90 other cases, and 10,234 receiving outdoor relief.

Contracts were agreed with the following suppliers of goods to be supplied to the workhouse and the auxiliary houses from 25 March 1849 to 25 March 1850:

Margaret Berry - New milk, imperial quart one penny three farthings.

John Griffin - Black tea @ 4/= per lb. Jamaica sugar @ 5d per lb. Best coffee @ 1/10 per lb. Loaf sugar 8d per lb. Starch 7d per lb. Dipped candles 6½ d per lb. Mould candles 8d per lb.

Michael Gowane - meat @ 2¾d per lb.

William Livingston, Westport, to supply depots in the union from week ending 31 March to week ending 30 June 1849, with: best yellow Indian meal @ £9.2.6d per ton. best rye meal @ £8.11.0d per ton and barley meal @ £8.10.0d per ton. Three weeks supply to be kept in the union, to be paid in cash at the end of each fortnight. Orders were to be given to Mr Livingston's agent in Clifden who was to receive payments and issue receipts.[15]

As the number of deaths in the workhouse averaged ten to twenty per week, some of the officials and staff became ill. D.V. O'Leary was now absent from board meetings for almost three months and Hamilton Smith was replaced by his assistant, William Gallagher. Smith was suffering from a severe pain in his side and chest 'brought on by long confinement and close application in the discharge of my duties for some months past.'[16] He was advised by his doctor to 'try a change of air for a few weeks,' but was unable to take up the advice because he had not been paid for some time and was without funds. His salary should have been paid out of the Poor Rate. The Poor Law Commissioners wrote to Sir Charles Trevelyan, in the Treasury, requesting permission to pay Smith his overdue salary out of the government grants to the union. They were informed that:

> their Lordships regret that they do not feel themselves authorized to pay the balance of salary owing to the clerk of the Clifden Union, out of funds which have been granted by Parliament for the relief of extreme destitution in the distressed Unions in the West of Ireland.[17]

The Master at Clifden, Patrick Joyce, was given one month's leave of absence to recover from his illness: he eventually retired, and was replaced by his brother Peter Joyce. In the middle of all this sickness, John Winter, the recently appointed assistant master, and Sarah Barrett, the assistant matron at Hildebrand's store, both resigned.[18]

Cholera Epidemic

As the numbers of dead, both inside and outside the workhouse, continued to mount, reports of cholera in other parts of the country were causing alarm. In January and again in March the Commissioners had issued the vice-guardians with instructions on how to treat choler, should it appear in the workhouse. However, it was 17 April before the Union Minute Book recorded cholera having reached the workhouse and even then choler cases were not always recorded separately from fever cases.

On week ending 14 April there were 1,325 inmates in the workhouse and auxiliaries. There were 168 patients in the fever and workhouse hospitals; 108 of these were recorded as fever cases and 60 other cases. A total of 17 deaths had taken place that week, 75 persons were discharged and 11,505 persons received outdoor relief. The exact houses in which the deaths had occurred were again not shown, but the accounts of that week listed a Burial Account, and two cheques for coffins were issued, one of £1.7.0d to a John Flaherty and another, for coffins to Roundstone auxiliary, amounting to £2.15.6d made out to a Pat Kelly.

The following week, 22 deaths were recorded and on the week ending 28 April, for the first time, a separate entry was made showing 34 cholera cases among the 217 patients in the workhouse and fever hospitals. Rice and white bread were added to the diet of cholera victims in the workhouse. Cholera victims on outdoor relief were also given extra rations.

Christopher James Payne M.D., was appointed medical officer for Roundstone on 24 April, replacing Dr Gannon, at a salary of £30 per annum. He was also appointed to attend all cholera patients in the district around Roundstone and Ballindoon at 10/- per day. Dr Morgan was appointed to attend cholera cases in Clifden town and neighbourhood, at the same wage.

STATE of the WORKHOUSE for the Week ending Saturday, the _14_ᵗʰ day of _April_ 1849.

Number of Inmates for which accommodation is provided:—	Aged and Infirm.		Able-bodied.		Boys.	Girls.	Children under 2 years.	Born.		Total.	RETURN OF SICK AND LUNATICS.			OBSERVATIONS.
	Males.	Fem.	Males.	Fem.				Males.	Fem.		Number In Hospital on the above date.	No. of Lunatics and Idiots in Workhouse on the above date.		
Workhouse, 600 / Temporary Buildings, 250 / Permanent Fever Hospital, / Fever Sheds, 66 / Total, 1306											In Workhouse Hospital, 60 / In Fever Hospital 105	In separate Wards, / In Wards with other Inmates,		
Remaining on previous Saturday, as per last Return,	8	4	272	527	268	262	10	2	1		1349	Total, 168	Total,		
Admitted during the Week,	..	..	26	24	11	5	2	..	..		68				
TOTAL,	8	4	298	551	274	267	12	2	1		1417				
Discharged during the Week	..	..	29	17	13	15	1	..	..		75				
Died,	..	..	1	5	8	2	1	..	..		17	_Fever Cases 108_ } 168			
Total Discharged and Dead	..	..	30	22	21	17	2	..	..		92	_Other Cases 60_			
REMAINING ON THE ABOVE DATE,	8	4	268	529	253	260	10	2	1		1325				

RETURN of DESTITUTE PERSONS relieved out of the Workhouse, as by Relief Lists, for the last Week ended Saturday, the _7_ᵗʰ day of _April_ authenticated and laid before the Board of Guardians at this Meeting.

RELIEF DISTRICT.	Destitute Persons relieved out of the Workhouse under 10 Vict. c. 31, s. 1.		Destitute Persons relieved out of the Workhouse, but not comprised in Sec. 1.		Total relieved out of the Workhouse.		RELIEF DISTRICT.	Destitute Persons relieved out of the Workhouse under 10 Vict. c. 31, s. 1.		Destitute Persons relieved out of the Workhouse, but not comprised in Sec. 1.		Total relieved out of the Workhouse.	
	Number of cases relieved.	Number of Persons, including Applicant and Family, dependent on him or her.	Number of cases relieved.	Number of Persons, including Applicant and Family, dependent on him or her.	Cases.	Persons.		Number of cases relieved.	Number of Persons, including Applicant and Family, dependent on him or her.	Number of cases relieved.	Number of Persons, including Applicant and Family, dependent on him or not.	Cases.	Persons.
No. I.	1009	2649	74	131	1083	2780	Bt. forward						
No. II.	596	1542	38	67	634	1609	No. X.						
No. III.	402	1115	9	21	411	1136	No. XI.						
No. IV.	530	1520	57	38	557	1558	No. XII.						
No. V.	405	1018	42	71	447	1089	No. XIII.						
No. VI.	1620	3202	81	131	1701	3333	No. XIV.						
No. VII.							No. XV.						
No. VIII.							No. XVI.						
No. IX.							No. XVII.						
Car. forward	4562	11046	271	459	4833	11505	TOTAL,						

COPY of MINUTES of Proceedings of the Board of Guardians, at a Meeting held on _Tuesday_ the _17_ᵗʰ day of _April_ 1849

PRESENT: In the Chair,

Other Guardians:

State of the Workhouse for the week ending Saturday 14 April 1849.
Taken from Minute Book Clifden Union, September 1848 - July 1849.

The Commissioners complained that they were receiving insufficient information on the running of the union and official forms were not being filled in correctly. They requested details from the medical officers on cholera cases they had attended and the 'particulars of each case of death from destitution' from the vice-guardians. The medical officers were also instructed to make a weekly report to the Board.

The vice-guardians, 'in consequence of cholera being in the workhouse', decided to hold all future board meetings outside the workhouse. The Commissioners disagreed with their actions and ordered them to transfer all books and papers belonging to the union back into the workhouse as soon as possible.

The numbers of deaths continued to rise, reaching a peak on 8 May with 54 deaths recorded. Burial expenses for the week came to £17.16.0, covering the cost of coffins supplied by P Kelly to Roundstone and W Gallagher to the Clifden workhouse and Electoral Division. In each district of the union a person was employed 'to cleanse and enforce cleanliness', to prevent the spread of the disease, and medical officers were given an assistant to distribute medicine.

Dr.Suffield was reported unwell and William Gallagher, acting secretary, was taken ill and replaced by John Moran. 'In consequence of the spread of cholera, and the want of medical assistance at Kylemore auxiliary workhouse', it was decided to limit the intake of inmates there and to delay the opening of Bunowen Castle for a fortnight. Lack of medical assistance in Kylemore eventually forced the closure of the workhouse in June and all furniture and inmates were removed to Clifden.

Bunowen Castle was 'open to paupers' on 4 June and a Roman Catholic chaplain was appointed, at £40 per annum, to attend to the spiritual needs of the inmates. The following day, 5 June, the medical officers reported to the Board that 'Cholera had quite subsided in the town of Clifden.' Temporary hospitals were closed and the staff paid off.

Two weeks later, at the Board meeting on Tuesday 19 June, Hamilton Smith was back as secretary and it was recorded in the minutes that cholera had 'wholly disappeared from the workhouse and auxiliaries and had almost totally subsided in the country districts of the union.' The vice-guardians praised the medical officers, Dr. Suffield, Dr. Morgan and Dr Payne, stating that the

zealous, judicious and effective measures adopted by these gentlemen in their several departments, as well as their readiness to co-operate with them in every way for the public good,

had succeeded in eliminating cholera from the union.

The figures for the week show the workhouse and auxiliaries having a total of 1,537 inmates. There were 70 patients in the workhouse infirmary and 42 in the fever hospital. Five deaths were recorded and 28 persons discharged. The number on outdoor relief, however, had been steadily increasing over the previous weeks and now stood at 13,203. The cost of provisions and necessaries for the workhouse and auxiliaries was £106.9.5d and the cost of outdoor relief £275.15.2d. Again, as so often in the previous weeks, there was no rate collected that week, but a cheque for £500 was received from the Treasury through the Poor Law Commission.

The number of deaths recorded in the workhouse and auxiliary work-houses between 14 April and 16 June came to 208.[19]

Vice-Guardians Step Down

Throughout the country the potato crop of 1849 was for the most part healthy and there were only isolated reports of blight. The Famine had officially come to an end. To normalize conditions as quickly as possible, the vice-guardians were removed and the administration of the union was returned to a Board of Guardians on 1 November 1849.

The vice-guardians were originally sent into the union to clean up the administrative chaos created by the board, to collect all outstanding rates and to administer relief efficiently and economically. During their term in office the country had experienced yet another crop failure and the num-bers seeking relief had swamped the system. Their efforts to collect the poor rate from bankrupt landlords and impoverished farmers met with little success and the union was even more in debt when they left than it had been when they had entered.

When the vice-guardians took up office on 7 February 1848 the union was £564 in debt, at the time of their removal that debt had increased to £6,898. Outstanding rates, which stood at £2,035 on 7 February 1848, amounted to £5,233 on 1 November 1849. The total expenditure of the union under the vice-guardians came to £46,231, £34,840 of this being grants received from the government[20]. The number of persons relieved during their second year in office, year ending 28 September 1849, at 6,126 indoor and 20,426[21] outdoor, was high when one takes into account the vice-guardians constant revision of the relief lists along with their close observation of the Quarter-Acre Clause. Death and emigration had also reduced numbers.

Financially the union may not have been in as healthy a condition as the government would have liked. However, the vice-guardians were also sent in to make the Poor Law effective and in that they had been successful.

Under the vice-guardians a structured implementation of the Poor Law had taken place. With the restructuring of the Relief Districts and the increase in workhouse accommodation in February 1849, the union was made more efficient than ever before. The vice-guardians were an extremely hard working team of dedicated men, but even they found it impossible to run the union as efficiently as they would have wished. Their attempts to administer relief and restructure the union were impeded at every step by the lack of funds.

Their reports to the Poor Law Commission on the conditions in the union were less emotional than those received from the Board of Guardians, which makes their content all the more poignant. Their notes of despair, pointing out the impossibility of feeding a large starving population on the proceeds of the rate alone, were all the more real coming from men sent into the union to make the system work. Their desperation, and at times real panic, at being left with large numbers of starving people and with no food to feed them, forced them on occasions to purchase supplies out of their own pocket, thus attracting the criticism of the Poor Law Commission.

Their leaving seems to have attracted little attention or comment, as with the departure of John Deane some months before. However, the records show that, although required to administer a cold and harsh system of relief in an area which had suffered severely before and during their term in office, they did so as efficiently and humanely as possible.

CHAPTER 12

RECKLESS DESPERATION

In the years before the Famine the people of Connemara were recognized as peace-loving, friendly and hospitable. Every man's property was considered safe and outbreaks of unrest and serious acts of violence were almost unheard of. In 1846 Rev Duncan described the people as being the most patient in the world. But just how much would their patience endure?

Driven by starvation and the need to provide for their dying children the poor turned on each other, stealing from the homes of their neighbours and slaughtering their animals on the hill sides. They put their freedom and their very lives at risk as they stole the landlord's sheep from his land, then quickly destroyed the skin before the arrival of the police, who were never too far behind. The depth of despair reached by the starving people is evident in the many examples of the lengths they were driven to in their struggle to survive.

Clifden Bridewell
Courtesy of the National Library of Ireland

As the Famine advanced and the conditions of the people deteriorated it was the feeling of the authorities that it was only a matter of time before organized acts of outrage would take place. With the transport of large quantities of food, the setting up of government food depots and the increased stores held by local merchants, attacks on supplies were considered to be inevitable.

Heavy security was provided and a close watch was kept on the people by the staff of the Board of Works, the police and the Resident Magistrate.

However, the anticipated riots and organized plunder of supplies never took place. Throughout the Famine there were no reports of secret societies or subversive individuals orchestrating attacks on food stores or private property. The acts of outrage and violence which did occur appear to have been carried out by individuals, or by family groups, and were recognized by the authorities as individual acts of desperation driven by need rather than political motivation.

The only show of strength which would seem to indicate the influence of some society or group, although there is no reference to this in the newspapers or official reports of the time, was that displayed on 23 September 1846. On that day a large crowd from all over the union gathered in Clifden to pressurise the assembled ratepayers to seek adequate works under the Labour Rate Act and thereby give employment to the suffering poor. Violent threats were made but the crowd dispersed peacefully at the end of the session.

Two days earlier a group had assembled on the lawn of Clifden Castle to voice their distress before Hyacinth D'Arcy. But following this there were no large gatherings of protesters and even where large groups were brought together, such as on the public works and at the soup kitchens, their conduct was reported by Board of Works staff as 'subordinate in the extreme'. Weakened by starvation, fever and dysentery and thankful at having obtained a place on the works, these people would do little to jeopardise that place.

The only real show of organized resistance was displayed by the ratepayers in resisting the collection of the Poor Rate in 1847. Yet, even then, opposition to the collection of rates and rent was confined to a quick response to the actions of the day. When the rate collector arrived with his bailiffs to distrain stock the farmer put up a fight and, backed up by friends and neighbours, was usually successful in driving him off. However, the government's insistence that a police escort accompany the collectors soon brought an end to such displays.

Police Duties Increased

In 1845 Quarter Sessions were held in Clifden, Oughterard, Tuam and Galway. Petty Sessions were held in Clifden, on the second Thursday of every month, Renvyle on the first Tuesday and Roundstone on the second Thursday[1]. The Magistrates were members of the local landed gentry and the Resident Magistrate for the Barony had recently died and had not yet been replaced.

The head of the local constabulary was Sub-Inspector James Ireland. He was appointed on 17 April 1841 his headquarters was at Clifden and his district included Roundstone and Letterfrack. The head constable in Clifden was John Reilly, he took up his appointment on 1 September 1839 and William Wilks was appointed to Roundstone on 1 January 1843. [2]

In the early years of the Famine the protection of government and local relief committee food stores fell to the police force, greatly stretching manpower and causing staffing problems for Sub-Inspector Ireland. In November 1846 a detachment of the 49th Regiment, made up of sixty one men under the command of Lieutenant Seton, was sent to Clifden to assist the police in their duties. However, the following month six of the troops, a corporal and five privates, were arrested for plundering the government store at Clifden while under their protection.

The scarcity and high price of food and the difficulty in obtaining employment on the public works drove many to crime in the harsh winter of 1846/47. By January 1847 the numbers involved in crime stretched the resources of the police, courts and jails to the limit. The theft of sheep, cattle and food was a regular occurrence.

John Dopping R.M. 1800-1855

In early January warrants for a variety of charges were issued for forty persons to appear at the Roundstone Petty Sessions later that month. Those found guilty would be taken to the bridewell at Clifden, which would normally accommodate eighteen and which was then full to capacity. There, due to the absence of a Resident Magistrate in the district, they could expect to spend up to fourteen days before being bailed. However, such a short period of time in such crowded conditions was a threat to both health and life as the prisoners came into contact with fever and dysentery.

Sub-Inspector James Ireland complained that:

the force of the district is far from being able to efficiently discharge the duties required, or as I would wish, but I do my best, and so does every man under me.

He was answering criticism by Thomas Martin that the police were not acting fast enough on warrants and that their numbers were insufficient for the area. Ireland recommended that the force be increased and 'the service of a stipendiary magistrate in this very large locality would be absolutely required.'[3] Soon afterwards, John Dopping of Derrycasson House, Granard in County Longford, was appointed Resident Magistrate and moved with his family to Clifden where he leased Glenowen House from the D'Arcy family.

In March forty four prisoners were held in the Clifden bridewell awaiting transfer to Galway jail. As quickly as one lot were dispatched their places were filled with more petty offenders. The penalties handed down by the court varied, with some prisoners receiving six months hard labour for larceny of sheep while others were given transportation for seven years for the same crime. Larceny of purses received two months, larceny of teaspoons one month hard labour and theft of clothes three to six months.

Along with protecting the food depots, arresting thieves and escorting prisoners to the county prison in Galway, the police still had the investigation of more serious crime, such as murder, to attend too.

On 18 February a woman's body was discovered on the mountain at Cushatrower, about two miles from Roundstone. Head constable William Wilks had the remains removed to Roundstone where she was identified as Bridget Conneely, the daughter of Bartley Conneely of Ervallagh. Twelve 'respectable inhabitants' were then called on to view the body and Dr Kerran carried out an examination.

Bridget had left her home on Friday 5 February, to go to Clifden to buy fish and a shirt for her father, and was never seen alive again. The verdict of the inquest, held on 23 and 24 February, was that Bridget had been

recently ravished and afterwards strangled with a woollen kerchief tied about her neck by some person or persons to us at present unknown. Nor can we at this time say on what day the said murder was committed.[4]

People Growing Desperate And Daring

In January 1848 John Dopping reported to Under-Secretary Thomas Redington that:

poverty, destitution and crime are still on the increase - Deaths from actual starvation are becoming frequent and so desperate and daring have the people become that they not infrequently enter dwelling houses through the roof and steal what ever they can find, while the inhabitants are a sleep[5]

Hyacinth D'Arcy corroborated this statement in his letter two days later, where he stated that conditions in the district had deteriorated considerably and that there was a high rise in crime 'and the recklessness with which it is carried out.'[6] As a result, the number of persons brought before the courts had greatly increased; recent Petty Sessions in Roundstone went on for two days, the cases heard being for the most part burglary and larceny. Two prisoners were committed for stealing cash, three for stealing sheep, three for cow stealing, seven for burglary and robbery, one for stealing an anchor, one for stealing a cable and another for stealing a rope.

Clifden bridewell was crowded with prisoners awaiting transport to Galway jail and death from fever was common among the inmates of both. Dominick Kerrigan, the Keeper of the Clifden bridewell, reported to John Dopping that, although the bridewell was built to hold eighteen, it now held sixty nine:

> My bridewell was only intended for 18, having only six cells and a refectory cell for misdemeanants, the most I could put in each cell of six is three in each bed, having no further accommodation.[7]

At Galway jail the situation was the same. On 3 January 1848 the jail, intended to accommodate 110 prisoners, held 564 and one hundred more arrived from Clifden a few days later. John Dopping, informing his superiors of conditions in both places of detention, remarked that:

> The state of the prisoners under those circumstances can be easily imagined, and yet the poor people are most anxious to be committed, and look upon the gaol as an asylum.[8]

The police in Clifden were fully occupied escorting prisoners to Galway jail and John Dopping feared for the safety of the food depot and suggested that, given the present crisis, a company of infantry should be quartered in Clifden as a precautionary measure. Their presence would also, he felt:

> have the affect of inducing merchants to send large supplies to the town by giving confidence as to their safety...a feeling of reckless desperation has manifested itself amongst the portion of the people really in a state of starvation, and where instances are not wanting of depraved persons taking advantage of such a state of things, and wantonly plundering their neighbours.[9]

The request for a military presence was granted by the Lord Lieutenant later in the month.[10]

Dr Suffield inspected the bridewell on 8 February and found 70 prisoners in custody; four had fever and one, Pat King, was dying. Dominick Kerrigan and his wife were doing their best to attend to the sick but were finding the situation intolerable. Dr Suffield recommended that a hospital be set up and a nurse employed to care for the sick, and that proper food 'wine, broth and other necessaries' [11] be provided.

The strain of working under such conditions was having its effect on Kerrigan, who, in a letter to Dublin Castle, blamed Sub-Inspector Ireland for the overcrowding and went on to describe the inmates as:

Half starved, half naked beings in human form. If marched off when tried and convicted such would not be the case. But Mr Ireland does as he likes and would not be dictated to by anyone, my curse on him, he is the means of robbing me of the little portion of health which I possess after the fever...Roundstone sessions will be on the 9th and Clifden on the 10th and what an awful place my bridewell will be on Friday morning. May the Lord look to us in the midst of fever and dysentery, overcrowded with felons and beggars. Amen.[12]

The feeling of 'reckless desperation' was not only confined to those dying of starvation but was also evident among the beleaguered ratepayers, as shown in the verdict delivered at an inquest held into the death of James Ward of Emlaghmore.

Ward had, according to his widow Maria, 'lent several hundred pounds to the poor people in the neighbourhood' and because of the 'distressed condition of those people...he despaired of ever being repaid.' The strain of financial worries made him fearful of loosing his mind, 'like Mr Blake of Renvyle', Maria told the inquest. Henry Blake was in financial difficulty and his mental and physical health was causing concern for his family and friends.

The verdict delivered by twelve of his neighbours, all 'good and lawful men'[h], declared that on 20 February James Ward of Emlaghmore cut his throat:

with his own razor while labouring under an aberration of mind, brought on, as they (the jury) believe by the pressure of the present poor rate, and the fear of a new rate being struck.[13]

Sheep Stealing

Sheep stealing was taking place at an alarming rate; seventy nine people were committed to the county jail for that offence alone in the month of January. John Dopping told the under-secretary that he was finding it impossible to put an end to it in his district:

The persons engaged in this offence...are not always those in a state of destitution...The persons in absolute want seldom take any trouble to conceal their guilt, whereas the wanton offenders - taking advantage of the law, as it stands at present, by concealing such portions of the animal as are capable of identification...are frequently discovered with the carcases of sheep in their possession which they have not come honestly by, but for which they can not, under the existing law, be called on to account.[14]

[h]The twelve men listed were: John Robertson, George Nimmo, Thomas Hazel, Darby Hickey, Michael MacDonaugh, Mark Carr, Valentine Geralish, Thomas Flaherty, Patrick Kelly, John Mannion, Pat Kerby and Michael Foran.

He enclosed a letter from Major-General Thomson of Salruck requesting that the matter be brought to the attention of the authorities:

> What is to be done to stop the increasing sheep stealing that is going on in this neighbourhood it is frightful -they throw the skins and heads into the sea or into bog holes and sometimes burn them and tho' you find the mutton in their houses or even in their pots boiling they can not be convicted tho' there can not be a shadow of doubt that they came by it dishonestly - having no means whatever of getting it otherwise. Would it not be right to represent this fact to Government - let me know your opinion on the subject.[15]

Major-General Thomson of Salruck

Thomas was, however, successful in having four people caught in the act of killing one of his sheep on the night of 1 March. They were under suspicion for some time but no evidence could be found against them: 'I hope from the evidence now against them that they will be sent across the water'.

Thomas agreed with Dopping that the situation was out of control:

> the country is getting into a dreadful state of disorganisation they will have neither sheep or cattle in the country and shortly neither life or property will be safe fifty sheep have been stolen from Robert Fair within the last six weeks. Then Mr Eastwood's had 20 sheep stolen from there a few nights ago I have nothing but complaints from every quarter-.
>
> A search was made in Lettershanbally three nights ago and a great quantity of mutton was found in the house of a man of the name of Joyce which they could not take as they found nothing that they could identify...but the man, tho' there is not the smallest doubt of the mutton being stolen, still escapes.[16]

Spring Assizes 1848

At the Spring Assizes held in Galway in March 1848, members of the Galway Grand Jury complained that not one penny of 'public Cess levied on the Barony of Ballynahinch has been collected,' and yet the barony had sent more prisoners to the Galway jail than any of the other four baronies in the county, on one day alone 102 prisoners arrived from Connemara. Many of the prisoners were, on arrival, already in a 'dying state', and died soon after. Hyacinth D'Arcy, a member of the Grand Jury, informed the jury that no-one could be found to collect the Public Cess, 'owing to the distress and poverty of that part of the county and consequently the difficulty of collecting.'[17]

A large number of persons before the court were accused of cattle and sheep stealing and petty larcenies, all of whom pleaded guilty and were sentenced to prison for periods 'varying from one to two or three months from time of their committal.' A great many of the prisoners came from the Clifden union and the judge, Baron Lefroy, criticized John Dopping and the other magistrates from that district for 'crowding the gaol with whole families against whom there was only a pretext for committal,' when only one member was accused.

Dopping answered that 'it was the desire of those persons to be sent to gaol and in committing them he had only done what appeared to him necessary for the protection of property.' It was not uncommon for whole families to become involved in the theft of sheep from the mountain side, it was their desire to be transported together to Van Diemen's Land rather than be left behind to starve in Connemara. The judge observed that 'it was not right to gratify them at the expense of the county, and that the magistrates should have exercised more discretion.'

One of the first cases to come before the court was that of Michael Ward and Ellen Reilly, 'two wretched looking creatures,' from Derrigimlagh, indicted for stealing a foal, the property of Anne Kinealy, on 3 February 1848. Mathias Gordan testified to having witnessed the accused chase a mare and foal into a field, where they killed the foal and proceeded to skin it.

Gordan reported the incident to the police and Constable Robert Allen went to investigate. Allen found the remains of the foal and the skin hidden in a wall and fresh meat was discovered under a bed in the prisoner's house. The Constable was told by a steward on a relief scheme that the two prisoners would not work on the road 'and were consequently cut out of the relief list.'

The jury, without leaving the box, found the prisoners guilty, 'but recommended them strongly to the mercy of the court.' The Judge, taking into account information received from a local magistrate, 'that relief was not given in that very destitute locality', declared that he was happy to be in a position to pass a sentence 'which would enable the prisoners to receive it' and sentenced them to six weeks in prison.

Hyacinth D'Arcy then asked for permission 'to state briefly the wretched conditions' of the Clifden union and went on to cite the calamities that had befallen the union over the previous three years and the difficulties experienced by those trying to deal with the effects:

> For the last three years the people have beeen suffering unheard of misery. Their entire dependency was upon the potato and fishing, both of which failed them - for fishing too, has failed this year except very little...This year the fishermen go out and return without taking anything, and the people are therefore in most unheard of distress...the distress exceeds the power of description to convey the idea of it. Distress, too, is so prevalent, my lord, that I could name a whole townland where there is not a single house free from fever...Two doctors who were connected with the poorhouse have died, and the greater portion far of those receiving out-door relief are infected with disease. I will mention one instance...the sergeant of police - a most humane man, who gives most of his means to the poor, and knowing something of medicine, is of the greatest benefit to them - and he informed me that he had seen a family in fever in a hovel, and so distressed were they that when he threw some crackers to the children - for he was afraid to enter - the mother attempted to take them from them...It was literally like throwing them into a den of wild beasts...my friend Captain Dopping apprised the government whenever a case of peculiar distress came before him. The magistrates in that district are in a most painful position, and when destitute persons charged with larcenies are brought before them, they are obliged to commit them for the protection of persons not much better off and such as are barely able to pay the poor-rate.[18]

The Judge sympathised with the magistrates:

> it was, no doubt a trying position to be placed in, but the Magistrates, however much persons might desire it, had no right to sent them to prison to be maintained at the expense of the county.

He suggested that a memorial be sent to the Lord Lieutenant requesting that Quarter sessions be held in Clifden in the future[i] , to save prisoners the long journey to Galway. For the time being, however, he recommended to the Board of Superintendence that prisoners from Connemara who had been discharged were to receive 'a couple of days food...to enable them to reach home.'[19]

---

[i] Even though Thom's Directory 1845-1853 continues to list the Quarter sessions as being held in Clifden throughout this period.

Mother Accused Of Cannibalism

On 11 March 1848 at 11 o'clock at night Dominick Kerrigan was awakened with a knocking on the bridewell gate. He got up and opening the gate found James Cooke, an overseer and the brother of the relieving officer for the Roundstone Division, a policeman and two prisoners outside. The prisoners, accused of stealing a calf belonging to James Cooke, were Bart Flaherty and his wife Honor:

> The wife appeared to me to be quite dead, upon which they dragged her out of the car like a dead sheep, and pulled her into the door and left her and the husband...in my custody...to my astonishment she never moved a hand or foot since that moment, and never uttered a word. Such cruel treatment of human beings is revolting to human nature. Her husband says that they were so treated that all their family died of starvation, and shocking to relate that the unfortunate victim, the deceased, cut off the feet from the ankles of one of the children and eat of them.

On receipt of this report from Kerrigan John Deane went immediately to Kilkieran to investigate. Deane and the vice-guardians were anxious to ascertain if the 'cause or consequences' of such an act could be found 'to have any relation to the out-door relief system' and could they somehow be held responsible.

On investigation it was discovered that Bart Flaherty, his wife and four children had been discharged from the workhouse on 9 December and had since then received his daily rations. Some meal was found in the house when the couple were taken prisoner, along with the meat of the calf 'alleged to be stolen.' Kilkieran at the time was overrun with fever and soon after returning home the whole family had become ill and three of the children, Martin, Mary and Pat, had died.

On the day before Honor's death James Cooke, accompanied by Mark Conneely, went to Bart Flaherty's house in search of a calf recently stolen from his land:

> Conneely and Cooke looked through an opening in the wall of the hut, and saw Bart Flaherty, his wife Honor, a woman named Bridget Marmion, and Margaret Flaherty, daughter of Bart Flaherty, lying on the floor, and the hide of the calf placed over them.

Cooke went to the police at Roundstone and had Flaherty arrested. The next morning he called for the arrest of Honor Flaherty also and she was taken into custody. Later that morning in bad weather and in an open cart the two made the twelve hour journey to Clifden:

> On Saturday morning, about 11 o'clock, the police took the prisoners to Clifden. For about 16 or 17 miles of the road they travelled on an outside

jaunting-car, and for the remainder of the distance on a common car.

The constable escorting the prisoners to Clifden later told the sworn inquiry that:

> the woman, Honor Flaherty, was in a very sickly condition when she was put on the car, and the day was extremely cold and severe...he did not hear the woman complain during the journey: she was offered bread by her husband but refused to eat it.

Deane and the vice-guardians were satisfied that the woman's death was not caused by starvation:

> There can be no doubt whatever that her death was caused by exposure to cold and wet during a journey of 40 miles.

Dr Suffield investigated the husband's allegations that his wife had eaten the flesh of her child, found a grave

> a short distance outside (the cabin), covered merely with a sod and a few stones, lying on the surface of the ground, where the bodies of two of the children. They had been dead, according to his evidence, about two months. It was impossible...for any medical man to come to a conclusion as to whether the flesh of the legs had been torn or cut, the bodies being far advanced in decomposition.

Following his inquiry Deane was of the opinion that there was no truth in Flaherty's 'disgusting statement'. And after examining several of his neighbours 'one and all testified to the fact of his being a recipient of relief, and of their disbelief of his statement.'

The vice-guardians were critical of James Cooke and dismissed him from their service:

> From the inhumanity of James Cooke, exhibited by having brought the poor creature on a most inclement day in an open cart, without even straw to protect her from the injuries of a long journey, we felt coerced to dismiss him at once from any service under our Board.[20]

The following month the *Galway Vindicator* reported on the case of a Connemara man, John Conneely, being brought before the court for sheep stealing. John Conneely pleaded guilty to the charge and the Judge passed a sentence of three months hard labour.

Then, according to the newspaper, before Conneely was taken away, John Dopping stood up and spoke in his defence stating that when this case first came to his attention:

> he had been told that the prisoner and his family were starving when this offence had been committed - one of his children died, and he had been credibly informed that the mother eat part of its legs and feet after its death. He had the body exhumed, and found that nothing

but the bones remained of its legs and feet.

A thrill of horror pervaded the court at this announcement. There was deep silence for several minutes, during which time many a tear trickled down the cheeks of those present...The prisoner was instantly discharged.[21]

The similarities between the two cases seem incredible and leaves one to suspect that the newspaper report is a misinformed account of the Flaherty story.

Buried Alive

The Dopping family were themselves feeling the effects of famine-related diseases when in April Dopping reported to the under-secretary that his son was 'ill in Typhus fever and in a state of the most extreme danger, and I am myself far from well.'[22] Both father and son appear to have made a full recovery and Dopping was soon back on duty as Resident Magistrate.

In May he came across what must surely be the most poignant example of true victims of famine to be found among the many shocking stories coming before him at the time.

At about 9 o'clock on Monday morning, 29 May, Peggy Melia, a woman in a very week state, was seen by her neighbours walking in the direction of Roundstone. Later that afternoon her brother, Martin Melia, asked a neighbour, John Adley, for a shovel to bury his sister.

John, accompanied by his uncle Valentine Adley and several neighbours, went to where Peggy was lying on the sea shore. Martin began digging a hole in the sand, although the neighbours later stated that Peggy was still 'drawing her breath and groaning'. One neighbour, Barbara Ashe, asked Martin 'was he going to bury his sister alive'. He gave no reply and so Barbara turned and walked away. Martin told the Adley's that, 'she (meaning his sister) would die when she was put in the hole', and he placed his sister into the hole and covered her with sand and stones. 'He said he could not lose his rations by coming again to bury her', John Adley stated this in his sworn statement before John Dopping on 3 June 1848.[23]

Dopping was shocked to learn that such an occurrence had taken place in a christian country:

The wretched man could have had no object in the commission of the savage act but to save himself time and trouble or probably to put an end to the sufferings of his sister who must have been at the point of death...the persons looking on were scarcely less criminal in permitting the thing to be done - most of them women and children.

The place of the occurrence is within a mile of Roundstone, in a neighbourhood in which - as well as in other parts of Connemara, I regret to say some of the peasantry are scarcely human.[24]

Martin Melia was committed for trial. However, extensive research has failed to reveal the verdict.

The catalogue of petty crime continued throughout 1848 and 1849. In January 1849 the *Galway Vindicator* reported that the county jail was crowded with 'nearly naked and almost starving' prisoners, most of whom were from the rural districts. The jail 'intended for 110 prisoners, contained now over five hundred', 157 of whom were under sentence of transportation.[25]

However, following the successful harvests of 1849 and 1850 and a gradual improvement in the conditions of the people, crime was on the decline throughout the county. At the Spring Assizes in July 1851 the Lord Chief Justice declared that the county of Galway 'appears to be in a state of perfect peace.'[26] There were but a few cases of a serious nature before the court and the remainder were the result of poverty and vagrancy, two of the many legacies left by the Famine.

John Dopping was replaced as Resident Magistrate by Lieut-Col Robert Shaw in 1853. Just two years later, on 3 April 1855, at the age of fifty five he was drowned, along with three others, in a boating accident in Lough Gowna near Granard in County Longford.[27]

CHAPTER 13

IN THE WAKE OF A CALAMITY

The Board of Guardians which replaced the vice-guardians was made up of 13 elected and 11 ex-officio guardians. The Chairman was Hyacinth D'Arcy, Vice-Chairman Martin R Hart, Deputy Vice-Chairman Redmond Joyce, Treasurer, Dr W Suffield[j], Clerk and Returning Officer, H Smith. The master of the workhouse was George Workman and the matron was Anne Shannahan.[1] Dominick Kerrigan was replaced as Bridewell Keeper in 1850 by John Coneys.[2]

The Board took over a union in dept, with still a large number of the population dependent on them for relief and many of the ratepayers offering their estates for sale in the newly established Encumbered Estates Court.

For a time financial assistance would be provided under the new Rate-In-Aid Act; this Act spread the financial burden of the distressed union over the entire country. However, debts accumulated under the many relief Acts would take many years to clear and despite a successful harvest in 1849 there were, as can be seen from the following figures, still large numbers in need of relief.

Number relieved in workhouse, number of deaths and number receiving outdoor relief during the half year ending on 25 March 1847, 1848, 1849 and 1850.

Clifden.		Workhouse accomm. on 25/3	No relieved in workhouse during h.year.	No of deaths in h.year	No on outdoor relief.
25 March 1847		300	188	16	none
do	1848	410	1,500	309	13,098
do	1849	1,323	3,285	92	11,347
do	1850	1,906	3,927	195	3,570 [3]

Poverty would remain with the people for many years after the 'official' ending of the Famine and the number of destitute remained high when compared with other parts of the country. As late as July 1852 the number of inmates in the workhouse still constituted just under six per cent of the population of the union; far higher than the one per cent estimated by Joseph Burke when setting up the union.

On week ending 24 July 1852 there were 1,249 inmates in the workhouse. They divided up into the following categories: able-bodied males

[j]Dr William Henry Suffield lived out his life in Connemara until his death at the age of 57 on 23 June 1872.

and females, 531; boys and girls aged between five and nine, 129; infants and children, 78; and aged or infirm, 61. In September, 99 of the able-bod-ied were issued with clothing and discharged, there being an increase in the demand for casual labour it was expected that they would find work.[4] However, if no permanent work could be found, or if they failed to raise the price of a ticket to England or America, the unfortunate man or woman could expect to be back in the workhouse within a couple of months.

An alternative to the workhouse was to 'take the soup'. To accept food and clothing from the Irish Church Mission, a proselytising Society active-ly seeking converts among the Roman Catholic community in Connemara at this time.

Proselytising Clergy Cause Division

The Society for Irish Church Missions to the Roman Catholics was formed on 29 March 1849, but its work, 'to give the Roman-thought people of Ireland the Gospel with its bearing on and rejection of Roman error'[5], had already begun amid strong support from the landlords and clergy in Connemara. Rev Alexander Dallas, the Society's founder, was welcomed into Connemara by Rev Anthony Thomas the Rector of the Ballynakill Union. Rev Thomas was recognized as an evangelical churchman and had acted as Rector of Ballynakill Union since 1822, when he succeeded his uncle Rev Charles Seymour.[6]

The Society's aim was to convert the Roman Catholics of Ireland to the Protestant faith and it had chosen to begin its work in Connemara, a region where only three Protestant clergymen ministered

> over a district which contained 40,000 souls. This, then, was the place for the first missionary effort on the new principle of open aggression on the errors of Rome.[7]

The zealous activities of proselytising clergymen were not new in Connemara. In 1836 Rev Thomas and his two curates, Rev Mark A Foster and Rev Brabazon Ellis, along with 'a few of the pious and influential lay-men in Connemara', formed the Connemara Christian Committee.[8] This Committee was set up to instruct and protect recent converts to the Protestant faith. Among the Committee's members were Hyacinth D'Arcy and his brother James. For many years the brothers were united in prayer for the 'spiritual awakening of the country'.[9]

The Connemara Christian Committee attempted to set up a colony on 600 acres of bogland outside Clifden, which they planned to drain and divide into small farms for distribution among recent converts. Major-General Thomson and Henry Blake made every effort to attract the colony on to their land[10], but without success. In the end the idea had to be aban-doned as no clergyman could be found to take up the work.[11]

Rev Dallas was Rector of Wanston in Hampshire and in the year before his arrival in Connemara he had succeeded in having 23,000 letters delivered by post to different parts of Ireland on 16 January 1846. The letters contained a tract written by Rev Dallas entitled 'A Voice from Heaven to the People of Ireland'[12] and were seen by the Society as the first step in their missionary work. Dallas was aided in this work by a small group of helpers, in particular two Dublin women, Miss Mason and Fanny Bellingham, and was financed by an Englishman, Enoch Durant.

Later in 1846 Rev Dallas visited Galway where he established his first mission at Castlekirke on the shores of Lough Corrib. On an invitation from Rev Thomas, Dallas came further west and was introduced to Hyacinth D'Arcy. The first meeting between Rev Dallas and Hyacinth D'Arcy was seen by both men as 'the confluence of two streams of prayer and effort'.[13] D'Arcy went on to be 'the leader in all the Mission work in the west',[14] and central to the success of the Society in Connemara.

Back in England Dallas pleaded for donations for his mission in Ireland and more than £10,000 was subscribed. A committee was formed, headed by the Duke of Manchester, and funds were sent to Connemara.

Having seen the success of the 'feeding' schools under the British Relief Association scheme, D'Arcy began establishing 'a large number of mission schools throughout the whole district of Connemara.' The children

Salruck school feeding hour 3 August 1850
by Fanny Bellingham

attending the schools received food and clothing and were encouraged, along with their parents, to attend Sunday service:

And this was the first beginning of that widely-spread system of Sunday and day-school teaching which had contributed so powerful-ly to the success of the Irish Church Mission.

All who attended Mr D'Arcy's schools were instructed in the Scriptures well and thoroughly; and these little ones often acted unconsciously as missionaries, by urging their parents and relatives to attend the services and preaching.[15]

Glenowen House, residence of Louisa Bagot D'Arcy after the death of her husband John D'Arcy (1839). Leased by John Dopping while acting as Resident Magistrate in the area. In 1854 the house was purchased by I.C.M.S. and converted into an orphanage for girls.

The Famine left a large number of children without parents, James A Tuke on his visit to Connemara in 1847 commented that:

> Nearly two-thirds of the inmates of the Union-houses of Connaught are...children, many of them orphans.[16]

D'Arcy and his supporters

> frequently found little children by the road-side fainting with hunger, their parents dead, and themselves utterly unprotected...An orphanage was planned and set on foot, first for girls only, then for boys also; and this was the beginning of the `Connemara Orphan Nursery',[17]

The girl's orphanage was set up at Glenowen House and the boy's at the old Glebe house at Kingstown.

Ballinaboy school 10 August 1850

Courtesy of the National Library of Ireland NLI R24,719

With the work well under way in Connemara, the Irish Church Mission Society was officially formed on 29 March 1849. The Society's headquarters, organisation and fund raising were all carried on in England but its main missionary work was carried on in Connemara and Dublin. The Society employed Irish speaking preachers and scripture readers and soon alongside the schools and the orphanages new churches and rectories were built.

Within a short time there were seven ordained missionaries, sixteen scripture readers and twelve schoolmasters and mistresses in Connemara.

Schools were opened at Fakeeragh, Clifden, Streamstown, Sellerna, Omey, Cleggan, Ballinaboy, Errislannan, Derrigimlagh, Aillebrack, Roundstone and Moyrus. Before long almost every village in Connemara had its mission station and services were frequently conducted in the Irish language.[18]

The society's access to funds gave it an advantage and the food, clothing and employment, in the construction of buildings etc, attracted many 'converts' from the ill clad, undernourished, unemployed masses of Connemara poor.

The missionaries' sermons were aimed at undermining the priests and discrediting their teachings. They attempted to provoke the priests into retaliation and were frequently successful in doing so. Violent acts against the missionaries were encouraged by local priests in their fight to maintain their flock and to dissuade the missionaries from continuing with their work.

The children from Rev Kilbride's school at Errislannan were attacked by boys from the monk's school on their way to 'tea and cake' at Clifden Castle in July 1850. Hyacinth D'Arcy was entertaining Rev Dallas and his new bride at the castle. The couple were on a tour of the Connemara mis-

Irish Service at Salruck schoolhouse Sunday 28 July 1850.
by Fanny Bellingham

sion and the following day, on their way to visit Sellerna school, their coach was stoned and a stone wall was built across the road to block their way. But the missionaries thrived on such obstacles and soon had the wall pulled down and continued on their journey.[19]

Rev Hyacinth D'Arcy

In July 1851, following the sale of his estates in the Encumbered Estates Court, Hyacinth D'Arcy was ordained and appointed Rector of Omey Union:

> His long standing influence in the country as a landed proprietor and a magistrate made this event an important step in the missionary progress.[20]

Dallas had been very instrumental in having him appointed:

> I proposed to the Bishop of Tuam to admit you to holy orders, either as a missionary or as curate of Clifden...The Bishop has determined to divide the union of Ballynakill and he wants an Incumbent for one division and proposes to present this living to the Rev H D'Arcy.[21]

In the years that followed Hyacinth D'Arcy changed from the sympathetic, caring man, as revealed in his many letters to Dublin Castle and the Relief Commission, to a zealous, authoritarian bigot. Rev D'Arcy became as strident in his criticism of the people's attachment to their religion as his leader Alexander Dallas. He preached provocative sermons in Clifden and elsewhere, many of these he had printed and distributed among the Roman Catholic population. He considered the entire population to be his flock and he would address them even against their wishes if necessary.[22] On 8 June 1852 D'Arcy married Fanny Bellingham, a strong supporter of Rev Dallas and one of two Irish women who had worked closely with him from the beginning:

> This remarkable woman, whose powers of organisation were as uncommon as her energy and quickness of judgment, now threw herself heart and soul into the Connemara work.[23]

Mrs D'Arcy's health, however, was fragile and she died childless after a short illness on 26 June 1854. Rev D'Arcy later married Mary Anne Newman and they had three daughters; Mary (b 1863), Isabella (b1864) and Anne (b1866).[24] He continued as Rector of Omey until his death in 1874.

The Society was successful in converting large numbers of the poor in the early years of its missionary work, and of housing many orphaned children. The Society's offer of food and employment was enticing. As already mentioned, the landed families were already enthusiastic supporters of the cause, and were after all the only other people offering employment in the area. To stand up against such forces would have been difficult.

But for those who chose to 'take the soup' there was the certainty of being ostracised by one's family and neighbours and of attracting the wrath of the priests.

However, many did 'take the soup' in the immediate years after the Famine. The exact number of converts is impossible to estimate as both sides tended to distort figures to suit their own purpose. But when conditions began to improve many 'converts' returned to the Roman Catholic Church and so became known as 'jumpers'; jumping from one religion to another[k] . The term 'souper' or 'jumper' often remained with a family for generations and caused untold suffering to those forced to take that course.

To counteract the activities of the Society the Convent of Mercy was opened in Clifden in 1855. The nuns opened two schools for girls and one for boys under five years of age. Three years later the nuns opened an orphanage next to the convent.[25]

The Irish Church Mission continued its activities in the region throughout the 1850's and 1860's, although with less aggression than in earlier years. Alarmed by this lack of aggression, Rev Dallas on his last trip to Connemara in 1869 urged his parsons not to abandon their crusading spirit.

However, with the disestablishment of the Church of Ireland and the death of Rev Dallas in 1869, followed by the death of Rev D'Arcy in 1874 and a general improvement of the conditions of the people, the Society no longer enjoyed the many advantages that had helped it to success. However, this particular legacy of the Famine lingered with the people of Connemara for many years. And up until the Society finally quit the region in the 1950's its members still managed, at certain periods in the history of the region, to incite bitterness and cause division among the people.[26]

James And Mary Ellis

In contrast to the activities of the Irish Church Mission Society was the very personal Christian mission taken by James and Mary Ellis. James and Mary were an English couple who came to Connemara to try, in what ever way possible, to bring a little comfort into the miserable lives of the people.

James Ellis and his wife Mary, on reading the reports of their fellow Quakers on the terrible conditions in the west of Ireland, decided to uproot themselves from their comfortable surroundings in Bradford, England and take up residence in Connemara. They made the move in 1849 and for the next eight years they 'spent their time and income there in trying to set an example of honest dealing and generous treatment of the poor Irish.'[27]

James Ellis had just months before retired from a successful milling business in Bradford. He and his brother-in-law had for many years

---

[k]The word 'jumper' is also believed to be an anglicised corruption of the Gaelic word *d'iompaigh*, meaning to turn. Phonetically, it may have been the case that 'jumpers' were *'na daoine a d'iompaigh'* - the people who 'turned'.

enjoyed 'a monopoly of the right of milling and malting' for the town. However, 'having adopted total abstinence principles,' they decided to sell off the more lucrative malting side of the business: 'a trade which caused so much misery,'[28] and instead invest in the worsted trade. They were again successful in this trade and the Ellises enjoyed a comfortable life surrounded by their family and fellow members of the Society of Friends until James's retirement in 1848.

They first visited Connemara in July 1848 and Mary wrote to her sister, Esther Seebohm in Bradford: 'it made our hearts ache as we have passed along to see our fellow-creatures so depressed'.[29]

The following year, on 6 April 1849, James Ellis leased 959 acres at Letterfrack from Francis Graham, at a yearly rent of £80. More land was added later bringing the holding to over a thousand acres.[30]

Letterfrack was not James's first choice, but the title to other property which attracted his attention was so unsound that he was

> obliged to look for land where I could get it with a good title, rather than for that which had merely a good position.[31]

Ellis began immediately to drain the land and prepare it for crops. To do this he needed to employ a large number of men, forty at first, later rising to eighty. From the beginning he ran into trouble with neighbouring landlords for offering too high a wage. His wife Mary, who kept up a regular correspondence with her sister Esther, wrote:

> James finds there are complaints at his giving his labourers even eight pence a day. He thinks their labour is worth more, but supposes it will not do to advance further while his neighbours give only sixpence.[32]

Ellis was full of praise for his workforce. The Irish were at the time frequently referred to in English newspapers as an 'indolent race', but James told a *Daily News* correspondent visiting the area:

> These men...work cheerfully from six in the morning to six in the evening, with proper intervals for breakfast and dinner, for wages varying according to their several capacities from 7d to 9d a day. They are paid regularly in money wages and they show themselves not only contented, but grateful...There is no better work-people in the whole world if they only feel assured that they will be paid fairly for all they do.[33]

The site chosen by the couple for their house was rocky:

> but he blew up the rocks with gunpowder, and used the stone for making fences and for building portions of the premises. Upon this spot he has now a very elegant villa, surrounded by a garden which is well fenced in. The house faces the bay upon the west...on the south there are gardens, which extend to the foot of a range of hills, and

which are watered by a stream which forms a natural cascade, within 100 yards of the windows of the drawing-room. A prettier situation can scarcely be imagined. It combines views of sea, lake and mountain, without participating in the inconveniences of either.[34]

The house took only five months to complete, the speed with which the job was done was seen as a miracle among the local people.

In the garden Ellis grew beans, carrots, cabbage, turnips and strawberries. He experimented with imported and home produced fertilizers and found the seaweed collected locally to be the most successful. Ellis was anxious 'to show the people that pretty things will grow here' too and so flower seeds were sent by friends in Bradford and eleven thousand trees and shrubs from Ballinrobe.[35]

The Ellises were well thought off by the people and while crime continued in the neighbourhood: 'pilfering there is and must be, in the present state of things.' They felt safe and secure, and 'though we leave things about in a way which would be perfectly unsafe in Bradford.' They felt nothing had been taken from them 'to the value of a peppercorn.' They even went so far as to 'venture our few sheep on the hills through the night, though I believe no others do.'[36]

While her husband tended to the land, Mary took care of the

widows, orphans, and the sickly. One poor man I found, a fortnight since, had been for months confined to his bed for want of a shirt to put on. So the gift of a few garments led him forth directly to the mountains to take willows for turf baskets, and he seems unwilling to take anything for them.[37]

Mary Ellis was impressed by the poor who surrounded her; she wrote to her sister:

A finer race of people no one could wish to see - gentle, polite, cheerful and easily made happy; rather gumptionless for want of practice, at some things, but by no means idle.[38]

Running a household in Connemara was cheaper than running one in Bradford and as their first year in residence advanced they found that:

what we expended at Bradford we find very well keeps our family and fifty others, besides leaving enough to educate one hundred and twenty children.[39]

To keep families out of the workhouse they gave employment where ever possible. James increased his labourers to eighty while Mary took in knitted stockings and food:

It seems such a shame that a people craving employment should not be able to get it.[40]

They opened a shop in the village, offering 'butter, eggs etc., goslings, fowls and lambs,' and built cottages, a school and later a dispensary.

The Ellises were highly critical of the local gentry:

> The dissoluteness of the 'upper classes' is the ruin of this part of the land.[41] James is still in no way discouragèd about the country or the poor with whom he has to do; but people talk as though things cannot mend till the race has died out. It goes to one's heart to hear it. I believe it would be a blessing if some Irish landlords could be extirpated. They would leave the better part *behind* them.[42]

They complained that the local landlords could not give employment

> because the money, which should be employed in cultivating the ground, is spent in hunting and sporting, drinking and waste. The 'gentry', who live in the neighbourhood, seem to spend nothing hardly.[43]

The Ellises were under suspicion by the Roman Catholic Church, as it was feared that their acts of charity would be accompanied by attempts at proselytising. But time proved those fear to be unfounded; there was no hidden agenda with the Ellises. They were simply offering schooling for the children, an honest wage for an honest day's work to the parents and a little charity to those who were unable to work or for whom no work could be found.

After more than a year of continuous hard work and charitable acts Mary wrote to her sister on 6 June 1850:

> we seem to be getting into favour with the Roman Catholic priests. James got highly extolled from the pulpit about a fortnight since; - set, I believe, in contrast with the rest of the masters here, who 'keep back the hire of the labourers'...Yesterday, John of Tuam [the Roman Catholic Archbishop] stopped his carriage to pay a visit to the school with two other priests, expressed his satisfaction in it, thought it was much better to be learning arithmetic etc., than spending the time over the catechism; remarked that the children looked so much better than those where they got 'feeding'.[44]

The 'feeding' schools referred to were those belonging to the Irish Church Mission Society. The bitterness aroused by the proselytising activities of the Society were causing difficulties for those wishing to live out a true Christian life. The Ellises had to fight to defend their stand and their opinion of the Society is evident in the following extract, again taken from one of Mary's many letters to her sister:

> John of Tuam has been about all this week, confirming, etc., and drawing crowds after him, and raising ill feelings, so that the 'Church missionary' has thought fit to arm himself; but this does not move us,

except we fear a party feeling may be getting up, and Christianity be banished still further away...yet still we fancy our presence rather stems the tide of evil...Far more, we think, than Popery, Episcopalianism wants to lord itself over all, and over us too; and we have had to wage a stiff battle just now against our clergyman taking possession of our schoolroom to deliver in it his controversial lectures, which we think have little tendency to promote real Christianity.[45]

In 1857, due to James's ill health, the Ellises left Letterfrack and retired to Thornton, near Pickering in England. The property was sold to John Hill, a supporter of the Irish Church Mission Society and their schoolroom became a Church of Ireland church and later a Roman Catholic chapel.[1] Back in England James's health was partially restored, but sadly, within a very short time, his wife became ill and died on 1 August 1857. James himself died in 1869.

Encumbered Estates Court

The shooting, hunting and fishing referred to by Mary Ellis came to an end for many of the landed families in the Encumbered Estates Court in the 1850's. Here in the years following the Famine almost all of Connemara came under the hammer. In the Barony of Ballynahinch 181 townlands out of a total of 278 were put up for auction. The sales brochures for the estates carried wonderful descriptions of Connemara, pointing our its untapped resources and potential:

a soil capable of producing all kinds of crops, and possessing inexhaustible supplies of seaweed, coral sand, and limestone manures, a climate remarkable for its mildness, and salubrity. The vicinity of excellent harbours...rivers and lakes abounding in salmon and trout, considerable sea-frontage...and offering numerous opportunities for establishing fishing stations and conducting the deep sea fisheries...The numerous rivers and lakes afford a considerable command of water power and great facilities are presented for extensive irrigation. There is an abundance of excellent turbary.

The opening of the Midland Great Western Railway at Galway on 1 August 1851, brought 'Dublin within four hours...Holyhead within nine hours and London within eighteen.'[46] Who could resist such an enthusiastic sales pitch? Almost everyone, it would seem.

It was the government's hope that men of capital would be attracted into the region and invest in land reclamation, agriculture and fisheries and, in time, help to turn a backward land into a productive one. However, all over the country heavily indebted estates were coming on to the market and, because of the large number on offer, they were attracting very low prices.

---

[1] The Ellis house later became a Christian Brothers monastery and Industrial School for boys.

Despite its idyllic scenery, the under developed, pauper-ridden estates of Connemara held little to attract potential buyers. The Law Life Assurance Company foreclosed their mortgage on the 196,540 acre Martin estate in November 1848. In August of the following year the property was put up for sale in London but failed to attract a buyer. Attempts were made by a group of men to put a company together and purchase the estate, but this eventually fell through.[47]

In March 1849 the property was again on the market. It was hoped that the estate would attract 'a purchaser with means, who would be followed by many similar men who would convert Connaught into a productive province'[48] Lot after lot was put forward only to attract too small a bid or no bid at all. Some small lots were sold, but almost all of the property was returned to the vendor. The company then installed Lieutenant-Colonel Edward Archer as agent.

To facilitate the sale of the many indebted estates throughout the country the Encumbered Estates Act was passed in 1848. Under this Act the Encumbered Estates Court was set up and it was in this Court that the Connemara estates were eventually sold.

The Martin Estate

In July 1852 the Martin estate was again put up for sale, this time in the Encumbered Estates Court. Again it failed to attract any buyer and was eventually purchased by the mortgagees, the Law Life Assurance Company, for £180,000, a price considered to be well below its value.

Mary Martin and her husband Arthur Gonne Bell Martin emigrated to Belgium. She had, in 1845, published a novel '*St Etienne*' which was well received at the time. In 1850 while living abroad she published a second, '*Julia Howard A Romance*'. However, this story was said to have little merit. In the same year, with the financial assistance of friends and family, Mary and her husband set sail for New York, her destination being Canada. However, on board ship Mary suffered a miscarriage and it appears she did not recover. Ten days after landing in New York, Mary, the one time 'Princess of Connemara', died at the Union Place Hotel on 7 November 1850.

D'Arcy Estate

The D'Arcy Estates were offered for sale in the Encumbered Estates Court on three occasions, November 1849, April 1850 and July 1852.[49] Sections of the estate were purchased in small lots. But by far the largest section, including the town of Clifden, was purchased by the mortgagees, Thomas and Charles Eyre, of Bath in England, for £21,245.[50]

Hyacinth D'Arcy entered the ministry of the Church and became Rector of Omey in 1851 and lived out his life in Connemara until his death in 1874.[51] However, it was his proselytising activities, rather than his work on the relief committee and Board of Guardians, that went down in Connemara folklore.

O'Neill Estates

The estates of Faul, Ardagh and Bunowen, covering 12,914 acres, the property of John Augustus O'Neill, was offered for sale on 9 July 1852. The estates consisted of the following townlands: Faul, Ardagh, Munga, Beaghcauneen, Slieveburke, Dolan, Callow, Emlaghmore, Doohulla, Foorglass, Ballyconneely, Bunowen Beg, Bunowen More, Aillebrack, Keerhaun More, Leaghcarrick, Silverhill, Creggoduff, Doonloughan and Truska.[52]

Again sections of this estate were purchased in individual lots. However, almost eight thousand acres, including Bunowen castle, was purchased by Valentine O'Connor Blake of Towerhill, County Mayo[53], a cousin of the Blake family of Renvlye.

Graham Estate

The Graham Estate in Ballynakill went up for sale in the Court on 1 July 1858. Many of those holding long leases took this opportunity to purchase them. However, by 1871 Francis Graham was shown to be still in possession of 8,641 acres.[54]

Blake Estate

The Blake family lived on at Renvlye, although the estate was greatly reduced in size, up until the early years of the twentieth century.

Thomson Estate

Down through the years sections of the Thomson estate were sold off privately and to the Congested Districts Board. However, the descendants of Major-General Alexander Thomson of Salruck, the Willoughbys, are the only landed family from the Famine period to continue to occupy the same property today.

New Owners

With the breakup of the old estates, new names became associated with Connemara. The majority of the new owners had properties and interests elsewhere and devoted even less time to their Connemara estates than had their predecessors. The Connemara castles became summer residences for families like the Eyres, the Blakes and the representatives of the Law Life Assurance Company. Others built hunting and fishing lodges on their newly purchases estates, it would seem that the 'shooting, fishing and hunting' was set to continued[m].

Over the years some land was reclaimed and on many estates holdings enlarged and livestock took the place of tenants. It was not always necessary to remove tenants to make way for stock; that had already been done through death, emigration and the implementation of the Quarter-Acre Clause, which forced the people to abandon their holding in order to qualify for entry to the workhouse.

However, the expenditure of large sums by the new owners never materialized and the new landlords were no more eager to employ labourers than were their predecessors. Henry Coulter, in his book on the west of Ireland published ten years after the Famine, criticized the Law Life Assurance Company, now the largest property owners in the region, for

> their want of spirit and enterprise in not employing the people in the improvement of the land and the development of its great natural resources.[55]

The Remaining Tenants

With the reduction in tenant numbers many holdings were enlarged making them more viable for the occupant. Every effort was made to encourage the tenants to grow a variety of crops and although other crops were grown the people still continued to depend heavily on the potato. Indian meal remained on as a substitute for the potatoes during the *hungry months* and during times of crop failure.

The *hungry months* would remain with the people for some time to come and crop failure, mainly due to bad weather, continued to be a feature of their lives. Crop failure caused severe hardship in the 1860's and again in the late 1870's. However, the improved circumstances of the people and the prompt response of government and private relief agencies kept famine at bay. For the majority of tenants, however, there was only one option for the future, emigration.

Emigration

The census of 1851 recorded the population of the Barony of Ballynahinch at 21,349. This showed a loss of 12,116 over the previous census taken ten years before in 1841. How many of this number died and how many emigrated, it is impossible to distinguish.

[m]The history of Connemara in the years following the Famine is continued in, Kathleen Villiers-Tuthill, Beyond The Twelve Bens: A history of Clifden and District 1860-1923.

In 1835 John D'Arcy and his fellow landowners reported to the Commission inquiring into the conditions of the poorer classes in Ireland that there was almost no emigration from this region. On 12 January 1850 the *Illustrated London News* reported that the number of emigrants who embarked from Galway during the year ending 31 December 1849 amounted to 3,934: 1,958 males, 1,832 females, with 144 cabin passengers.[56] Again, how many of those were from Connemara, it is impossible to say. But the irreversible trend of emigration from the barren fields of Connemara to the crowded streets of English and American cities had begun.

The emigrants left behind them the graves of loved ones and the living skeletons that were family and friends. Many were themselves no better than skeletons. Disease-ridden and impoverished some would never survive the journey to the new land, but those who did carried with them bitter memories of hunger, nakedness and pauperism.

They would go on to endure further humiliation in their new homeland, as they strove to improve their lot and educate their family for a better life. They would at the same time pass on their bitter memories to their children and their children's children, leaving the blame for their suffering firmly at the door of the Irish landlords and the British Government.

Over the years the money sent home by these emigrants saved many a family from further hunger. It helped many a father to extend his holding, purchase cattle and reduce his dependency on the potato crop. But all too often the money sent went towards the purchase of a ticket for the next member of the family to join his brothers and sisters in America. And so it continued, emigration assisted by family remittance, charitable donation and by landlords intent on land clearance, thinning out the population, leaving empty homes and deserted villages.

Those who remained considered themselves the unlucky ones and would endeavour, whenever possible, to scrape together the passage to escape the poverty they saw waiting for them among the barren rocks of Connemara.

However, among some there was already a new consciousness dawning, or perhaps just a fresh call to an old cause. The following article, which appeared in the *Galway Vindicator* of the 7 November 1849, called the people to abandon any hope for equality in a United Kingdom and instead embark on a path of self reliance which would, in time, make the country a nation:

> From England we have nothing to expect save oppressive laws, mockery and insult. Irishmen must fall back on their own resources, and the sooner they close their ranks - fill up the gaps made by foolish dissension and cowardly desertion - and show a bold front to their old foe, the better it will be for themselves and the interests of their common country...we are now thrown on our own resources - left to sink

or swim by those who held the country up by the chain until it fretted down into the waters of pauperism. Let us in God's name strike out boldly and trust to our own strength alone - we have been too long supporting ourselves on the corks of a spurious loyalty. Let us cast them from us and breast the waves like men. If we are not up and stir-ring in our united endeavour to make our country a nation...our doom is sealed - our race extinct.[57]

EPILOGUE

From the outset Connemara was ill-equipped to face the onslaught of the Great Famine. Disadvantaged as it was by its remoteness, its large population of potato dependent poor, its bankrupt landlords and lack of food importers, employers and solvent ratepayers, left its fate in the hands of a detached bureaucracy. Scheme after scheme set in place by the government to alleviate the conditions of the people failed to do so. Inept relief committees and an incompetent Board of Guardians added to the difficulty of making inadequate government policies succeed. The result was years of suffering borne by the people with patient endurance. The Great Famine was a period unequalled in our history for human suffering. No section of the population of the region escaped unscathed.

The census of 1851 reveals a population loss of 12,116 for the Barony of Ballynahinch since 1841. From the extract reproduced in Appendix 4 it is possible to examine the impact of the Famine, townland by townland, by comparing the population figures of 1841 with those of 1851. Almost every townland registers a loss.

What we cannot measure is the impact of the Famine on the minds of the people themselves. Having witnessed the death of children, parents, siblings and loved ones, they endured deep humiliation to prevent the same happening to themselves. Entire communities devastated, entire villages deserted, those that remained would be anxious and ever watchful for the return of the dreaded blight.

Many survivers coped with the trauma of what they had witnessed by simply pushing the experience to the back of their minds, never to be resurrected in their lifetime. For the emigrant it was a memory left behind in the old country. Those who remained rarely talked of those years to family or friends, and if they did they failed to pass on the true horror of that experience; it was something they survived, but not to be dwelt on. For others it prompted a political awareness which would lead to action in the years to come.

For today's generation the famine represents a period of great complexity and confusion and I can only hope that this work goes someway towards illuminating this dark episode. Even today the very landscape of Connemara still bears testimony to the Famine.

The shaded tracks of the lazybeds, where the potatoes were once grown, can be traced on the slopes of the hills. The Famine graves are left unmarked but still identifiable to the farmer. Part of the workhouse wall now forms a boundary between houses and factories. The children's auxiliary workhouse in Clifden is now, appropriately enough, a children's playground. The auxiliary workhouse at Kylemore was pulled down and replaced by a hotel and the workhouse at Roundstone is now a private house. The only building still in use today is the courthouse. And even that is under threat, as I write.

The jail, an abandoned ruin, still dominates the southern approach to Clifden, its narrow cells, yards and high external walls, have managed to retain an atmosphere of severity and hardship. It is easy to imagine a cart load of prisoners, huddled together in the winter rain, passing through the now blocked gate on their way to the Galway court. And to see Honor Flaherty's body being dragged across the yard 'like a dead sheep'. The low voices of the inmates can be heard moaning in their fever induced delirium and Dominic Kerrigan, ever present, trying to create order where there is only chaos.

Shedule Of Tenants On The Clifden Estate
30 May 1847

No	Denomination	Tenants names	Arrears Struck off	No	Denomination	Tenants names	Arrears Struck off
	Aughrushmore				Bayleek	Chrisr. Boskin	15..12..4
21	"	Thos. Conroy	20..5..9	57	"	Thomas Coyne	3..3..6½
22	"	Pat Cahill dead	16..18..1	58	"	Pat Davis Mother	8..17..3½
23	"	Rich. Dishone	14..19..8	59	"	Michl. Corbett	5..0..11½
24	"	Math Davis & Bror	15..13..10	60	"	Pat Connely	3..17..1
25	"	John Mangan	22..3..9	61	"	Michl. Joyce	5..17..1
26	"	John Mangan	23..1..6	62	"	Florence Poole	5..16..10½
27	"	Owen King	17..5..6	63	Ardmore	John King	22..2..6
28	"	Edmond Corbett	15..14..8		"	Pat Madden	20..12..2
29	"	Messr. Thos. Conry and Lowy	30..9..10	64	"	Luke Madden now Michl. Corbett	12..3..0½
30	"	Michl. Mulkern	9..1..5	65	"	Chrisr. Boskin	24..3..11
31	"	John King	15..17..17	66	"	Thomas Coyne	5..5..10
32	"	Simon Halloran	6..10..4	67	"	Pat Davis Mother	11..11..11
33	"	Thos. Flaherty	9..9..7	68	"	Michl. Corbett	14..4..5½
34	"	Widow Heffron	15..4..0	69	"	Pat Connely	4..14..11
35	"	Path Mangan dead	14..15..0	70	"	Michl. Joyce	6..0..10
36	"	Michl. King Pat d	8..9..6	71	"	Terence Poole	7..2..11½
38	"	Michl. Cashow	25..0..10	72	Clifden		
39	"	Pat Flaherty dead	5..1..5½	73	"	Path Browne	5..2..10½
40	"	Michl. Flaherty	7..16..11½		"	Thos. Mongan	1..0..3
41	"	John Murphy	14..7..7½	95	"	James Connely	8..4..7
42	"	Pat Flaherty dead	11..0..0	96	"	The Quinns	7..12..3
	Barnarushen			110	"	Pat McClean dead	4..13..9
43	"	Wm Davis	11..9..1	129	"	Thos. Burk	9..18..7½
44	"	Patrick Conry	10..14..6½	144	"	Widow Graham	3..14..0
45	"	Path Baker dead	6..12..8½	145	"	Thos. Connely Quenrs	1..16..6
46	"	Barbara Gordon	8..4..5½	146			
47	"	Widow Flaherty	9..7..0½	148	Glenowen		
48	"	Bror Flaherty & Pat Conr	24..17..11½	165	"	Martin Mannion	8..4..10½
49	"	Michl. Toole dead	6..19..0½	167	"	Path Connely	3..18..6
50	"	John Molloy	14..0..9	168	"	Anthony King	5..19..9
51	"	Peter Mealand &		169	"	Michl. Neal	2..14..0
52	"	John Conry	7..4..5		Clochenard		
		John Conry	6..13..9	173	"	Edwr. Staunton	6..5..11
	Bayleek			175	"	Widow Staunton	8..2..0
54	"	John King	10..10..6	176	"	John Staunton	8..14..0
55	"	Pat Madden	7..4..2½				
56	"	Luke Madden now Michl. Corbet	9..3..3½			5	Forward

Schedule Continued

No	Denominations	Tenants Names	Arrears Struck off	No	Denominations	Tenants Names	Arrears Struck off
177	Clochencard	Wm Flaherty Patt	4 . 11 . 10½		Emlough		
178	"	Thady Flaherty	7 . 0 . 0	210	"	Feetus Davin Walsh	16 . 12 . 8
181	"	Martin Hamilton dead	9 . 16 . 1	211	"	Lawce Foole Stephen	9 . 4 . 9
				212	"	A. Earkin and Patt Cloghirty	3 . 12 . 0
	Derreen			213	"	John Maley	15 . 10 . 5½
184	"	John Corbett	15 . 7 . 9	214	"	Austin Maley	15 . 7 . 1
185	"	James Cowen and David Laghten	23 . 0 . 6	215	"	Jas McDonnell	7 . 4 . 1½
				216	"	Patt Maley	5 . 2 . 0½
186	"	King and Navin	12 . 4 . 3½		Fakeragh		
187	"	Patt Derivy	5 . 3 . 8	219	"	Widow Thady Paw & John Fohn	9 . 8 . 11
188	"	Patt Corbett in Arth	7 . 7 . 2	220	"	Peter McLoghlin	3 . 2 . 4
189	"	Patt Corbett Junior	10 . 11 . 3		Part Knockdane and Toureen		
190	"	George Corbett	3 . 15 . 10				
191	"	James Cowen & Patt Corbett Senior	15 . 6 . 3	229		Mr Mat Duane	32 . 6 . 0
	Derrylee				Gortdrough		
192	"	Michl Joyce	12 . 1 . 2	232	"	Michl Prendergast	16 . 16 . 0½
193	"	Roger Lyden	7 . 17 . 5	235		Michl Nee	5 . 11 . 1½
194	"	Patt & Wm Pye	28 . 19 . 5	236	"	Pat Wheelan	6 . 4 . 10½
				239	"	Walter Joyce	12 . 6 . 4
	Derryshane			240	"	Thos Joyce	21 . 1 . 2½
195	"	John Joyce	5 . 17 . 11	243	"	Martin Joyce	10 . 5 . 2½
196	"	Edwd Maley	11 . 14 . 2	244	"	Walter Keely and Brother John	7 . 4 . 6½
	Emlough			245		Edwd & Bno Eams	11 . 7 . 1½
		Jno Connolly dead	3 . 16 . 4½		Knockbane		
198	"	Mark Lowrey	7 . 1 . 0	247	"	Thos Davin & John	5 . 0 . 11½
199	"	Jno & Phelim Foole	9 . 17 . 8	250	"	John Liddane	3 . 3 . 6
200	"	Stephen Foole	8 . 18 . 8	251	"	Wm & Pat Wards	6 . 12 . 1
201	"	Michl Burke dead	13 . 18 . 0	252		Corbett & Brown	10 . 11 . 1
202	"	Edwd Connelly	7 . 0 . 6		Kilvoughane		
203	"	Jas Foole Stephen's	23 . 17 . 1½	257	"	Mrs Guere	4 . 6 . 8
204	"	Pat McDonnell	12 . 7 . 3	259	"	Michl King	4 . 2 . 8½
205	"	Michl Davin dead	10 . 4 . 11	260	"	Daniel King	6 . 8 . 11
206	"	John Farrell dead	12 . 4 . 11		Knockawally		
	"	Lawce Foole dead	10 . 14 . 11	262	"	Pat Davin	10 . 0 . 7½
	"	Edwd Halleran	10 . 15 . 5	263	"	Jas Corley	11 . 16 . 6½
				264	"	Mathias King	16 . 7 . 3½
		forwd £				forwd £	

Schedule Continued

No	Denominations	Tenants Names	Arrears struck off	No	Denominations	Tenants Names	Arrears struck off
	Knockawally				Tullavoheen		
265	"	William Price	14 . 1 . 5½	312	"	Widow Connolly than	3 . 6 . 3½
266	"	George Corbett	11 . 0 . 5½	314	"	John Coyne	2 . 0 . 6
267	"	Michl Murray	10 . 0 . 0	317	"	Michl Gannon	18 . 6 . 11
268	"	Pat Berry dead	9 . 3 . 4½		Gannoughs		
269	"	Denis & Bro Holland	6 . 12 . 7½	320	"	Michl King	6 . 3 . 8
271	"	Denis Conry	8 . 2 . 0½	321	"	Patt Roach	7 . 0 . 11
272	"	Austin Holland	9 . 15 . 6	322	"	Patt Cunnane	7 . 4 . 5½
273	"	Pat King dead	5 . 5 . 0	323	"	Michl Davis	18 . 18 . 10
274	"	George Price	2 . 16 . 0	324	"	Patt Conry	7 . 6 . 5½
275	"	Michl Noone	4 . 14 . 7½	325	"	John Conry	5 . 6 . 4½
278	"	"	5 . 19 . 0½	326	"	John Davis	9 . 10 . 5½
279	"		15 . 3 . 5	327	"	Michl King dead	22 . 1 . 4
280	"	Denis Conry	6 . 10 . 1½	328	"	James King Dead	20 . 3 . 2½ the
				329	"	Joseph Connolly	9 . 2 . 7
286	Lettermush	Patt Corbitt	9 . 18 . 4	330	"	Bartld Lacy	9 . 8 . 4½
288	"	Widow Maley Bro		331	"	Michl King Ned	22 . 4 . 0½
		now Martin Hart	28 . 19 . 10	332	"	Festus Conry	10 . 14 . 3
	Mowneen			333	"	James Flaherty	8 . 19 . 0
290	"	Pat Burke	25 . 8 . 1½		Tolls & Customs		
291	"	Bro Sullivan	17 . 17 . 10	334	"	Frans Mullens and Corbitt	54 . 5 . 0
294	"	Widow Roach	6 . 0 . 3		Derryler		
295	"	Thos Nanne	7 . 10 . 0		as noted in 1st Return		
	Rusadlisk				"	Owen Darcy	12 . 18 . 0
298	"	Mathias Halloran	14 . 14 . 6	335	"	Richd Joyce	6 . 12 . 0
299	"	Edwd Halloran	14 . 9 . 0½	339	"	Mark Connoly	6 . 0 . 0
300	"	John Halloran	9 . 18 . 4½	340	"	Martin Guare	11 . 5 . 0
301	"	Thos Murray	11 . 7 . 4½	341			
302	"	Pat Gannon &	14 . 18 . 8½				
303	"	Widow Toole	9 . 9 . 4½				
304	"	John Clomeen	8 . 1 . 3				
	Tullavoheen						
307	"	Pas Coyne now Conry Corbitt	6 . 7 . 0				
308	"	Thos Connoly	14 . 6 . 0				
309	"	James Flaherty	5 . 10 . 9				
310	"	Michl Flaherty	5 . 15 . 3½				
11	"	Bro Connoly tend 2	1 . 18 . 6				

Pawnbroker's Returns

During the Famine years there was one pawnbroker operating in the union. The following are his returns for the years 1844-1848, accompanied by the comments of Henry Harrison Briscoe, Poor Law Inspector.

PLEDGES RECEIVED

Month.	1844	1845	1846	1847	1848
January	425	400	450	600	200
February	325	423	375	500	100
March	525	425	450	450	50
April	525	450	525	200	50
May	400	375	675	150	50
June	450	475	950	100	50
July	575	575	850	50	50
August	450	475	500	150	50
September	300	325	450	200	50
October	325	325	700	100	50
November	325	325	600	150	100
December	400	375	650	150	50
Total:	5025	4950	7175	2800	850

Year:	No of articles pawned.	Amount lent on the articles.
1844.	5,025	£813.0.3
1845.	4,950	£837.5.4
1846.	7,175	£1,071.6.4
1847.	2,800	£426.16.2

The pawnbroker kept no account of pledges returned, but states that in 1847 the number was about half; in 1848, very few indeed.

That in 1848 the quantity of clothes offered for pawn was so great that his premises, if they were double the size, would not have held them, but refused, fearing infection, to take them.

The people of this union are wretchedly clad; nothing can be worse.

There is a perceptible difference between the manner in which the peasantry used to be dressed on Sundays, and the manner in which they are so dressed now.[1]   *January 1849*

One Week In The Workhouse

The following is a breakdown of administrative costs, expenditure and receipts of the Clifden Union for one week: week ending Friday 29 September 1848, taken from the Union Minute Book September 1848 - June 1849.

There were 585 inmates in the workhouse that week, officially it could only accommodate 300. The workhouse hospital held 20 patients and the Fever hospital 32. The number admitted during the week amounted to 147: 28 males, 48 females, 42 boys, 27 girls and 2 children under two years of age. One male died and 50 persons were discharged. In the same week there were 6,696 persons receiving outdoor relief.

The cost of provisions and necessaries consumed in the workhouse for the week was £49.18.7½d. The average cost of an inmate 1/7½d, the average cost in the infirmary 3/= and the average cost in the Fever hospital 3/4d.

The Rate collected for the week amounted to £7.17.6 and £387.17.6 was received from the Poor Law Commission.

The Master's estimate of provisions and necessaries required for the ensuing week read as follows:

Bread 230lbs	Salt 70lbs	Pepper 1lb
Meat 280lbs	Tea 3.quarts of a lb	Onions 28lbs
Oatmeal 268lbs	Indian meal 2352lbs	Fish 1doz
Sweetmilk 1400qt	Rice 356lbs	Soap 20lbs
Starch 2lbs.		

The relieving officers' list of requirements for the week:

A.G. Kearns: 85 cwt Indian meal, £46.15.0. 1 Cwt flour, £1.0.0. 14lbs sugar, 7/=. 7lbs cocoa, 4/8d. 100qts milk, 12/6d.

Mathias Maley: 90Cwt Indian meal, £50.12.6. 2stone oatmeal, 4/=. 100qts milk, 12/6d. 68lbs bread, 11/4d.

Peter Joyce: 130 Cwt, Indian meal, £71.10.0. 1 cwt rice, £1.0.0. 1 Cwt oatmeal, 16/=.

John Corbett: 90cwt Indian meal, £50.12.6.

John Joyce: 30cwt Indian meal, £16.17.6d. half cwt flour, 10.0d. 50qts milk, 6/3d.

Thomas Cooke: 50cwt Indian meal, £28.2.6.

James Dooner: 40cwt Indian meal, £22.10.0.

Richard Burke: 60cwt Indian meal, £33.15.0.

Patrick Evans: 80 cwt Indian meal, £44. 1cwt oatmeal, 16/=.

The Master stated requirements for the workhouse were:

12 lino brushes, 6 sweeping brushes, 6 clothes baskets, 100 tin measurers, 100 tin plates, 1 gross Iron spoons, 6 tubs, 12 buckets, 2 cwt chloride lime, 6 Turf Baskets, 12 Bath Bricks, 8 stone washing soda, 2 hundred nails.

Six month contractors, up to 25 March 1849, were granted to the following suppliers:

Margaret Berry: new milk at 2.5d per quart.

John Griffin: oatmeal 16/= per cwt, best brown sugar 5/= per lb tea 4/= per lb. dipped candles 6.5d per lb. mound candles 8d per lb. blue 1/3d per lb. soap, best quality, 3 farthing per lb. vinegar 3/= per gallon.

John King: rice at 2/7d per lb. salt 2/3 per cwt.

Thomas Lydon: sweeping brushes and lino brushes.

B Bodkin: washing soda 4/= per stone. Blacklead 8d per lb. oil 5/= per gallon.

John Flaherty: coffins 3 sizes 3/=, 1/4d, 1/= respectively.

H Buttler: bread (white) 2d per lb, bread (brown) 1¾d per lb, for three months.

In the week that followed cheques, as listed below, were issued:

On the report and recommendation of the Finance Committee, the following bills having been duly examined, and found to be correct, and in accor-

dance with the several Orders were directed to be paid, the checks for the several amounts were duly drawn on the Treasurer, and signed, namely:

No of cheque		Amount
Clothing Account.		
44 Stephen Wallace	leather	£5.1. 9
Establishment Account.		
45 Peter Kneafsey	ward master Payment	£4.0 3
46 H. Smith	payment for assistant clerks	£2.12.6
47 H. Smith	Clerk Act. salary	£10.0.0
48 Bryan Powell	rent Letterfrack depot	£1.12.6
49 Wm. Davis	Depot distributor Claddaghduff	£7.0.0
50 Samuel Freyer	do Cleggan	£5.0.0
51 John Mullin	Porter, wages to 29th Sept.	£4.3.4
52 Bridget Joyce	rent Cloonacartan depot	£3.10.0
53 John King	car lime (clerks)	£ 17.0
54 A J Crighton	fitting up schoolhouse	£5.0.0
55 J McSwiney	lime	£4.2.0
56 Michael Burke	turf, Cloonacartan.	£1.10.0
57 Denis F O'Leary	V-G. salary 24 Sept.	£32.10.0
58 Joseph Jackson	V-G. salary 24 Sept	£32.10.0
Workhouse Invoice Account		
59 James Butler	Bread.	£19.13.3
60 Michael Lydon	Ind. meal	£ 3.0 .6
61 John Griffin	Ind. meal delivery.	£11.15.4
62 Thomas Joyce	Meat	£1 .17.6
63 Patrick D'Arcy	Milk	£12.12.4
64 John King	Rice & Salt	£3 .1 .3
65 John Elbite	Turf	£2. 2 .0
Outdoor Relief Invoice Account.		
66 John Robertson	Ind. meal	£95.1 .8
67 John King	do	£5.10.0
68 Wm. Joyce	Milk to sick poor	£2.18.10
69 John Griffin	Ind. Meal	£68.12.0
70 Wm. Livingston	do	£85.5 .0
71 Rush & Palmer	do	£27.10.0
72 J Butler	supplied to R.Officers	£2.5.0
73 Bryan Powell	do orders.	£12.6
74 Henry Hildebrand	Ind. meal	£130.0.0
75 Andrew Connelly	on R.Off orders.	£4.14.11
76 Richard McDonough	milk & flour	£16.0
Fever Hospital Accounts		
77 John Griffin	supplies to Ballindoon.	£2.3.0
78 John Griffin	do Ballynakill	£1.1.0
79 J. Butler	do Ballindoon	£3.13.0
Valuation Expenses		
80 William H Poole	Act. revision.	£30.0.0

Appendix No 4

1851 Census Barony Of Ballynahinch

BARONY OF BALLYNAHINCH.

PARISHES, TOWNLANDS, AND TOWNS.	AREA.	POPULATION IN 1841.			POPULATION IN 1851.		
		Males.	Females.	TOTAL.	Males.	Females.	TOTAL.
BALLINDOON P. :							
Aillebrack,	601 3 33	208	190	398	184	185	369
Ardagh,	1,052 3 22	119	122	241	74	81	155
Ballinaboy,	298 1 12	80	101	181	71	82	153
Ballinaleama,	121 1 11	15	20	35	15	11	26
Ballyconneely,	1,339 1 26	317	342	659	243	263	506
Beagbcauneen,	664 3 35	26	29	55	23	15	38
Boolagare,	543 0 27	5	4	9	.	.	.
Bunowen-beg,	566 1 18	108	122	230	94	96	190
Bunowen-more,	243 2 11	24	22	46	4	8	12
Callow,	997 1 15	118	115	233	91	97	188
Creggoduff,	145 2 31	2	2	4	9	14	23
Curhownagh,	91 1 4	25	15	40	13	12	25
Derrigimlagh,	2,636 1 6	472	451	923	211	213	424
Derryeighter,	116 2 15	25	22	47	13	13	26
Dolan,	1,084 0 37	92	83	175	118	95	213
Doohulla,	887 2 39	108	101	209	62	58	120
Doonloughan,	186 2 26	30	23	53	33	19	52
Drimmeen,	257 1 15	145	155	300	120	116	236
Drinagh,	393 2 0	45	44	89	5	11	16
Emlagharan,	398 1 14	93	102	195	59	59	118
Emlaghmore,	1,178 2 11	62	58	120	45	54	99
Foorglass,	222 2 7	60	69	129	42	40	82
Keerhaunmore,	163 3 25	40	37	77	46	31	77
Keerhaun, North,	100 0 3	19	15	34	17	18	35
Keerhaun, South,	185 3 22	56	55	111	27	24	51
Kill,	289 3 15	56	49	105	32	27	59
Knock,	46 1 19	9	2	11	7	3	10
Leaghcarrick,	211 2 3	53	48	101	22	15	37
Lehid,	190 2 39	34	26	60	19	13	32
Mannin-beg,	326 0 11	84	103	187	32	41	73
Mannin-more,	578 1 32	150	132	282	85	76	161
Maum,	304 0 20	45	45	90	36	48	84
Munga,	902 3 12	3	1	4	2	2	4
Pollrevagh,	158 1 39	40	22	62	19	13	32
Shannanagower,	139 3 25	.	.	.	2	4	6

Parishes, Townlands, and Towns.	Area.	Population in 1841.			Population in 1851.		
		Males.	Females.	Total.	Males.	Females.	Total.
Silverhill, . . .	159 2 22	20	13	33	14	15	29
Slieveburke, . .	1,400 3 38	1	1	2	.	.	.
Truska, . . .	415 0 19	22	25	47	13	10	23
Islands:							
Ardillaun, . .	8 2 30	.	.	.	.	.	.
Calf Island, . .	1 3 23	.	.	.	.	.	.
Chapel Island, .	10 3 24	.	.	.	.	.	.
Duck Island, .	13 3 16	.	.	.	.	.	.
Fox Island, . .	3 2 10	.	.	.	.	.	.
Glassillaun Islands,	1 3 11	.	.	.	.	.	.
Horse Island, .	13 3 5	.	.	.	.	.	.
BALLINDOON P.—*con.*	A. R. P.						
Islands:							
Illaunaleama, .	20 3 5	.	.	.	.	.	.
Illaunamenara, .	5 1 32	.	.	.	.	.	.
Illaunamid, . .	29 0 15	16	14	30	13	16	29
Illaunane, . .	11 2 13	.	.	.	.	.	.
Illaunrush, . .	2 2 38	.	.	.	.	.	.
Illaunurra, . .	21 2 39	.	.	.	.	.	.
Inishdawros, . .	22 1 19	3	5	8	2	4	6
Inishdugga, . .	42 1 20				3	2	5
Inishule, . .	6 3 20	.	.	.	.	.	.
Inishkeeragh, . .	24 3 39	.	.	.	.	.	.
Lyal-beg, . .	5 0 11	.	.	.	.	.	.
Lyal-more, . .	14 1 29	.	.	.	.	.	.
368 other Islands, .	169 0 34	.	.	.	.	.	.
	20,033 0 32	2,830	2,785	5,615	1,920	1,904	3,824
Auxiliary Workhouse,	. . .	.	.	.	242	369	611
Total, . .	20,033 0 32	2,830	2,785	5,615	2,162	2,273	4,435
BALLYNAKILL P. :							
Addergoole, .	2,658 3 25	24	22	46	8	2	10
Ardkyle, . .	209 0 31	64	75	139	30	47	77
Ardnagreevagh, .	161 2 32	150	122	272	74	92	166
Attirowerty, .	498 2 7	36	35	71	40	38	78
Ballynew, . .	493 3 16	152	146	298	53	60	113

PARISHES, TOWNLANDS, AND TOWNS.	AREA.	POPULATION IN 1841.			POPULATION IN 1851.		
		Males.	Females.	TOTAL.	Males.	Females.	TOTAL.
Baunoge,	933 3 15	67	55	122	44	54	98
Bundouglas,	88 0 15	91	103	194	12	8	20
Bunowen,	1,452 1 28	46	31	77	31	25	56
Cartron,	241 0 24	40	40	80	17	22	39
Cashleen,	350 1 39	55	41	96	61	63	124
Cleggan,	889 1 1	127	124	251	58	63	121
Cloon,	342 2 31	69	53	122	48	47	95
Clooncree,	79 2 33	27	23	50	13	19	32
Cloonederowen,	100 2 23	41	42	83	4	3	7
Cloonlooaun,	832 3 16	134	137	271	94	109	203
Crocknaraw,	884 1 2	60	51	111	3	8	11
Culfin,	324 0 25	67	62	129	48	58	106
Curragh,	103 1 25	117	105	222	.	.	.
Curry wongaun,	644 3 36	22	27	49	28	31	59
Dawros-beg,	170 1 27	84	73	157	63	69	132
Dawros-more,	612 2 4	157	173	330	86	82	168
Derryherbert,	552 1 15	49	35	84	50	49	99
Derryinver,	867 2 37	130	126	256	53	59	112
Derrylahan,	67 2 5	7	8	15	7	8	15
Derrynacleigh,	1,058 3 30	56	62	118	17	23	40
Dooneen,	24 0 29	12	14	26	2	3	5
Finnisglin,	1,086 0 29	22	19	41	11	8	19
Foher,	623 3 6	79	86	165	10	18	28
Garraunbaun,	171 3 10	67	73	140	20	17	37
Glassillaun,	322 0 9	87	85	172	34	46	80
Glencraff,	1,562 3 24	32	24	56	19	21	40
Gleninagh,	657 2 25	.	.	.	5	3	8
Gorteennaglogh,	283 0 28	69	76	145	84	79	163
Illion,	477 3 10	8	4.	12	5	8	13
Kanrawer,	70 1 12	12	5	17	.	.	.
Keelkyle,	1,006 3 23	35	49	84	43	50	93
Knocknahaw,	72 0 22	42	53	95	5	9	14
Kylemore,	5,034 1 32	66	61	127	46	43	89
Lecknavarna,	1,275 3 6	8	2	10	16	13	29
Lemnaheltia,	736 0 3	4	3	7	3	5	8
Letterbeg,	231 2 34	11	8	19	.	.	.
Letterbreckaun,	1,610 3 13	11	7	18	6	11	17
Letterettrin,	399 2 26	4	4	8	2	3	5
Letterfrack,	1,239 1 6	91	98	189	101	87	188
Lettergesh, East,	2,180 2 28	123	96	219	36	28	64
Lettergesh, West,	1,186 0 0	99	90	189	17	30	47
Lettermore,	236 3 8	57	56	113	22	22	44
Lettershanbally,	1,382 0 10	32	29	61	2	2	4
Luggatarriff,	526 1 7	5	8	13	3	3	6
Maumfin,	107 1 25	27	41	68	7	7	14
Moyard,	1,172 1 4	78	86	164	110	107	217

PARISHES, TOWNLANDS, AND TOWNS.	AREA.			POPULATION IN 1841.			POPULATION IN 1851.		
	A.	R.	P.	Males.	Females.	TOTAL.	Males.	Females.	TOTAL.
BALLYNAKILL P.—*con.*									
Mulinghglass,	874	1	37	123	129	252	59	74	133
Mweelin,	652	3	39	4	5	9	3	3	6
Pollacappul,	1,077	0	36	6	2	8	5	2	7
Roscrea,	122	3	25	32	41	73	17	16	33
Rosleague,	218	3	2	66	75	141	59	48	107
Rosroe,	296	2	18	80	70	150	58	74	132
Ross,	138	1	26	92	105	197	15	15	30
Rusheenduff,	287	3	23	55	51	106	4	10	14
Salrock,	238	3	28	26	20	46	25	28	53
Shanaveag,	207	1	39	3	3	6	1	1	2
Shanboolard,	283	1	14	53	49	102	25	25	50
Sheeauns,	666	2	11	55	53	108	5	12	17
Tievegarriff,	118	3	36	52	40	92	41	48	89
Tievemore,	48	2	12	29	23	52	6	4	10
Tonadooravaun,	259	3	7	54	57	111	36	37	73
Tooreen,	757	1	38	45	38	83	26	26	52
Tooreena,	885	3	33	129	119	248	20	28	48
Toorcenacoona,	539	3	1	4	5	9	.	.	.
Tully-beg,	167	0	39	16	10	26	28	21	49
Tullyconor,	424	3	4	1	3	4	.	.	.
Tully-more,	345	3	27	89	75	164	58	43	101
Ungwee,	655	1	37	36	29	65	17	21	38
Islands:									
Braadillaun,	4	2	8	.	.	.	.	.	.
Crump Island,	63	1	18	13	3	16	5	3	8
Freaghillaun, North,	9	3	10	23	19	42	.	.	.
Freaghillaun, South,	49	0	24	.	.	.	5	7	12
Freaghillaun, South,	7	3	20	.	.	.	.	.	.
Glassillaun,	2	0	35	.	.	.	.	.	.
Inishbarna,	19	3	28	.	.	.	3	4	7
Inishbroon,	12	0	4	.	.	.	.	.	.
Roeillaun,	36	2	7	8	9	17	8	13	21
Roeillaun,	3	1	20	.	.	.	.	.	.
Shanvallybeg,	10	3	28	.	.	.	.	.	.
74 other Islands,	25	2	16	.	.	.	.	.	.
	47,962	2	33	4,047	3,881	7,928	2,080	2,225	4,305
Auxiliary Workhouse,	.	.	.	.	.	.	205	298	503
Total,	47,962	2	33	4,047	3,881	7,928	2,285	2,523	4,808

PARISHES, TOWNLANDS, AND TOWNS.	AREA.	POPULATION IN 1841.			POPULATION IN 1851.		
		Males.	Females.	TOTAL.	Males.	Females.	TOTAL.
MOYRUS P. :							
Aillenarally,	339 2 4	41	49	90	18	12	30
Ardbear,	390 0 7	185	196	381	142	149	291
Ard, East,	217 2 32	132	123	255	96	103	199
Ardmore,	497 3 23	111	125	236	63	80	143
Ard, West,	405 0 7	100	91	191	83	87	170
Arkeen-beg,	302 1 33	12	8	20	6	11	17
Arkeen-more,	518 3 12	.	.	.	.	.	.
Athry,	1,613 3 20	42	45	87	25	33	58
Ballinafad,	871 1 1	44	37	81	18	21	39
Ballynahinch,	790 1 32	26	23	49	19	19	38
Barnanang,	1,199 2 19	4	1	5	2	4	6
Barnanoraun,	895 1 21	15	19	34	2	3	5
Beagha,	847 1 26	5	2	7	.	.	.
Boheeshal,	2,542 2 25	11	13	24	5	3	8
Bunnahown,	671 3 29	86	85	171	41	47	88
Caher,	747 1 28	10	11	21	8	7	15
Callaneruck,	1,032 3 24	16	14	30	12	12	24
Callowfinish,	803 3 10	107	96	203	56	67	123
Canower,	271 3 15	25	38	63	2	2	4
Cappaghoosh,	2,160 2 39	39	30	69	24	18	42
Carna,	1,080 1 32	61	73	134	42	52	94
Cashel,	1,281 2 21	59	65	124	40	43	83
Cloonbeg,	330 2 15	9	11	20	5	2	7
Cloonisle,	904 0 11	54	45	99	10	11	21
Cloonnacartan,	1,569 2 36	20	19	39	25	29	54
Cuilleen,	676 2 30	43	61	104	69	67	136
Cushatrower,	1,028 0 37	72	69	141	52	50	102
Derryadd, East,	421 3 27	6	5	11	9	6	15
Derryadd, West,	1,414 3 16	97	91	188	69	68	137
Derryclare,	2,531 1 21	6	3	9	3	3	6
MOYRUS P.—con.	A. R. P.						
Derrycunlagh,	2,128 1 37	5	4	9	.	.	.
Derrylea,	1,634 1 1	47	27	74	23	17	40
Derrynavglaun,	1,362 0 23	23	21	44	15	7	22
Derryneen,	221 3 4	3	5	8	11	5	16
Derryrush,	1,634 0 30	72	60	132	24	23	47
Derrysillagh,	137 0 12	28	23	51	17	13	30
Derryvealawauma,	1,434 3 23	23	21	44	6	4	10
Derryvickrune,	852 1 8	8	8	16	3	4	7
Derryvoreada,	740 1 37	15	16	31	12	11	23
Dooletter, East,	739 1 0	.	.	.	.	.	.

Parishes, Townlands, and Towns.	Area.			Population in 1841.			Population in 1851.		
				Males.	Females.	Total.	Males.	Females.	Total.
Doolctter, West,	527	3	31	8	6	14	8	9	17
Doonreaghan,	158	3	39	59	52	111	28	22	50
Dooycher,	347	2	2	195	163	358	177	176	353
Emlaghdauroe,	750	2	7	38	31	69	17	10	27
Emlaghmore,	1,736	0	3	22	19	41	15	18	33
Errisbeg, East,	1,471	1	6	196	185	381	76	81	157
Errisbeg, West,	1,120	2	19	86	82	168	87	88	175
Ervallagh,	353	1	8	187	214	401	129	132	261
Faul,	185	2	24	73	63	136	50	52	102
Garroman,	1,936	2	11	48	47	95	36	47	83
Glonarnid,	550	3	13	5	7	12	.	.	.
Glencoaghan,	3,139	1	27	27	18	45	25	23	48
Glencrees,	95	2	6	.	.	.	.	.	.
Gleninagh,	2,654	1	24	21	24	45	4	2	6
Glennaun,	397	0	26	.	5	5	.	.	.
Glinsk,	1,161	2	25	87	83	170	88	84	172
Gowla,	3,167	2	26	53	53	106	11	18	29
Gowlan, East,	3,942	2	22	} 50	46	96	{ 6	4	10
Gowlan, West,	768	0	39						
Halfmace,	119	0	27	33	26	59	42	39	81
Illion, East,	1,531	0	2	8	10	18	5	4	9
Illion, West,	662	0	4	13	6	19	4	4	8
Kilkieran,	2,255	0	33	223	221	444	221	210	431
Killeen,	429	1	34	.	.	.	.	.	.
Killymongaun,	491	0	14	59	62	121	31	39	70
Knockboy,	914	2	0	.	.	.	.	.	.
Kylesalia,	1,484	1	1	138	134	272	73	76	149
Lehanagh, North,	662	1	7	6	7	13	2	4	6
Lehanagh, South,	922	1	24	146	125	271	80	91	171
Letterard,	840	3	9	248	297	545	122	135	257
Lettercaumus,	351	0	13	31	42	73	38	33	71
Letterdeskert,	282	2	8	40	41	81	28	32	60
Letterdife,	1,590	2	20	111	124	235	64	78	142
Letterpibrum,	607	3	7	12	12	24	6	5	11
Lettershea,	629	0	14	15	18	33	15	16	31
Lettershinna,	4,396	1	34	42	37	79	22	38	60
Lettery,	951	1	32	29	28	57	22	23	45
Lissoughter,	1,386	0	13	21	20	41	17	16	33
Loughaconeera,	1,434	2	26	65	85	150	45	44	89
Loughawee,	1,100	3	36	.	.	.	.	.	.
Mace,	251	2	20	81	76	157	88	78	166
Moyrus,	1,313	0	37	200	192	392	49	51	100
Murvey,	1,087	0	32	146	177	323	59	72	131
Rosroe,	1,049	3	9	111	119	230	29	26	55
Roundstone,	210	3	6	36	41	77	32	25	57

PARISHES, TOWNLANDS, AND TOWNS.	AREA.	POPULATION IN 1841.			POPULATION IN 1851.		
		Males.	Females.	Total.	Males.	Females.	Total.
Rusheennamanagh, .	926 1 20	195	216	411	102	109	211
Rusheenyvulligan, .	103 3 34	5	8	13	3	3	6
Scrahallia, .	191 1 12	23	21	44	26	23	49
Shannadonnell, .	530 3 7	1	1	2	.	.	.
Shaunakeela. . .	1,907 2 34	36	30	66	37	37	74
Shannawirra, . .	796 1 2˙	5	1	6	.	.	.
Tawnaghbaun, . .	259 . .	50	59	109	9	15	24
Tawnaghmore, . .	600 2 33	10	6	16	11	9	20
Tievebreen, . .	1,561 2 31	.	.	.	.	.	.
Toombeola, . .	461 3 14	51	41	92	43	37	80
Tullaghlumman-beg, .	394 1 31	.	.	.	.	.	.
Tullaghlumman-more,	787 1 31	.	.	.	.	.	.
Islands:							
Ardnacross Island,	2 2 36	.	.	.	.	.	.
Avery Island, .	2 3 37	.	.	.	.	.	.
Beaghy Island, .	9 2 18	.	.	.	.	.	.
Beaahu. North. .	6 3 24						
MOYRUS P.—con.							
Islands:							
Birbeg Island, .	2 3 11	.	.	.	.	.	.
Birmore Island, .	32 1 30	.	.	.	.	.	.
Carra Island, .	2 2 38	.	.	.	.	.	.
Colt Island, .	4 0 0	.	.	.	.	.	.
Croaghnakeela Island	141 3 29	.	.	.	.	.	.
Croghnut, . .	15 2 14	.	.	.	.	.	.
Deer Island, . .	4 3 8	.	.	.	.	.	.
Finish Island, .	153 2 12	37	29	66	26	24	50
Freaghillaun, .	39 0 17	.	.	.	.	.	.
Greeve Island, .	1 3 8	.	.	.	.	.	.
Flat Island, . .	1 1 8	.	.	.	.	.	.
Illaunnacroagh-beg,	2 3 3	.	.	.	.	.	.
Illaunnacroagh-more	12 1 38	.	.	.	.	.	.
Illaunacroghnut, .	23 3 26	.	.	.	.	.	.
Illaunaknock, .	3 3 26	.	.	.	.	.	.
Illaunard, . .	12 3 33	.	.	.	.	.	.
Illaunmaan, . .	1 1 24	.	.	.	.	.	.
Illaunnakirka, .	8 3 6	.	.	.	.	.	.
Illaunfadda, . .	2 0 16	.	.	.	.	.	.
Illaungorm, North,	33 0 19	.	3	3	.	.	.
Illaungorm, South,	12 1 11	.	.	.	.	.	.
Illaungurruig, .	3 0 0	.	.	.	.	.	.
Inishbigger, . .	8 2 3	.	.	.	.	.	.
Inishlackan, . .	129 1 36	68	58	126	67	58	125
Inishmuskerry, .	18 2 18	.	.	.	.	.	.

Parishes, Townlands, and Towns.	Area.	Population in 1841.			Population in 1851.		
		Males.	Females.	Total.	Males.	Females.	Total.
Inishnee,	856 1 7	232	223	455	12	9	21
Inishtravin,	190 1 21	45	48	93	46	49	95
Inishtreh,	10 1 21	.	.	.	.	.	.
Inishtroghenmore,	11 3 32	.	.	.	.	.	.
Joyces Island,	1 2 0	.	.	.	.	.	.
Kinnelly Island,	3 0 30	}					
Kinnelly Island,	1 3 30		.	.	.	.	.
Kinnelly Island,	0 3 38	}					
Mason Island,	92 0 26	50	48	98	43	31	74
Mutton Island,	1 2 16	.	.	.	.	.	.
Mweenish Island,	572 0 29	329	320	649	241	230	471
North Island,	11 1 13	.	.	.	.	.	.
Oghly Island,	12 2 16	.	.	.	.	.	.
Red Island,	3 0 32	.	.	.	.	.	.
Red Island,	1 2 13	.	.	.	.	.	.
Rusheennacholla,	78 2 36	25	28	53	13	11	24
St. Macdara's Island	60 2 9	4	5	9	6	6	12
104 other Islands,	56 2 35	.	.	.	.	.	.
	100,981 3 20	5,797	5,776	11,573	3,593	3,649	7,242
Roundstone T.,	. . .	194	202	396	237	234	471
Auxiliary Workhouse,	. . .	.	.	.	351	494	845
Total,	100,981 3 20	5,991	5,978	11,969	4,181	4,377	8,558
OMEY P. :							
Aillenaveagh,	964 1 9	.	.	.	.	.	.
Ardmore,	58 0 10	3	3	6	.	.	.
Atticlogh,	392 3 30	.	.	.	.	.	.
Attigoddaun,	183 2 18	52	61	113	44	51	95
Aughrus-beg,	443 1 30	118	109	227	81	85	166
Aughrus-more,	482 1 15	160	154	314	111	128	239
Barnahallia,	85 3 12	.	.	.	1	2	3
Barnanoraun,	366 2 28	.	.	.	6	9	15
Belleek,	312 2 21	94	78	172	73	66	139
Boolard,	372 2 27	45	44	89	24	21	45
Claddaghduff,	416 2 10	107	99	206	42	55	97
Clifden,	310 0 17	46	37	83	.	.	.
Clifden Demesne,	206 0 29	16	9	25	5	3	8
Cloghaunard,	208 0 17	50	58	108	62	78	140
Coolacloy,	129 0 18	60	56	116	47	46	93
Couravoughil,	398 2 24	38	39	77	17	19	36
Courhoor,	531 3 33	3	2	5	7	9	16
Cregg,	1,304 3 30	4	2	6	.	.	.
Cushatrough,	501 1 7	94	98	192	37	28	65
Derreen,	198 1 28	20	30	50	26	33	59

PARISHES, TOWNLANDS, AND TOWNS.	AREA.			POPULATION IN 1841.			POPULATION IN 1851.		
	A.	R.	P.	Males.	Females.	TOTAL.	Males.	Females.	TOTAL.
OMEY P.—*con.*									
Doon, . . .	554	0	0	89	89	178	35	35	70
Emlagh, . . .	313	1	12	149	118	267	67	82	149
Eyrephort, . .	142	3	39	1	3	4	5	3	8
Fahy, . . .	204	1	35	74	71	145	72	65	137
Fakeeragh, .	137	1	4	47	54	101	57	60	117
Fountainhill or Knock-avilra, . . .	143	0	11	31	20	51	16	15	31
Gannoughs, . .	233	3	32	170	171	341	67	65	132
Glen, . . .	291	2	32	44	48	92	14	19	33
Glenbrickeen, . .	567	2	19	88	90	178	43	43	86
Gortrummagh, .	283	3	22	77	69	146	60	71	131
Grallagh, . . .	160	0	35	33	20	53	16	17	33
Kill, . . .	274	0	15	77	81	158	10	9	19
Kingstown Glebe or Ballymaconry, .	78	1	37	25	36	61	38	47	85
Knockavally, .	202	0	38	97	86	183	28	30	58
Knockbaun, .	99	1	37	55	44	99	20	21	41
Knockbrack, .	195	1	33	147	155	302	90	108	198
Laghtanabba, .	207	0	11	.	.	.	.	.	.
Leagaun, . . .	122	2	30	31	45	76	25	29	54
Letterdeen, .	278	0	38	78	79	157	56	74	130
Letternoosh, . .	397	1	16	60	44	104	50	64	114
Lettershanna, .	189	2	27	32	41	73	8	9	17
Loughauna, .	1,050	2	20	14	9	23	1	2	3
Maw, . . .	424	3	37	.	.	.	.	.	.
Moorneen, .	276	3	25	30	35	65	47	55	102
Patches, . .	153	3	15	45	57	102	14	9	23
Rossadillisk, .	185	2	34	141	128	269	110	95	205
Rusheen, . .	61	0	5	18	16	34	16	16	32
Shanakeever, .	259	3	35	3	2	5	7	3	10
Shinnanagh, .	639	0	20	5	8	13	8	12	20
Streamstown or Barra-trough, . .	1,000	3	8	155	168	323	120	136	256
Tievebaun, .	1,136	2	20	16	14	30	.	.	.
Tooraskeheen, .	715	0	16	40	38	78	20	23	43
Tooreen, . .	148	0	31	46	40	86	24	25	49
Townaloughra, .	261	3	22	.	.	.	.	.	.
Trean, . .	105	1	10	38	32	70	28	31	59
Tullyvoheen, .	364	2	36	77	84	161	83	81	164
Islands :									
Ardmore Island, .	1	1	34	.	.	.	.	.	.
Boolard Island, .	12	2	30	.	.	.	.	.	.
Cruagh, . .	82	2	38	.	.	.	.	.	.

PARISHES, TOWNLANDS, AND TOWNS.	AREA.	POPULATION IN 1841.			POPULATION IN 1851.		
		Males.	Females.	TOTAL.	Males.	Females.	TOTAL.
Eeshal Island,	12 2 8	.	.	.	.	.	.
Friar Island,	24 3 20	.	.	.	.	.	.
Hog Island,	9 0 28	.	.	.	.	.	.
High Island,	82 3 21	.	.	.	.	.	.
Inishturk,	132 2 1	45	39	84	48	49	97
Malthooa,	5 3 23	.	.	.	.	.	.
Omey Island, Cartoorbeg,	73 3 26	44	43	87	20	26	46
„ *Cloon,*	94 2 5	30	23	53	2	4	6
„ *Gooreen,*	145 2 17	53	43	96	38	35	73
„ *Gooreenatinny*	117 0 28	16	12	28	4	3	7
„ *Sturrakeen,*	91 0 24	67	66	133	35	38	73
Roeillaun,	3 1 12	.	.	.	.	.	.
Turbot Island,	147 2 19	74	72	146	82	87	169
213 *other Islands,*	67 2 34	.	.	.	.	.	.
	20,835 2 38	3,272	3,172	6,444	2,067	2,229	4,296
Clifden T.,	. . .	727	782	1,509	740	862	1,602
Workhouse,	. . .	.	.	.	285	354	639
Bridewell,	. . .	.	.	.	8	3	11
Total, .	20,835 2 38	3,999	3,954	7,953	3,100	3,448	6,548

Introduction

1   Census of Ireland for the years 1821 and 1841.

2   *First Report from His Majesty's Commissioners for inquiring into the condition of the poorer classes in Ireland, with appendix and supplement*, 1835 [369], xxxii, part 1. evidence of John D'Arcy, landlord.

3   *Her Majesty's Commission of Inquiry into the State of the Law and Practice in respect to the Occupation of Land in Ireland*, (Dublin 1847), (Devon Commission), Digest of Evidence taken before above Commission, 1844 Part 11, witness 493, Henry Kearney, shopkeeper Clifden, p471. (hereafter Devon Commission).

4   *First report from His Majesty's Commissioners for inquiring into the condition of the poorer classes in Ireland, with appendix and supplement*, 1835 [369], xxxii, part 1, pp484-487, evidence of Thomas Martin M.P. landlord.

5   *Devon Commission*, witness 491, Major-General A Thomson, pp466-467.

6   *First report of His Majesty's Commissioners for inquiring into the condition of the poorer classes in Ireland*, 1836, xxxiii, Supplement to Appendix F. p4.

Chapter 1

1   National Archives, Letter-Books of Joseph Burke, Assistant Poor Law Commissioner. 1838-55, Book 1839-40, No 61, *Formation of the Clifden Union*, Burke to Poor Law (P.L.) Commissioners, 22 July 1840. (hereafter Letter-Books).

2   Letter-Books, No 325, Burke to P.L.Commissioners, 25 April 1842.

3   *The Connaught Journal*, 24 September 1840.

4   Kathleen Villiers-Tuthill, *History of Clifden, 1810-1860*, (Galway 1982).

5   Letter-Books, No 61, Burke to P.L.Commissioners, 22 July 1840.

6   ibid.,

7   Shevawn Lynam, *Humanity Dick Martin 'King of Connemara' 1754-1834*, (Dublin 1989).

8   Kathleen Villiers-Tuthill, *Beyond The Twelve Bens, History of Clifden and District 1860-1923*, (Galway 1986) pp123-124; *Galway Archaeological and Historical Society Journal Vol.2 1902*, An account of the Castle and Manor of Bunowen by Martin J Blake.

9   The Blake Family, *Letters from the Irish Highlands*, Introduction by Dr. Kevin Whelan, (Gibbons 1995) pxvii; Tully Cross Guild, Irish Countrywomen's Association, *Portrait of a Parish, Ballynakill, Connemara*. Tully Cross I.C.A. 1985, pp27-30.

10 Tully Cross Guild, Irish Countrywomen's Association, *Portrait of a Parish, Ballinakill, Connemara*, pp35-39; Mr and Mrs S.C. Hall, *Ireland: Its Scenery, Character etc.*, 3 vols, (London 1841-3), Vol 111, p489; Devon Commission, witness 491, Major-General Alexander Thomson, pp465-467.

11 Villiers-Tuthill, *Beyond The Twelve Bens*, pp138-139.

12 *Devon Commission*, witness 498, Francis John Graham, landlord, Ballinakill, p477.

13 Blake, *Letters from the Irish Highlands of Connemara*, Introduction by Dr. Kevin Whelan, pviii; Thomás S. O'Conaola, Society and Settlement in Pre-Famine Connemara, *Galway Roots, Journal of the Galway Family History Society*, Vol.iv, pp56-60.

14 *Devon Commission*, witness 498, Francis John Graham, landlord, Ballinakill, p477

15 *Devon Commission*, witness 496, James O'Dowd, shopkeeper, Clifden, pp475-476.

16 ibid., witness 497, Martin R Hart hotelier Clifden, p 476.

17 ibid., witness 499, Anthony Mullins, farmer, Cloghaunard, Clifden, p478.

18 ibid.,

19 ibid., Evidence of Major-General Thomson, p467.

20 ibid., witness 500, Henry Hildebrand, merchant, farmer and agent, p480.

21 Census of Ireland for the year 1841.

22 *First report of commissioners for inquiring into the condition of the poorer Classes in Ireland*, 1836 [36] xxxi, Appendix D. Rev P Fitzmaurice P.P. Clifden, p4.

23 ibid.,

24 *The Third Annual Report Of The Commissioners Of Public Works re The Fisheries Of Ireland*, 1845 xxvi.

25 *Correspondence from July 1846 to January 1847 relating to the measures adopted for the relief of the distress in Ireland (Commissariat Series)* 1847, 1847 [761] li, Assistant Commissary-General Millikin to Sir Randolph Routh, 8 December 1846.

26 *Devon Commission*, witness 494, Fr Flannelly, p473.

27 ibid., witness 500, Henry Hildebrand, p479-480.

28 ibid., witness 496, James O'Dowd, p475.

29 ibid., witness 500, H Hildebrand, p480.

30 *First report of commissioners for inquiring into the condition of the poorer Classes in Ireland*, 1836 [36] xxxi, Appendix D, Father Fitzmaurice P.P. Clifden, p4.

31 ibid., Reverend Anthony Thomas, Ballinakill, p4.

32 *First report of His Majesty's Commissioners for inquiring into the condition of the poorer classes in Ireland*, 1836 [37] xxxii, Appendix E, Rev P Fitzmaurice P.P. Clifden, p4.

33 *Devon Commission*, witness 501, Matthew Lewis Coneys, farmer and shopkeeper resident at Clifden, pp480-481.

34 *First report of commissioners for inquiring into the condition of the poorer classes in Ireland*, 1836 [36] xxxi, Appendix D, Henry Blake, Renvyle, p4.

35 ibid., Rev A Thomas, Ballynakill, p4.

36 Letter-Books, No 61, Burke to P.L.Commissioners, 22 July 1840.

37 *First Report from His Majesty's Commissioners for inquiring into the condition of the poorer classes in Ireland, with appendix and supplement*, 1835 [369] xxxii, part 1, pp484-487, evidence of Patrick Lidden, butcher.

38 ibid., evidence of John Kelly, mason.

39 *First report of His Majesty's Commissioners for inquiring into the condition of the poorer classes in Ireland*, 1835 [369] xxxii, Appendix B, Part 11.

40 *Abstracts of the most serious representations made by the several medical superintendents of public institutions (fever hospitals, infirmaries, dispensaries etc.,) in the provinces of Ulster, Munster, Linster and Connaught*, 1846 [120] xxxvii.

41 Letter-Books, No 61, Burke to P.L.Commissioners, 22 July 1840.

42 ibid.,

43 *Report from the select committee of the House of Lords on the laws relating to the relief of the destitute poor together with the minutes of evidence taken before the committee*, 1846 [694] xi, part 1, Evidence of Edward Gulson, Assistant Poor Law Commissioner, p32.

44 Registry Of Deeds.

45 Letter-Books, No 296, Burke to P.L.Commissioners, 18 February 1842.

46 *Report of the commissioners for inquiring into the execution of the contracts for certain union workhouses in Ireland with appendices*, 1844 xxx.

47 *Report from the select committee of the House of Lords on the laws relating to the relief of the destitute poor together with the minutes of evidence taken before the said committee*, 1846 [694] xi, part 1, Evidence of Edward Gulson, Assistant Poor Law Commissioner.

48 *The Dublin Almanac And General Register Of Ireland*, 1848.

Chapter 2

1 National Archives, Relief Commission Papers, Incoming Letters, Ballynahinch Barony; *Further returns showing the progress of disease in the potatoes, the complaints which have been made, and the applications for relief, for the week ending the 4 April 1846*, 1846, [213] xxxvii.

2 *Devon Commission*, witness 500, Henry Hildebrand, p479.

3 ibid., witness 496, James O'Dowd, shopkeeper Clifden, pp475-476.

4 Samual Lewis, *A Topographical Directory of Ireland*, 2 Vol, (London 1837), p339.

5 *Devon Commission*, witness 500, Henry Hildebrand, p479.

.6 *Correspondence explanatory of the measures adopted by Her Majesty's Government for the relief of distress arising from the failure of the potato crop in Ireland* 1846 [735] xxxvii. Sir Randolph Routh to Charles Trevelyan, 31 July 1846.

7 ibid.,

8 National Archives, Chief Secretary's Office Registered Papers, Distress Papers 1846, D1406, Henry Blake to Lord Lieutenant, 19 May 1846. (hereafter Distress Papers).

9 *Correspondence explanatory of the measures adopted by Her Majesty's Government for the relief of distress arising form the failure of the potato crop in Ireland, 1846* [735] xxxvii. Captain Helpman to Sir James Dombrain, 19 May 1846.

10 Distress Papers 1846, D1413, Hyacinth D'Arcy to Under-Secretary, 22 May 1846.

11 ibid.,

12 Distress Papers 1846, D1445, Fr Peter Curran P.P. to Lord Lieutenant 23 May 1846, with reply from P.L.Commissioners.

13 ibid.,

14 Distress Papers 1846, D1444, Relief Commission to Roundstone Committee, May 1846.

15 *Correspondence explanatory of the measures adopted by Her Majesty's Government for the relief of distress arising from the failure of the potato crop in Ireland, 1846* [735] xxxvii, p235.

16 ibid., Captain Perceval to Charles Trevelyan, 22 June 1846.

17 ibid.,

18 ibid., Sir R Routh to Commissary-General Howetson, 23 June 1846.

19 ibid., Helpman to Routh, 14 July 1846.

20 ibid., Treasury Minute, 16 June 1846.

21 ibid., p338 & p357.

Chapter 3

1 National Archives, Relief Commission Papers, Incoming Correspondence, Ballynahinch Barony, 5111, Hyacinth D'Arcy to Relief Commission, 5 August 1846.

2 *Correspondence from July 1846 to January 1847 relating to the measures adopted for the relief of the distress in Ireland. (Commissariat Series), 1847* [761] li, Routh to Trevelyan, 14 January 1847, p479. *(hereafter Commissariat series)*

3 *Commissariat series*, Captain Perceval to Charles Trevelyan, 20 August 1846.

4 *ibid.,* Routh to Lister, 14 August 1846.

5 ibid., Lister to Routh, 25 August 1846.

6 ibid.,

7 ibid., Lister to Routh, 31 August 1846.

8 ibid., Lister to Routh, 25 August 1846.

9 ibid., Lister to Routh, 31 August 1846.

10 ibid., Dombrain to Routh, 5 September 1846.

11 ibid., Treasury Minute, 8 September 1846.

12 ibid., Dombrain to Routh, 18 September 1846.

13 National Archives, Chief Secretary's Office, Registered Papers (CSORP), Hyacinth D'Arcy to Chief Secretary, 21 September 1846.

14 *Galway Vindicator*, 30 September 1846.

15 ibid., 3 October 1846.

16 ibid., 30 September 1846.

17 National Archives, Relief Commission Papers, Incoming Correspondence, Ballynahinch Barony, D5681, Dr Suffield to Central Board of Health, 5 September 1846.

18 *Correspondence from July 1846 to January 1847 relating to the measures adopted for the relief of the distress in Ireland, (Board of Works Series)*, 1847 [764] l, p123.

19 National Archives, Relief Commission Papers, Incoming Correspondence, Ballynahinch Barony, Dr Suffield To Relief Commission, 3 October 1846.

20 Distress Papers 1846, D6470, D'Arcy to Lord Lieutenant, 9 October 1846.

21 National Archives, Relief Commission Papers, Incoming Correspondence, Ballynahinch Barony, 6124, Roundstone Committee to Relief Commission, 5 October 1846.

22 ibid., 6271, 10 October 1846.

23 ibid., Clifden Board of Guardians to Chief Secretary, 13 October 1846.

24 ibid., D6471, D'Arcy to Chief Secretary, 13 October 1846; D6308, D'Arcy to Relief Commission, 13 October 1846.

25 *Board of Works series*, p211.

26 *Board of Works series*, Presentments and Recommendations from 10 December 1846 to 8 January 1847.

27 National Archives, Relief Commission Papers, Incoming Correspondence, Ballynahinch Barony, 6557, Dr Suffield to Relief Commission, 21 October 1846.

28 *Board of Works series*, Commissioners of Public Works to the Lords of the Treasury, 12 November 1846.

Chapter 4

1 National Archives, Relief Commission Papers, Incoming Correspondence, Ballynahinch Barony, 6557, Dr Suffield to Sir Routh, 18 October 1846.

2 *Galway Vindicator*, 28 October 1846.

3 *Commissariat series*, p230.

4 National Archives, Relief Commission Papers, Incoming Correspondence, Ballynahinch Barony, 6870, Rev Duncan to Lord Lieutenant, 28 October 1846.

5 *Commissariat series*, p222.

6 ibid., Routh to Trevelyan, 2 November 1846.

7 ibid., D8483, Clifden Relief Committee to under-secretary, 23 November 1846.

8 ibid., 7786, Relief Commission to Hyacinth D'Arcy, 1 December 1846.

9 National Archives, Relief Commission Papers, Incoming Correspondence, Ballynahinch Barony, 7781, Ballynakill Committee to Routh, 27 November 1846.

10 *Commissariat series*, p384.

11 ibid., 7883, Clifden Relief Committee to Relief Commission, 11 December 1846.

12 ibid., Routh to Trevelyan, 24 December 1846.

13 ibid., The Secretary of the Admiralty to Trevelyan, 28 December 1846.

14 ibid., p428; National Archives, Relief Commission Papers, Incoming Correspondence, Barony of Ballynahinch, 8236, Routh to Clifden Committee, 17 December 1846.

15 ibid.,

16 Commissariat series, Parker to Routh, 19 December 1846, p396.

17 National Archives, Relief Commission Papers, Incoming Correspondence, Ballynahinch Barony, Clifden Committee to Relief Commission, 26 December 1846.

18 ibid., Ballynakill Relief Committee Minute, 29 December 1846.
19 *Galway Vindicator*, 30 December 1846.

Chapter 5

1 National Archives, Relief Commission Papers, Incoming Correspondence, Ballynahinch Barony, Roundstone Relief Committee to Relief Commission, D336, 19 January 1847.
2 *Correspondence from January to March 1847, relating to the measures adopted for the relief of the distress in Ireland. (Board of Works Series) Second Part*, 1847 [797] lii, Report of Captain Hutchinson, 23 January 1847; Mr Ffennell to Mr Mulvany, 23 February 1847. (Hereafter *Board of Works series, second part*.)
3 National Archives, Relief Commission Papers, Incoming Correspondence, Ballynahinch Barony, D493, Guardians to Chief Secretary with reply from Relief Commission, 7 January 1847; 9493, Clifden Relief Committee to Relief Commissioners, 23 January 1847.
4 *Commissariat series*, p474.
5 National Archives, Relief Commission Papers, Incoming Correspondence, Ballynahinch Barony, Ballynakill Committee to Relief Commission, 17 January 1847.
6 ibid., Relief Commission to Clifden Relief Committee, 21 January 1847.
7 Distress Papers 1846-7, Clifden Relief Committee to Lord Lieutenant, 22 January 1847.
8 ibid., Hyacinth D'Arcy to Chief Secretary, 24 January 1847.
9 *Board of Works series*, Treasury Minute, 23 October 1846, p136.
10 *Board of Works series second part*, Extract from journal of Capt Hutchinson, 13 February 1847.
11 ibid., p49.
12 ibid., Report of William Pierce, 3 March 1847.
13 ibid., Captain Hutchinson Report, 23 January 1847, p118.
14 ibid., Report of William Pierce, 3 March 1847, p213.
15 ibid., Extract for Journal of Captain Hutchinson, 13 February 1847, p268.
16 ibid., Commissioners of Public Works to the Lord of the Treasury, February 1847, p39.
17 ibid., Extracts from journal of Capt Hutchinson, 6 February 1847, p267.
18 *Correspondence from January to March 1847, relating to the measures adopting for the relief of the distress in Ireland. (Commissariat Series) second part*, 1847 [796] lii, Deputy Assistant Commissary-General F Parker to Routh, 5 February 1847, p125. (Hereafter *Commissariat series second part*.)
19 *Commissariat series second part*, Routh to Trevelyan, 11 February 1847, p123.
20 ibid., Rev Mark Foster to Bishop of Tuam, January 1847, p11.
21 Society Of Friends, *Distress In Ireland 1846-'47*, Narrative of William Edward Forster's Visit In Ireland From The 18th To The 26th January 1847.
22 ibid.,

Chapter 6

1 *Commissariat series second part*, Trevelyan to Captain Hamilton, 18 February 1847, p148.
2 National Archives, Relief Commission Papers, Incoming Correspondence, Ballynahinch Barony, 10538, Roundstone Relief Committee to Relief Commission, 6 February 1847.
3 ibid., 16507, 21 March 1847.
4 *Fifth, sixth and seventh report of the Relief Commissioners constituted under the Act 10 Vict., cap.7. and correspondence connected therewith, with appendices*, 1847-8 [876] xxix, p32.
5 Society Of Firends, *Distress In Ireland 1846-'47, Narrative of R Barcley Fox's Visit To Some Parts Of The West Of Ireland, March and April 1847*, p4.
6 *Galway Vindicator*, 3 August 1847, p2.

7 Archer E S Martin, *Genealogy of the family of Martin of Ballynahinch Castle*, (Winnipeg 1890).

8 *Galway Vindicator*, 22 May 1847.

9 *Second Report of the Relief Commissioners constituted under the Act 10 Vic., cap.7, with appendices*, 1847 [819] xvii, Appendix D, p24.

10 *Third report of the Relief Commissioners constituted under the Act 10th. Vic., cap.7, with appendices*, 1847 [836] xvii, Appendix C, p27.

11 *Fourth report of the Relief Commissioners constitute under the Act 10 Vic., cap.7. with appendices*, 1847 [859] xvii, Appendix 1.

12 *Fifth, sixth and seventh reports of the Relief Commissioners constituted under the Act 10 Vict., cap. 7, and correspondence connected therewith, with appendices*, 1847-8 [876] xxix, p7.

13 ibid.,

14 National Archives, CSORP, Clifden Magistrates to Lord Lieutenant, 17 June 1847.

15 *Fifth, sixth and seventh reports of the Relief Commissioners constituted under the Act 10 Vict., cap. 7, and correspondence connected therewith, with appendices*, 1847-8 [876] xxix, Lists of orders on certificates from the Central Board of Health in Ireland.

16 ibid.,

17 *Board of Works series second part*, Extract from Journal of Captain Hutchinson, 13 February 1847, p268.

18 Salruck Papers SP/159b, Henry Blake to Henry Labouchere, Chief Secretary, 28 April 1847.

19 D'Arcy Family Records, Joseph Scott Moore, Solicitor, to the Lord High Chancellor of Ireland, 1848, Report of Thomas Scully, Receiver to Clifden Estate.

20 *Reports of the Board of Public Works in Ireland, relating to measures adopted for the relief of distress in March, April and May 1847*, 1847 [834] xvii, Commissioners to the Lords of the Treasury, 6 April 1847, p6.

21 National Archives, CSORP, Clifden Magistrates to Lord Lieutenant, 17 June 1847.

Chapter 7

1 *Fifth, sixth and seventh reports of the Relief Commissioners*, p9.

2 National Archives, Outrage Reports 1847, County Galway, Sworn statement of Joseph McDonnell before Mr Burke, Poor Law Inspector, 20 September 1847.

3 ibid., 18270, D147, 5 July 1847.

4 ibid., 30094, D147, 23 September 1847.

5 ibid., J Dopping to Lord Lieutenant, 2 October 1847.

6 ibid., Joseph McDonnell's sworn deposition before Mr Burke, Poor Law Inspector, 20 September 1847.

7 National Archives, Outrage Reports 1848, County Galway, 11/837, Poor Law Commissioners to T Redington, under-secretary, 25 September 1847.

8 National Archives, Outrage Reports 1847, County Galway, Sworn evidence of John Lydon, 7 December 1847.

9 National Archives, Outrage Reports 1848, County Galway, 11/54, 11 January 1848; 11\134, evidence of Constable Bennett, 26 January 1848.

10 ibid., 11/82, John Dopping to under-secretary, 23 January 1848.

11 ibid., Theabold McKenna to John Dopping, January 1848.

12 ibid., 11/108, John Dopping to under-secretary, 24 January 1848.

13 ibid., 11/134, Evidence of Constable Bennett, 26 January 1848.

14 National Archives, Outrage Reports 1847, County Galway, Thomas Davis sworn deposition before J Dopping, 16 November 1847.

15 ibid., Francis Graham to J Dopping, 16 November 1847.

Chapter 8

1 *Papers relating to the relief of the distress and state of the unions and workhouses in Ireland, Fourth series*, 1847-48 [896] liv, Deane to Commissioners, 2 November 1847. (hereafter *Relief of distress, fourth series.*)

2 ibid.,

3 ibid., P.L.Commissioners to Deane, 26 November 1847.

4 ibid., Deane to P.L.Commissioners, 22 November 1847.

5 *First Annual Report Of The Poor Law Commission.* 1848.

6 *Relief of distress, fourth series*, Deane to P.L.Commission, 9 November 1847.

7 ibid.,

8 *Papers relating to proceedings for the relief of distress and state of unions and workhouses in Ireland, Fifth Series*, 1848 [919] lv, Deane to P.L.Commissioners, 29 November 1847. (hereafter *Relief of distress, fifth series.*)

9 *Relief of distress, fourth series*, Dr Bodkin to John Deane, 2 November 1847.

10 ibid., Deane to P.L.Commissioners, 9 November 1847.

11 *Relief of distress, fifth series*, Deane to P.L.Commissioners, 25 December 1847.

12 ibid., Deane to P.L.Commissioners, 27 December 1847.

13 James A Tuke, *A Visit to Connaught in the Autumn of 1847*, A letter addressed to the Central Relief Committee of the Society of Friends, Dublin 1848, Second Edition, p14.

14 *Relief of distress, fifth series*, Deane to P.L.Commissioners, 20 December 1847.

15 Tuke, *A Visit to Connemara*, p40.

16 *Relief of distress, fourth series*, Deane to P.L.Commission, 16 November 1847.

17 *Relief of distress, fifth series*, Deane to P.L.Commissioners, 3 December 1847.

18 ibid., Deane to Count Strzelecki, 28 January 1848.

19 *First Annual Report of the Poor Law Commission.* 1848.

20 *Papers relating to relief of distress and state of unions in Ireland, Seventh Series*, 1848, 1847-48 [999] liv, Count Strgelecki to the Commissioners, 31 July 1848.

21 *Relief of distress, fifth series*, P.L.Commissioners to Deane, 30 December 1847.

22 ibid, Deane to Commissioners, 1 January 1848.

23 ibid, Commissioners to Deane, 4 January 1848.

24 ibid., Deane to Commissioners, 3 January 1848.

25 ibid.,

26 ibid.,

27 ibid., Dr Suffield to Deane, 11 January 1848.

28 ibid., Deane to P.L.Commissioners, 23 January 1848.

29 ibid., Deane to Commissioners, 20 January 1848.

30 ibid., Deane to Commissioners, 23 January 1848.

31 *Papers relating to proceedings for the relief of distress and state of unions and workhouses in Ireland, Sixth Series*, 1848, [955] lvi, Vice-Guardians to Commission, 22 February 1848. (hereafter *Relief of distress, sixth series.*)

32 *Relief of distress, fifth series*, Richard Burke, Poor Law Inspector to P.L.Commissioners, 31 January 1848.

33 ibid., D'Arcy to Deane, 2 February 1848.

34 ibid., Major-General Thomson to Deane, 2 February 1848.

35 ibid., Commissioners to Clerk of Clifden Union, 5 February 1848.

Chapter 9

1 *First Annual Report Of The Poor Law Commissioners,* 1848.
2 *Returns showing the financial state of each union in Ireland at the time of the appointment of paid guardians and at their removal,* 1850 [251] l.
3 *Returns showing the financial state of each union in Ireland at the time of the appointment of paid guardians and at their removal, 1850. [251], l; Relief of distress, sixth series, Deane to P.L.Commissioners,* 21 February 1848.
4 *Relief of distress, sixth series,* 1848 [955] lvi, Deane to P.L.Commissioners, 9 February 1848.
5 ibid., Deane to P.L.Commissioners, 15 February 1848.
6 ibid., Deane to P.L.Commissioners, 28 February 1848.
7 ibid., Deane to P.L.Commissioners, 21 February 1848.
8 ibid., Deane to P.L.Commissioners, 7 March 1848.
9 ibid., Deane to P.L.Commissioners, 21 February 1848.
10 ibid., Deane to P.L.Commissioners, 13 March 1848.
11 ibid., Vice-Guardians to P.L.Commissioners, 28 February 1848.
12 ibid., Vice-Guardians to P.L.Commissioners, 7 March 1848.
13 ibid., Vice-Guardians to P.L.Commissioners, 2 March 1848.
14 ibid., Deane to P.L.Commissioners, 7 March 1848.
15 ibid., O'Leary, Vice-Guardian to P.L.Commissioners, 22 March 1848.
16 ibid., P.L.Commissioners to Deane, 21 March 1848.
17 ibid., Deane to P.L.Commissioners, 7 March 1848.
18 ibid, Vice-Guardians to P.L.Commissioners, 16 March 1848.
19 ibid., Deane to P.L.Commissioners, 8 March 1848.
20 ibid., Dr Phelan to P.L.Commissioners, 27 March 1848.
21 ibid., Dr Phelan to P.L.Commissioners, 27 March 1848.
22 ibid., O'Leary, Vice-Guardian to P.L.Commissioners, 29 March 1848.

Chapter 10

1 *Relief of distress, sixth series,* 1848, Deane to P.L.Commissioners, 13 March 1848.
2 ibid., O'Leary, to P.L.Commissioners, 29 March 1848.
3 ibid., Vice-Guardians to P.L.Commissioners, 22 February 1848.
4 ibid., Deane to P.L.Commissioners, 27 March 1848.
5 National Archives, Outrage Reports 1848, County Galway, J B Kernan to under-secretary, 21 April 1848.
6 *First Annual Report of The Poor Law Commissioners.* 1848.
7 *Papers relating to relief of distress and state of unions in Ireland, Seventh Series,* 1848, 1847-48 [999] liv, Deane to Commissioners, 11 August 1848. (hereafter *Relief of distress, seventh series*).
8 ibid.
9 *Papers relating to the aid offered to the distressed unions in the west of Ireland 1849,* 1849 [1010] xlviii.
10 Minute Book Clifden Union, 3 October 1848.
11 ibid
12 ibid, 7 November 1848.
13 see Coilín Hernon, 'Johnny Seoighe', *Journal of the Galway Family History Society,* Volume 111, pp113-114; Minute Book Clifden Union, p336.
14 *Minutes of evidence before select committee on the operation of the Irish Poor Law,* 1849 xvi, evidence Lieut-Col. E Archer 10 May 1849, p922

15 Minute Book Clifden Union, 10 October 1848.

16 Minute Book Clifden Union, P.L.Commissioners to Vice-Guardians, 14 October 1848.

17 ibid., 3 October 1848.

18 ibid., 31 October 1848.

19 ibid., 10 October 1848.

20 ibid., Masters report 14 November 1848.

21 ibid.,

22 *Further papers relating to the aid afforded to the distressed unions in the west of Ireland* 1849, 1849 [1010] xlviii, Vice-Guardians to the P.L.Commissioners, 10 November 1848.

23 ibid., Copeland to the Commissioners, 11 November 1848.

24 ibid., Deane to P.L.Commissioners. 11 November 1848.

25 ibid., Vice-Guardians to P.L.Commissioners, 25 November 1848.

26 ibid., James Dooner to Vice-Guardians, 25 November 1848.

27 ibid., Home Secretary to P.L.Commissioners, 6 December 1848.

28 Minute Book Clifden Union, 2 December 1848.

29 *Further papers relating to the aid afforded to the distressed unions in the west of Ireland 1849, 1849 [1010] xlviii, P.L.Commissioners to Sir George Grey, Home Secretary, 18 December 1848.*

30 ibid., H Briscoe to P.L.Commissioners, 3 January 1849.

31 ibid., P.L.Commissioners to Home Secretary, 30 December 1848.

32 ibid, Home Secretary to P.L.Commissioners, 13 January 1849.

33 Minute Book Clifden Union, 2 January 1849.

34 ibid., 25 October 1848.

35 ibid., 31 October 1848.

36 *Galway Vindicator*, 26 June 1847.

37 Minute Books Clifden Union, Dr Suffield's report to the Board, 12 December 1848.

38 ibid., 19 December 1884.

Chapter 11

1 *Papers relating to proceedings for the relief of the distress and state of unions and workhouses in Ireland, Eighth Series*, Vice-Guardians to P.L.Commissioners, 22 January 1849, p23.(hereafter *Relief of distress, eighth series*).

2 ibid., H Briscoe to P.L.Commissioners, 21 January 1849, p23.

3 ibid., Vice-Guardians to P.L.Commissioners, 22 January 1849.

4 ibid., H Briscoe to P.L.Commissioners, 16 January 1849, p22.

5 *Further papers relating to the distressed unions in the west of Ireland, 1849*, 1849 [1023] xlviii, H Briscoe to P.L.Commissioners, 8 February 1849, p8.

6 *Fourth report from the Select Committee of the House of Lords appointed to inquire into the operations of the Irish Poor Law and the expediency of making any amendment to its enactments*, 1849 xvi, p664.

7 *Further papers relating to the aid afforded to the distressed unions in the west of Ireland,*1849, 1849 [1010] xlviii, H Smith to P.L.Commissioners, 21 December 1848, p36.

8 *Galway Vindicator,* 20 January 20 1849, p1.

9 Minute Book Clifden Union, 9 January 1849.

10 ibid., 23 January 1849.

11 ibid., P.L.Commissioners to Vice-Guardians, 12 January 1849.

12 *Further papers relating to the aid afforded to the distressed unions in the west of Ireland*, 1849, 1849 [1010] xlviii. Briscoe to P.L.Commissioners, 16 January 1849.

13 Minute Book Clifden Union, 13 February 1849.

14 ibid.,

15 ibid., 20 March 1849.

16 *Further papers relating to the aid afforded to the distressed unions in the west of Ireland*, 1849, 1849 [1010] xlviii, Smith to P.L.Commissioners, 14 May 1849.

17 ibid., Treasury Minute to P.L.Commissioners, p31.

18 Minute Book Clifden Union, September 1848 - June 1849.

19 ibid.,

20 *Returns showing the financial state of each union in Ireland at the time of the appointment of paid guardians and at their removal*, 1850 [251] l.

21 *Returns of the expenditure of Poor Rates of each union in Ireland for the year end 29 September 1849, and the number of persons relieved in and out of the workhouse in each union during same period*, 1850 [313] l.

Chapter 12

1 *The Dublin Almanac and General Register of Ireland*, 1845.

2 *Constabulary List and Directory, 1844. Dublin.*

3 National Archives, Outrage Reports County Galway 1847, Sub-Inspector Ireland's Report, January 1847.

4 ibid., Head Constable W Wilks report, February 1847.

5 National Archives, Outrage Reports County Galway 1848, 11/62, John Dopping to Under-Secretary Thomas Redington, 14 January 1848.

6 National Archives, CSORP, Hyacinth D'Arcy to Chief Secretary, 16 January 1848.

7 National Archives, Outrage Reports County Galway 1848, Dominick Kerrigan to John Dopping, 14 January 1848.

8 ibid., John Dopping to Under-Secretary Thomas Redington, 14 January 1848.

9 ibid, John Dopping to Under-Secretary, 17 January 1848.

10 National Archives, Outrage Reports County Galway, 1848, 11/837 Routh to P.L.Commissioners, 27 January 1848.

11 Distress Papers 1848, Dr W Suffield to Chief Secretary, 8 February 1848.

12 ibid., Dominick Kerrigan to Chief Secretary, February 1848.

13 National Archives, Outrage Reports County Galway 1848, 11/209, John Dopping to under-secretary, 22 February 1848.

14 ibid, 11/314, John Dopping to under-secretary, 4 March 1848.

15 ibid, 11/164, Major-General Thomson to John Dopping, 8 February 1848,

16 ibid, 11/314, 2 March 1848.

17 *Galway Vindicator*, 18 March 1848, p2.

18 *Galway Vindicator*, 25 March 1848, p3.

19 ibid,

20 *Relief of distress, sixth series*, 1848 [955] lvi, pp305-309.

21 *Galway Vindicator*, 1 April 1848, p3.

22 National Archives, Outrage Reports County Galway 1848, Dopping to under-secretary, 19 April 1848.

23 ibid, Sworn evidence given by Michael Ashe, Barbara Ashe, John O'Connell, John Adley before John Dopping, 3 June 1848.

24 ibid, 11/523, Dopping to under-secretary, 5 June 1848.

25 *Galway Vindicator*, 24 January 1849, p3.

26 *Galway Vindicator*, 30 July 1851.

27 *Burkes Landed Gentry*, 1899.

Chapter 13

1 *Thom's Irish Almanac*, 1850.

2 ibid., 1851.

3 *Comparative statement of the workhouse accommodation, the numbers relieved and the deaths, in each of the workhouse's in the province of Connaught during the half-year ending 25 day of March 1847, 1848, 1849, 1850 respectively. Also the numbers in receipt of out-door relief at the close of each of these periods*, 1850 [727] l.

4 Minutes Book Clifden Union, July-December 1852.

5 A.E. Hughes, *Lift Up A Standard, One Hundred Years With The Irish Church Missions*, p21.

6 The Rev Joseph D'Arcy Sirr D.D., *A Memoir of the Honorable and Most Reverend Power Le Poer Trench Last Archbishop of Tuam* (Dublin 1845).

7 Mrs Dallas, *Incidents In The Life And Ministry Of The Rev A R C Dallas* (London 1871), p352.

8 Sirr, *A Memoir of the Honorable and Most Reverend Power Le Poer Trench Last Archbishop of Tuam*.

9 *The Sunday At Home*, A family magazine for Sabbath reading, Religious Tract Society London, issue 1083, 13 February 1875, p103.

10 Salruck Papers, SP/80, Rev Ellis to Thomson, 30 October 1838.

11 Sirr, *A Memoir Of The Honorable And Most Reverend Power Le Poer Trench*, p651.

12 Hughes, *Lift Up A Standard*, p20.

13 Dallas, *Incidents In The Life And Ministry Of The Rev A R C Dallas*, p351.

14 ibid., p22.

15 *The Sunday At Home*, p156.

16 Tuke, *A Visit To Connaught In The Autumn Of 1847*, p16.

17 *The Sunday At Home*, p156.

18 *A Mission Tour Book In Ireland*, (London 1860), Published by the Society For Irish Church Missions; Villiers-Tuthill, *History Of Clifden* 1810-1860, pp67-72.

19 Dallas, *Incidents In The Life And Ministry Of The Rev A R C Dallas*, pp390-393.

20 ibid., p401.

21 ibid., p402.

22 see Villiers-Tuthill, *History Of Clifden 1810-1860* pp67-72; Villiers-Tuthill, *Beyond The Twelve Bens, A History Of Clifden And District 1860-1923*, pp16-19.

23 *The Sunday At Home*, p157.

24 Burkes Landed Gentry Of Ireland, 1871.

25 Villiers-Tuthill, *History Of Clifden* 1810-1860, pp75-76.

26 see Kathleen Villiers-Tuthill, Religious Conflict in Claddaghduff, *Connemara, Journal of the Clifden and Connemara Heritage Group*, Vol.2 No 1, 1995, pp7-13.

27 *Private Memoirs of B And E Seebohm*, Edited By Their Sons (London 1873), pp18-19.

28 ibid.,

29 ibid., p357.

30 National Archives, Landed Estates Court Rentals, July - November 1858, Vol 53. (hereafter LEC Vol 53).

31 National Archives, Landed Estates Court Rentals, May 1852, Vol 15, p26, Descriptive Particulars by George Preston White. (Hereafter LEC Vol 15).

32 *Private Memoirs of B and E Seebohm*, p359

33 LEC Vol 15.

34 ibid.,

35 *Private Memoirs of B and E Seebohm*, p365.

36 ibid., p364.

37 ibid., p366.

38 ibid., p359

39 ibid., p372.

40 ibid., p362

41 ibid., p373.

42 ibid., p361.

43 ibid., p362

44 ibid., p369.

45 ibid., pp372-373.

46 LEC Vol 15, p26.

47 Archer E S Martin, *Genealogy of the Family of Martin of Ballynahinch Castle*, (Winnipeg 1890).

48 *Galway Vindicator*, 7 November 1849, p2.

49 National Archives, Landed Estates Court Rentals, 1850, Vol 1.

50 Villiers-Tuthill, *History of Clifden 1810-1860*, pp57-64.

51 ibid., pp34-36.

52 LEC Vol 15, p26.

53 Villiers-Tuthill, *Beyond The Twelve Bens A History Of Clifden And District 1860-1923*, p125.

54 *Land Owners Of Ireland*, 1871; Villiers-Tuthill, *Beyond The Twelve Bens History of Clifden and District 1860-1923*, p116, pp138-139.

55 Henry Coulter, *The West Of Ireland: Its Existing Condition and Prospects* (Dublin 1862), p95.

56 *The Illustrated London News*, 12 January 1850.

57 *Galway Vindicator*, 7 November 1849, p2.

Appendix 2

1 *Papers relating to proceedings for the relief of the distress and state of unions and workhouses in Ireland, Eight Series*, 1849 [1042] xlviii.

BIBLIOGRAPHY

PRIMARY SOURCES

National Archives, Dublin.
Chief Secretary's Office, Registered Papers.
CSORP, Distress Papers
Letter-Books of Joseph Burke, Assistant Poor Law Commissioner, 1839-1855.
Relief Commission Papers, Incoming Correspondence, Ballynahinch Barony.
Outrage Reports County Galway 1847-8.
Landed Estates Court Rentals:
    1850, Vol 1
    May 1852, Vol 15
    July-November 1858, Vol 53.
Census of Ireland for the years 1821, 1831, 1841 and 1851.

Newspapers

Connaught Journal
Galway Vindicator
Illustrated London News

Minute Book Clifden Union, September 1848-July 1849.
Minute Book Clifden Union, July-December 1852.
First Annual Report Of The Poor Law Commission. 1848.
D'Arcy Family Papers.
Salruck Papers.

British Parliamentary Papers

First Report from His Majesty's Commissioners for inquiring into the condition of the poorer classes in Ireland, with appendix and supplement, 1835 [369] xxxii, part 1; 1835 xxxiii; 1836 [36] xxxi; 1836 [37] xxxii.

Her Majesty's Commission of Inquiry into the State of the Law and Practice in respect to the Occupation of Land in Ireland, (Dublin 1847), (Devon Commission), Digest of Evidence taken before above Commission, 1844 Part 11,

Third Annual Report Of The Commissioners Of Public Works re The Fisheries Of Ireland, 1845 xxvi.

Abstracts of the most serious representations made by the several medical superintendents of public institutions (fever hospitals, infirmaries, dispensaries etc.,) in the provinces of Ulster, Munster, Linster and Connaught, 1846 [120] xxxvii.

Report from the select committee of the House of Lords on the laws relating to the relief of the destitute poor together with the minutes of evidence taken before the committee, 1846 [694] xi, part 1,

Report of the commissioners for inquiring into the execution of the contracts for certain union workhouses in Ireland with appendices, 1844 xxx.

Further returns showing the progress of disease in the potatoes, the complaints which have been made, and the application for relief, for the week ending the 4 April 1846, 1846 [213] xxxvii.

Correspondence explanatory of the measures adopted by Her Majesty's Government for the relief of distress arising from the failure of the potato crop in Ireland, 1846 [735] xxxvii.

Correspondence from July 1846 to January 1847 relating to the measures adopted for the relief of the distress in Ireland. (Commissariat Series), 1847 [761] li.

Correspondence from July 1846 to January 1847 relating to the measures adopted for the relief of the distress in Ireland, (Board of Works Series), 1847 [764] l.

Correspondence from January to March 1847, relating to the measures adopted for the relief of the distress in Ireland, (Board of Works Series) Second Part, 1847 [797] lii.

Correspondence from January to March 1847, relating to the measures adopting for the relief of the distress in Ireland, (Commissariat Series) second part, 1847 [796] lii.

Second Report of the Relief Commissioners constituted under the Act 10 Vic., cap.7, with appendices, 1847 [819] xvii.

Third report of the Relief Commissioners constituted under the Act 10th. Vic., cap.7, with appendices, 1847 [836] xvii.

Fourth report of the Relief Commissioners constitute under the Act 10 Vic., cap.7. with appendices, 1847 [859] xvii.

Fifth, sixth and seventh reports of the Relief Commissioners constituted under the Act 10 Vict., cap. 7, and correspondence connected therewith, with appendices, 1847-8 [876] xxix.

Reports of the Board of Public Works in Ireland, relating to measures adopted for the relief of distress in March, April and May 1847, 1847 [834] xvii.

Papers relating to the proceedings for the relief of the distress and state of the unions and workhouses in Ireland, Fourth Series, 1847-48 [896] liv.

Papers relating to proceedings for the relief of distress and state of unions and workhouses in Ireland, Fifth Series, 1848 [919] lv.

Papers relating to the proceedings for the relief of distress and state of unions and workhouses in Ireland, Seventh Series, 1848, 1847-48 [999] liv.

Papers relating to proceedings for the relief of distress and state of unions and workhouses in Ireland, Sixth Series, 1848, 1848 [955] lvi.

Papers relating to the proceedings for the relief of distress and state of unions and workhouses in Ireland, Seventh Series, 1848, 1847-48 [999] liv.

Returns showing the financial state of each union in Ireland at the time of the appointment of paid guardians and at their removal, 1850 [251] l.

Papers relating to the aid offered to the distressed unions in the west of Ireland 1849, 1849 [1010] xlviii.

Minutes of evidence before select committee on the operation of the Irish Poor Law, 1849 xvi.

Papers relating to proceedings for the relief of the distress and state of unions and workhouses in Ireland, Eighth Series, 1849 [1042] xlviii.

Further papers relating to the distressed unions in the west of Ireland, 1849, 1849 [1023] xlviii.

Fourth report from the Select Committee of the House of Lords appointed to inquire into the operations of the Irish Poor Law and the expediency of making any amendment to its enactments, 1849 xvi.

Returns of the expenditure of Poor Rates of each union in Ireland for the year end 29 September 1849, and the number of persons relieved in and out of the workhouse in each union during same period, 1850 [313] l.

Comparative statement of the workhouse accommodation, the numbers relieved and the deaths, in each of the workhouse's in the province of Connaught during the half-year ending 25 day of March 1847, 1848, 1849, 1850 respectively. Also the numbers in receipt of out-door relief at the close of each of these periods, 1850 [727] l.

Eighth report of the commissioners for inquiring into the numbers and boundaries of Poor Law Unions and Electoral Divisions in Ireland, 1850 [1149] xxvi.

SECONDARY SOURCES

Blake Family, *Letters from the Irish Highlands*, Introduction by Dr. Kevin Whelan (Galway 1995).

Bowen, Desmond, *Souperism: Myth or Reality?, a study of Catholics and Protestants during the Great Famine* (Cork 1970).

Burkes Landed Gentry Of Ireland, 1871 and 1899.

Constabulary List and Directory, 1844 (Dublin 1844).

Corville Scott, Thomas, *Connemara After The Famine: Journal of a Survey of the Matrin Estate, 1853, Edited & Introduced by Tim Robinson (Dublin 1995).*

Coulter, Henry, *The West Of Ireland: Its Existing Condition, and Prospects* (Dublin 1862).

Dallas, Mrs, Incidents In The Life And Ministry Of The Rev A R C Dallas (London 1871).

Dublin Almanac and General Register of Ireland, 1845-8.

Eiriksson, Andres, and Ó Gráda, Cormac, (eds), *Estate Records Of The Irish Famine, (Dublin 1995).*

Galway Archaeological and Historical Society Journal Vol.2 1902, An account of the Castle and Manor of Bunowen by Martin J Blake.

Goodbody, Rob, *A Suitable Channel: Quaker Relief in the Great Famine* (Dublin 1995).

Hall, Mr and Mrs S.C. *Ireland: Its Scenery, Character etc.*, 3 vols (London 1841-3).

Hernon, Coilin, 'Johnny Seoighe', *Galway Roots, Journal of the Galway Family History Society*, Volume 111.

Hughes, A.E., *Lift Up A Standard, One Hundred Years With The Irish Church Missions (London 1948).*

Irish Church Missions, *A Mission Tour Book In Ireland* (London 1860).

Kinealy, Christine, *This Great Calamity: The Irish Famine 1845-52* (Dublin 1994).

Land Owners Of Ireland, (Dublin 1871).

Lewis, Samual, *A Topographical Directory of Ireland*, 2 Vol (London 1837).

Lindsay, Deirdre, and Fitzpatrick, David, (eds), *Records Of The Irish Famine*, (Dublin 1993).

Lynam, Shevawn, *Humanity Dick Martin 'King of Connemara'* 1754- 1834 (Dublin 1989).

Martin, Archer E S, *Genealogy of the Family Of Martin of Ballynahinch Castle* (Winnipeg 1890).

Martineau, Harriet, *Letters from Ireland* (London 1852).

Póirtéir, Cathal, *The Great Irish Famine, The Thomas Davis Lecture Series* (Dublin 1995).

O'Conaola, Thomás S., Society and Settlement in Pre-Famine Connemara, *Galway Roots, Journal of the Galway Family History Society*, Vol IV.

Ó Gráda, Cormac, *The Great Irish Famine* (Dublin 1989).

Ó Gráda, Cormac, *Ireland Before And After The Famine: Explorations in economic history, 1800-1925* (Manchester 1988).

Ó Tuathaigh, Gearóid, *Ireland Before The Famine* 1798-1848 (Dublin 1972).

Robinson, Tim, *Connemara Part 1 & 2* (Galway 1990).

Seebohm, *Private Memoirs of B And E Seebohm*, Edited By Their Sons (London 1873).

Sirr, Rev Joseph D'Arcy D.D., *A Memoir of the Honorable and Most Reverend Power Le Poer Trench Last Archbishop of Tuam*, (Dublin 1845).

Society of Friends, *Distress In Ireland 1846-'47*, Narrative of William Edward Forster's Visit In Ireland From The 18th To The 26th January 1847; Narrative of R Barcley Fox's Visit To Some Parts Of The West Of Ireland, March and April 1847.

Society of Friends, *Transactions of the Central Relief Committee of the Society of Friends during the Famine in Ireland 1846 and 1847 (Dublin 1996).*

Sunday At Home The, A family magazine for Sabbath reading, Religious Tract Society London.

Thom's Irish Almanac and Official Directory of Ireland, 1849-1853.

Tully Cross Guild, Irish Countrywomen's Association, *Portrait of a Parish, Ballynakill, Connemara* (Galway 1985).

Tuke, James A, *A Visit to Connaught in the Autumn of 1847*, A letter addressed to the Central Relief Committee of the Society of Friends (Dublin 1848).

Villiers-Tuthill, Kathleen, *History of Clifden, 1810-1860*, (Galway 1982).

Villiers-Tuthill, Kathleen, *Beyond The Twelve Bens, History of Clifden and District 1860-1923*, (Galway 1986).

Villiers-Tuthill, Kathleen, Religious Conflict in Claddaghduff, *Connemara, Journal of the Clifden and Connemara Heritage Group*, Vol.2 No 1, 1995.

Villiers-Tuthill, Kathleen, The Clifden Union, *Galway Roots, Journal of the Galway Family History Society*, Vol 111.

Woodham-Smith, Cecil, *The Great Hunger: Ireland 1845-9* (London 1962).

Terry Sweeney, E.J. King's, Clifden
Millars Connemara Tweeds Ltd, Clifden
G.M.T Ireland Ltd, Clifden
Guinness Ireland Group, Galway Office
Murphy Brewery, Galway Office

Lough Corrib Mineral Co, Oughterard
Securicor Omega Express, Dublin
Securicor Ltd, Dublin
Cashel House Hotel, Cashel, Connemara

Abbeyglen Castel Hotel, Clifden
Allied Irish Bank, Clifden
Ballynahinch Castel Hotel, Connemara
Bank of Ireland, Clifden
Casey Pharmacy, Clifden
Celtic Crafts Ltd, Clifden
Clifden Station House, Roybride Properties, Clifden
Connemara Fisheries, Clifden
High Moors Restaurant, Clifden
Ulick Joyce & Sons, Dawn Dairy Agents, Clifden
Michael Nee Coach Hire, Connemara
Peacockes (Keoghs Taverns Ltd.), Maam Cross, Connemara
The Quay House, Clifden
Rock Glen Manor House Hotel, Clifden
Gerard Stanley & Son, Clifden
Sweeney Oil Retail Ltd, Clifden
Tendafrost Foods Ltd, Galway
Tolan Food Service, Galway
Gertrude Tuthill, Cork

Connemara West PLC, Letterfrack